# In a Nutshell
Opinions & Articles during South
Sudanese Civil War
(2013 – 2016)

Chuar Juet Jock

DEDICATED TO

My Uncle Engineer. James Gatluak Lual Jock

My Mom Nyakong Lual Jock

My Dad Juet Jock Kuenywaar

# CONTENTS

# ACKNOWLEDGMENTS

My "in a nutshell" opinion articles on the Facebook wouldn't be a book today without the encouragement and the active participation of my friends and readers in Facebook and real life as well. Every 'in a nutshell" has been there because of the acceptance and the likes of its readers, the mirror where I reflect keenly whether such ideas and opinions has a positive impact or else. Most South Sudanese Facebook contributors believes that if our leaders do read what South Sudanese writes on their Facebook walls as reflection of what they think about their leadership, how they want them to be, how they dream of South Sudan of tomorrow, then, our leaders could have by far initiated a process change in both political and social endeavors that will probably meet their people expectations, however, this is far from being the case. All in all, it is worth noting that I am very grateful to all of you my Facebook readers of 'in a nutshell" and which the idea of this book originated and became a reality. It is better not to mention a particular name because all of you have helped in a way or another. Thank You

Chuar Juet Jock

# PREFACE

There is no doubt that the bloody massacres of 2013 have caught the majority of South Sudanese by surprise and ultimately, most of our perceptions and views on our own selves as a nation as well as to our political and national leadership were shaken in a way like never before. The December 15, 2013 political turmoil which started as a fierce power struggle within the top elite of South Sudan ruling party, the Sudan People's Liberation Movement (SPLM) and later to have spilled everywhere to involve the South Sudan Armed Forces or The Sudan People's Liberation Army (SPLA) and other regarded national security organs. What surprised us was the nature of 2013 war and how our national leadership turned tribal overnight and instead of staying the course of its national constitutional duty in protecting every South Sudanese regardless of tribe, religion, color, gender or any discriminatory ground prohibited by the 2011 transitional constitution of South Sudan, it sadly became the first violator and obstructer of the constitution. The defining line that will always resonate in our ears and minds is why the leadership of president Kiir Mayardit decided to wage the war as Dinka vs. Nuer, targeting one ethnic group in apparently well planned and calculated massacres despite that the conflict was purely an SPLM political wrangling within the top elite themselves? Was that because his main rival and challenger within the SPLM is a Nuer by tribe? The nature of massacres and killings didn't spare those who were supporters or relatives of his close political allies nor it didn't selectively target those who were deemed supporters of Dr. Riek Machar in fact it was generally aimed on Nuer ethnic group regardless and even those Dinka whose tribal marks were similar to Nuer were also targeted or narrowly escaped the killings.

What surprised us was that the government whom we thought it is the solution to our tribal disputes and wrangling here and there became in a matter of overnight the mastermind of tribal domination and tribal massacres. What surprised us was, how the then regarded liberation Army finally became the tool of slaughter and heinous atrocities to the very people it claimed to liberate and suppose to protect. What surprised us was how our national presidency turned overnight into a single tribe authority, using the capabilities and the national resources of the state of South Sudan to try to eliminate, dominate and subject others tribes to the rule of one single tribe. What surprised us was how our claims and credibility against Khartoum successive regimes which we have fought for the last five decades don't make any sense anymore and how we have proofed Khartoum claim right that we won't be able to rule ourselves and that we will wind up in endless pools of blood and tribal wars and unfortunately, in less the than 7 years, South Sudanese have run back in millions to Khartoum looking for safety as a refugees and foreigners this time and around. What surprised us was that, at the peak of the tribal war and competition, no one have looked back and asked these simple but serious questions, finally, is this what we have fought for the last 50+ years? Is this what our martyrs of around three million or more precious souls and lives sacrificed for?

Ironically enough, our tribal extremists were truly masters of art of defending their extreme views, dodging and twisting facts and realities in a way that was and still truly sickening. The truth and the way-out for the troubled South Sudan were all within their reach and sight but you wonder why they are still insisting on the wrong destructive path. South Sudanese have witnessed all sort of political domination, war side-effects and suffering for the last fifty years within united Sudan and if people really do learn by the hard way and bitter experience, those people should be South Sudanese. However, what happened and still happening after the hard-earned independence is still a horrible mystery looking for inclusive research and accurate answers.

Within these accumulated setbacks, the "in a nutshell" idea was born in the late 2013 several weeks after the 2013 massacres. First it started as status posts in Facebook as a personal reaction and opinion expression of the killings and destruction that was happening to innocent lives of South Sudanese as well as a personal contribution in defining and identifying the underpinning causes of 2013 political conflict and its aftermath bloody tribal war. That's in term of socio-economic, cultural and political aspects which could have a direct or indirect link to the conflict.

As a fundamental pillar of my beliefs, I do regard leadership to have a fundamental role in positioning the country and nation onto the path of peace, unity, prosperity and success and hence I have taken it to myself to identify the failure of President Kiir Mayardit leadership in all aspects that resulted in South Sudan to be a failed state and to be at war with itself. My criticism to President Kiir or any of his subordinate or other political leaders in South Sudan, Africa and the World was based on the role of responsible citizenship and fellowship and for the sake of better South Sudan, Africa and the World. It is never a personal grudge or hatred in anyway, in fact most of my Facebook debaters such as Cde Garang Gong and Mourter Majok are socially best of my friends, we chat, and laugh and debate honestly, agree and disagree and agree to disagree. I think in some cases I was even regarded as a liability to the opposition movement that cannot be trusted due to my close social approach to my political opponents. I believe in democratic debate, free expression and constructive criticism, I have a leaned respect to president Salva Kiir and Dr. Riek Machar, Dr. lam Akol, VP Wani Igga as elders but trust me, I would challenge them fiercely and constructively in their leadership scope and political opinions and my sole objective is that we should all be either part of solution or at worse, if we decided to stay silent, be part of the conflict. Hence, I do ask for each politician or leader or any person that I have challenged throughout my "in a nutshell" opinion articles not to take it personal, my love for South Sudan and the South Sudanese people has given me the courage to say and write what I see or consider right, in my opinion.

In conclusion, despite the setbacks, I am a firm believer that one day and not that long, we should reach the right form of state and political formula that should be the foundation of South Sudan of peace, unity, democracy, diversity and prosperity and where we should be at peace with ourselves and with the rest of the world.

Chuar Juet Jock

# CHAPTER 1

## 2013 ARTICLES

**December 23, 2013**

I know that this war was at store, that's why I never touch a foot on that state and also stopped writing on issues relevant to our country affairs when I have discovered that another monopoly is in the making. It was a war that has to be fought after independence to correct a wrong mentality that its results are what you see now. Living in state of denial or twist doesn't do us any good. This is not about Nuer even though this is the running propaganda right now, this is about the system and the state, and if there was any good system in place and country that was founded on fairness, just and equal distribution of power and resources, and then we wouldn't be in this mess. But those in the forefront of this system and state have been in complete resistance for calls and ideas to correct what we see as the origins of the state problems. They see it as an attempt of undermining their total control on the state and its resources. I was just wondering how really we have fought Khartoum and why just to find ourselves in a more oppressive system and state and this time in the name of tribe. If South Sudan has to be saved, then let us honestly point out where the problem lies

**December 26, 2013**
**In a Nutshell**

SPLA was never a national army and some of us know this ethnic cleansing was coming. Since its inception it has been a tool for subjection and submission to the authority of the few, a tool for tribal terror, revenge, intimidation and subjection to arbitrary arrests, torture of political opponents and tribal rivals.

The liberation war of South Sudan was a national cause and duty that every tribe, small or big has joint to fight against the oppressive systems in Khartoum. Yet it was also exploited to the maximum by a few tribal elites to form their own tribe dictatorship and rule and hence comes the defections and internal stripes.

In a nutshell, After the independence in 2011, it was kept in that name to satisfies a sick tribal ego even though a new army with a name of South Sudan Army or South Sudan People defense forces should be in place, an army that is well selected on national aspirations and balance of the diverse ethnic's structure of South Sudan, but to no avail, it didn't happen. South Sudanese will never speak up until they knew the ugly reality of the few who run this country as their own kingdom.

It is not in our national security interest in the long run to form a country on shaky foundation and bases such as it is now, it will fire back as it is now. There must be a system good enough to make sure this country could stand alone, prospers, live in peace with itself as well as with others. The victims of the dangers ahead are not the people who know that this country is wrong and are standing on the wrong footing but the victims are the one who don't know, lured in by fake country slogans while knowing nothing about what is really going on beneath the carpets and behind the curtains.

The few that are doing all these atrocities and monopoly in the name of Dinka may be so happy and in pride now that they have done whatever they ever wanted to do but also I believe someday they will pay a huge and a huge price for the very actions they are so happy and having pride for. Time will tell. Chuar Juet Jock

**December 29, 2013**
**In a Nutshell**

My concern is not those who have chosen the war and destruction to prove a sick tribal ego but it is those innocents whose peace and dreams has been destroyed.

Let us be realistic, this war won't go away with just a wish because those who control power and resources in our country has a very defiant mentality that's insisting the wrong must be right through lies, propaganda and conspiracy theories.

My prediction, the war will rage on and destroy the little that's left unless the defiant mentality has a healthy comeback from the insanity.

Accordingly, those UNMISS compounds are just a timing bombs and serious safety measures have to be taken such as relocation to a safer place, adequate protection and care.

The civil population is facing serious life threatening challenges, hunger, diseases and other safety concerns. We must actively alarm and engage the UN and international community to save our people.

The Juba regime is using those stranded in UN compound as a human shield protection for a possible attack and also a possible second genocide target. The UN here is alarmed and will be held accountable.

# CHAPTER 2

---

## 2014 ARTICLES

**April 24<sup>th</sup>, 2014**

### In a nutshell

By bringing in Paul Malong and Marial Nuor, president Kiir has formed a war government. A tribal war government. He brought what he thinks the best skilled in tribal hatred and killings and that's an okay for a more war and a more divide along the tribal line.

At least, if Nuer weren't fit to occupy some national ministerial posts due to mistrust and conflict of interest brought to surface by this war, Kiir should still insist in filling them with other South Sudanese nationals, Equatorians or others, at least, to keep the national face of South Sudan intact.

A state sponsored tribal war shouldn't find a single rational friend nor regionally or internationally and the South Sudanese with their diverse backgrounds should by all means reject this terrible direction. The international community should throw its weight in, by imposing arms embargo, economic sanctions and diplomatic pressure, these should be effective tools at least for now.

The tribal hawks are in the wait to finish the last hopes of South Sudan national identity. This shouldn't be left to happen at least if the latest cries of the international community about the recent massacres are genuine and not political.

The yet to unfold war scenario is much violent and merciless and it will for sure victimize the innocent South Sudanese in a more brutal fashion. The UNMISS should urgently relocate the IDPs to a more secure location, nearest neutral neighboring countries will be a great option and the sooner the better.

Power, ignorance and guns is a deadly combination add to that the sick tribal ego and pride. It is a sure hell that is going to finish this promising young country, hopefully not.

**May 3rd, 2014**

**In a Nutshell**

Every time the tribal government of dictator Salva Kiir captured a Nuer village or town it makes sure it burnt it all down to ashes and that every living thing from innocent civilians to all animals big and small are either killed, raped or uprooted

Last week it was Ayod and this week it is Ulang and the 30 days of Malong Awan genocidal march continue. Well, that's not a surprise to those who know the nature of ethnic war. It is a war that should destroy the other ethnic rival with all that it has at least from the destructive mindset of the tribalists.

What surprised us is how a government that claim and called itself a national government, using resources and capabilities of all the state and a nation including those whom is engaged shamefully in extermination will be the one in the seat of the tribal rival

How a government that is supposed to be the one restoring and ensuing law and order, protection of civilians and their properties. How on earth such a government should be the one doing the forbidden opposite, that's what, is surprising us and the rest of the world.

Why would a people's government burn towns down to ashes, engage in killing the very civilians, destroy the properties of the very civilians and spread the lawlessness and disorder? What is the objective of such a government? What are the nature and the color of such a government? Juba government should immediately change its name to some type of Kiir tribal Militia. It doesn't have any credibility left as a South Sudanese government, not a bit.

These are the lessons all South Sudanese need to learn from. You can't just turn a blind eye to how your country should be govern, managed and build because it is the very reasons some has taken this blindness to shamefully founded our country on a tribal ugly foundation.

Ulang, Ayod and every Nuer village will prevail but will never forget the atrocities committed by a bunch of tribal thugs enriching themselves in a name of national government.

## May 7th, 2014

### In a Nutshell

Rest assured that this rebellion can never be put down by either Paul Malong Awan or Kiir himself. The fall of Nasir shouldn't be viewed as the end of anything but in fact it is a fresh start of phase 2 of this war plus it is a direct and clear affirmative offensive on the latest peace efforts brokered by US secretary of state John Kerry.

Nasir has a unique meaning in the heart of Nuerland and I know how my Nuer people feel about its fall under Kiir genocidal forces. However, this is a war, many giant cities and people will definitely fall, villages erased and razed and the death will have befallen us, here and there. But my people stay strong and stay the course until victory. It is the nature of the war, cities will switch hands and captured and recapture, and that's definitely not the end, neither here nor there.

By capturing Nasir, Kiir is so keen on bringing himself and his regime to certain demise. Nasir will be recaptured, worry not, and every coward who has put his feet there will regret he never did. Nasir will be back only that the prospects for peace that the US and the international players has raised hopes about last week are deemed void and in serious jeopardy.

Juba is walking blindly and acting stupidly in an attempt to fulfill Mr. Malong's 30 days' military triumph upon the opposition and hence destroying along the way, all the chances and windows for peace and any political settlement for this war. However, Juba will never win this war militarily, time will witness my words.

**May 7th, 2014**

**In a Nutshell**

**On Machar- Kiir face to face Meeting**

Dr. Machar and president Kiir face to face meeting shouldn't mean anything rather than a meeting of two different visions that differ completely in how they can transform this country either into a peaceful united prosperous and democratic stable country or the current vision that is destroying our country and nation and the undisputed cause of this bloody conflict.

In fact, for Dr. Machar, it should be an opportunity to tell president Kiir that what you want is not a reward for a higher post or sort of accommodation in his current regime with its fragile and decayed structure, self-written constitution, exclusive system of governance, unfair power sharing and unequal distribution of resources and total lack of checks and balances system that separates both three branches of the government and prevent powers abuse, namely the executive, judiciary and legislature.

As we have seen from his many presidential degrees, Kiir in his current system is the president, the parliament and the supreme court of the land leave alone being the commander-in chief of the SPLA and the Chairman of SPLM, the country ruling party. It is totally a Kiir country; such powers are absolute and dangerous.

Dr. Machar should be clear and honest in addressing the need for restructuring the state of South Sudan from top to bottom. There is a need from the two leaders and from the people of South Sudan to confess that something is fundamentally wrong with the country foundation and pillars of governance. There is vital need to identify the problems in order to find the right solutions. Those who deny or dwell in the big lie that there are no problems; they are just mere opportunists who simply want the status quo to persist.

Hence, the two leaders in their face to face meeting should be honest enough and discuss the foundation and the future of this country and the nation of South Sudan in a good faith. They need to discuss what is wrong with our country, its foundation, its system of governance, its power sharing and resources distribution and above all the country constitution and the question of democracy, rotated presidency and federalism, just to mention few among many.

Dr. Machar and president Kiir could reenter the history and be forgiven of the scale and magnitude of the lost and suffering of their people triggered by this four months of bloody war and that's only if they could make this internal war the last that this nation will ever fought. They could make this war a justified one worthy of the entire lost and destruction only if they dedicated the face to face meetings and negotiations to a rebirth of this country and this nation into the best it could be.

Mr. President, surely do owe the masses of South Sudanese a lot of things he need to get corrected and get positioned right in this time of his life. We still claim we can read the heart, mind and the intentions of our president. By assuming that, if it wasn't the greed for power and the bunch of in-shadow advisors of confusion and troubles we could still say President Salva is a sounded minded leader, who loved this country, fought for it and raised its flag of independence and brought this nation together in a time of need. We still can assume he lost his temper, became impatient in a while and ordered his guards to carry out the orders of mass killings, at least we can assume that now he is back to his sanity, sober, good heart and clear thinking and that he is the driver now on the leadership seat of this country and not his advisors of confusion and troubles. Let us assume so, for the sake of peaceful South Sudan and given the benefit of doubt, president Kiir is here to prove otherwise.

For president Kiir and as head of state with vast powers and unchallenged executive decisions rights, he definitely could change the course of this country to one that could make South Sudan the country all its people dream about. On the other hand, our people need to give Dr. Machar a chance to translate what he is been fighting for since his first clash with the many odds within the SPLM/A. All his fights with the tribalism, marginalization, bad governance within the SPLM were all for the love of this country. However, in a confused state of affairs and tribal politics were the tribalism propaganda and interests do have the upper hand in our society, no matter how qualified or truthful you are, truth will be like a needle buried deep down in massive accumulation of lies. The man is mistakenly and politically being victimized and misplaced in a wrong position. Well, being a leader is not a joke; you got to take the bite, the risk and the blame for deeds you never wanted to occur.

Restructuring of the state of South Sudan from bottom top is the objective of this rebellion and president Kiir need to accept the simple fact that this whole thing is not about Nuer and Dinka contrary to the strategy he waged this bloody war upon. This whole thing is about the restructuring of the whole South Sudan with all its institutions and constitution.

## May 22, 2014

### In a Nutshell

President Kiir will definitely relinquish power at some point of time for a reason or another. However, the people of this country will still inherit a country without a good governance system neither working or effective independent institutions be them executive, judiciary or legislative.

We will still inherit a country with a one working political party which all sees as the only road to success and value. The slight idea that an alternative successful political program and model could come from nowhere but the SPLM seem to be nil and far from consideration and here why the fight around the control of historical party have taken many forms and shapes in different points of time until today, SPLM-Torit, SPLM-Nasir, SPLM-DC, Opposition and Juba and so on.

However, after the successful independence and liberation of our country, we should accept the reality that we need more than a one political party and more to that to adjust to the needs of change rather than to be imprisoned and kept ineffective by history.

I still believe that those who will genuinely fix and lays a right foundation to this country are those who are not hunting for positions in current or coming government, those who have no interest than seeing a great successful country, stable and peaceful and where every citizen can thrive and prospers.

Individuals' interests are short-lived but above all, individuals' successes should be a result of a just, fair and right overall spectrum not a result of marginalization and favoritism system. The focus than shouldn't be on just replacing a government rather than formulation of the right foundation for that successful state and nation.

That's, the system of governance need to change, our constitution need to be redefined, resources and powers sharing system need to be restructured and so on. It is after the successful agreement of the program of change that a qualified government should be in place to execute and implement the said programs of change. That's Dr. Machar's main point. We need a new country based on justice, freedom and democracy.

It is a high time for South Sudanese to be honest to themselves for a better future of their nation and country, recognizing the need for political dialogue as a mean to settle disputes and differences of one nation. Relinquishing the twist of truth and facts to fits and advance one's interest will be a great start. You decide.


**May 24, 2014**

**In a Nutshell**

This war has changed us and changed the dimensions of many social, personal and communal relationships. There is no single living conscience that would accept the systematic killings of innocent South Sudanese who are perishing on daily bases and by many direct and indirect means and methods.

Between years 2011 - 2014 the surge and disturbing increase in South Sudanese mortality rate is so alarming. It is unnecessary and unjustified and is for sure the saddest chapter we ever expected. It is a mere madness driven by a deep ignorance and sick tribal ego.

The pleasure of finishing each other's that we have noticed and observed from various South Sudanese who are involving in the ongoing conflicts is even much disturbing. Having a pride for humiliation, abuse and killing of each other is something the smart South Sudanese of just yesterday Sudan have never thought to be in for. We never expected to be at such point of stupidity at all.

Not like those days of old good South Sudan, the worst and ugly has come from who you were thinking are your brothers and countrymen. It is a complete nightmare for such a promising beautiful young country to slips down that road. I don't know how those who were severely affected by the current conflicts will ever look and sees South Sudan. If your think things will be just as they were than you better check your reading again.

War within sections of one nation whose social fabric has developed through many inter-tribal marriages and social relationships is never an option of the wise. Yet it is still seen as a necessary evil to keep or reach the seat in Juba or a way of a satisfaction to sick tribal ego and pride. It shouldn't be and it won't work. It is a counter-productive option and the consequences are dire if not seen now than definitely in the near future.

Our so-called leaders shouldn't be super occupied by personal ambitions for power and personal gains while our society is perishing. Something ugly is running unnoticed as a result of these bloody conflicts. Something that's destroying the very cohesive social fabric of this country and that will haunt this country next generations for time to come but above all it will haunts it very existence, to be or not be.

Trust is an essential factor for peaceful co-existence, nation building, country prosperity and stability. It is precious ingredient in whatever we do on daily bases as one nation. More killings and more divisions along tribal line the less trustful we will be to each other's and hence, the downfalls accordingly. But, who cares? So they say and so they think, unfortunately.

Well, the laws of nature do definitely cares and if you don't make them to work for you they definitely will work against you. Our so-called leaders need to wake up before the little remaining trust we have as a nation got consumed in unnecessary bloody conflicts that can be settled peacefully


## May 26, 2014

### In a Nutshell

Liars will always meet somewhere and they won't have even a bit of drop of shame to emphasis their lies as new realities, new facts and the ultimate truths.

Never felt like reading to Steve Paterno at any eyes meeting point with his so many biased articles or should we say books. But this time I was just curious about this piece of lie where he tried to connect the imaginary dots of claimed relationship between Dr. Riek Machar and Uganda LRA's Joseph Kony. Unfortunately, he failed miserably. His facts were swimming like drops of oil in stream of water with no cohesion whatsoever.

Nothing new his article has come with but more of the same propaganda against the inclusive mission and vision of Dr. Machar to South Sudan many governance shortcomings and paralyzed systems. Steve never in my opinion has ever stood with principles that can assures a path that would bring a great change to everyone in our country including the Equatorians themselves. However, he is entitled to his opinion, biased or else, it is his.

Dr. Machar mediation between the government of Yuri Museveni and LRA was for the sake of peace in Uganda as well as South Sudan. In fact, the later was even paying a huge price for the LRA atrocities. It wasn't a political move at all, it was a government of South Sudan effort to bring peace to the two affected regions but say what? The opportunist's eyes seem to have a different lens of seeing things. Steve should do and see better. Read Steve Peterno full article (http://www.sudantribune.com/spip.php?article51109)

On the other hand, the position of freed SPLM political detainees seems to be making controversial echoes here and there. Few controversial statements are said to be linked or said by who and who. Well, the current political game is by itself a multiple trends of approaches game of competition between the said politicians. There are no doubts they have different approaches for how to bring change to our country but at most everyone is trying to play it either smart, clean and safe by holding the rod from the middle, but know what, in a nutshell, it is either Kiir or Machar, so your better get lined up to whatever be your choice.

**May 27, 2014**

**In a Nutshell**

The claimed story of Mr. Pagan Amum controversial letter is a clear and good example of how the politics of propaganda, cooked lies and character assassination has been doing its damage to South Sudan peace and stability as well to its promising future leaders.

If there is any effective tool that has so killed thousands of South Sudanese in current tribal wars or the past during liberation days, it is the confusion created by the planned propaganda and lies. By now, we have as South Sudanese a well-established school and institution of propaganda that's becoming the source of death and destruction.

How we receive and react to whatever the architects and the cooks of such lies and destruction are also of higher impotence. We would be lucky enough if we were an informed and literate society that could distinguish and reasons before we react to such lies. The scale of damage and success of the lies and propaganda factory could have been reduced or prevented.

Unfortunately, it was the fabricated coup that brought this country down to its knees and it is the same propaganda that has killed thousands and thousands, sadly. Juba was always a place of coup stories and conspiracies until this last bloody one got believed.

Mr. Pagan Amum is man we know very well and his enemies know him very well too. He is a smart leader who read the political game and trends very accurately. Not in South Sudan alone but the whole entire region if not in international arena at large.

The Controversial letter is cheap attempt to pit the Nuer community against Pagan and any trends combined approach between the G11 and the SPLM/O. The source of those malicious letters and statements shouldn't be that much confusing. It should definitely be known.

I have said it before that the war on who will and should succeeds Kiir is the mother of all the fights. Kiir himself could be in this whole game a victim of smart guys in the shadows who are moving things toward the said goal.


**May 30, 2014**

**In a Nutshell**

Peace in South Sudan will definitely means new arrangements, new government and hopefully new direction and accordingly you can imagine how those whose interests and positions will be affected by the fact of realization of a final and just peace are acting and mobilizing their anti-peace efforts.

After the Kiir presidential decree that brought the whole government down last year and that turned the whole process upside down as old enemies becomes the new allies and vice versa. Juba ever since became a two ways route, an exit for the old allies and an entrance for the new ones. Accordingly, new political realities, coalitions and allies has emerged around Mr. Kiir and the kick start of the dirty games that ended with the majority of the SPLM Political Bureau being flushed out in that bloody fabricated coup of December of last year.

Boy and say what! It has been Kiir Mayardit game ever since, deciding who to be the government this time and who to be the rebel next time. David Yau Yau and Dr. Lam Akol are in, Dr. Riek Machar and Dr. Adwok Nyaba are out and you can just imagine who wanted to bite and humiliate who as much as they can.

Political revenge, envy and pry have been the dynamics of the game in effect in Juba that triggered all the bitter consequences the country is drowned in now. Hence, it is a pleasure to some to see Dr. Machar run for his life and becoming a rebel, Pagan Amum and Dr. Nyaba becoming prisoners and humiliated and the whole process becoming a hunt for personal grudges not a care for nation business.

While the country state of affairs is deteriorating both politically and economically and even worsening, Mr. Kiir has maintained the game and his current allies are in a fierce fight to prevent the possible peace and new arrangements that will bring the current rebels into the government and political plays otherwise they will find themselves back to the rebellion, the only language Mr. Kiir understands and rewards.

Well, who in Juba do really cares as all goes around and around in every political swaps except the master and center of the games, Kiir Mayardit himself. As every new government reshuffle means a new window and opportunity for some shortsighted so-called politicians who are upon themselves and not for the country long-term stability and interests.

However, where interests always defeat the truth and logic in our politics, chances are rare that our politicians will weighs in the higher interests of our nation and country and choose peace rather than dwells in endless costly political games and rivalries.

**June 2, 2014**
**In a Nutshell**

South Sudanese tribalists have something in common and that's their quick biased judgment upon anyone who slightly differs with them in their dead-end approaches and shortsighted solutions towards national issues and problems.

The time you become a traitor from the very tribalist viewpoints is the time you tell them that their shortsighted approaches to national matters would go nowhere far than their noses and that national issues and problems can never be solved through exclusive approaches and solutions rather than inclusive national approaches.

The very reasons Mr. Kiir systems are failing can't be applied by a movement who is seeking to be an alternative leadership and movement for South Sudan in its entirety. To win over Mr. Salva, you have to be better than him 10 times if not 100 times. That means a complete overhaul to whatever failed approach he applied there and here and a better vision to South Sudan's countywide, nationwide, regional and international policies and relations.

People should be above the biases that are hindering the success of South Sudan as a state. There is no need to mix personal grudges and rivalries with issues related to country destiny and future. There is a need to accept and recognize that every tribe, clan and individual permanent success and happiness relays in the overall success of South Sudan as a nation and country. South Sudan total destruction is surely our all sad demise with no exception whatsoever including those who has chosen to be bystanders and guests of dishonor in their own country's destiny and future.

But say what? You are like a doctor who is giving the life medicine to an ignorant patient, who will throw it away anyway and die anyway, if they didn't touch the fire then it is not a fir learning the bitter way, sadly.

## June 4, 2014
## In a Nutshell

How rogue regimes prosper and survive? Well, the thing is, any rouge regime is based on a wrong, unjust and unfair foundation but it is either through fear, terror or selfish interest-centered individuals that they do survives. It is making big money to some people, fulfilling their selfish interests and giving them the opportunity they might not get under right and fair play. As long as the wrong is backed by money than expects the wrong to be right and the wrong to rule, people are trying to inject and make sense to the senseless just because they are making big bucks out of it and so marketing the wrong to be right.

Not all the humanity has lost their conscience, sense and heart to the power of money and that is why there is still a little light of truth trying to make that hard resistance against the allure, the power and undeniable quest of the money.

However, in civilized and more matured societies, the scale and limit of human competition are set, played and conducted under fair laws, public safety and security procedures. That's whatever game it is, being those under economic fierce business competition or intensive political rivalries are to be played, ran and maintained under the laws. It is a crime to cross the line and endanger public safety and security regardless of who you are or whatever your motives or game maybe.

It was the failed political game within the ruling party the SPLM that brought the whole country into ruins and brink of collapse. If it was played safe, maintained within party without spilling it into public and security organs domains it could have ended their peacefully and saved the country from acute outcomes of political stupidity. But say what?

Some have sensed that the outcomes of peaceful democratic game within the SPLM were coming and not in their own favors and accordingly shifted the whole game to the realm of communist conspiracies, coups and whatever comes after fabricated coups and hence comes the mass killings of the innocent Nuer in the name of political figure, Dr. Riek Machar. Wasn't it a political game anyway that should, could be maintained as such?

The mass killings of Nuer were a collapse of South Sudan national security laws and institution. That a particular ethnic group could be targeted singled out for murder and genocide under the very watch of the president, national security institution and its laws is a complete failure of the said state leave alone that the president or those national security organs are the ones carrying out the killings.

The killings of innocent Nuer were also a collapse of South Sudan politics and its politician's morale, ethics and leadership substance. Starting from the Nuer politicians and those who's their constituents and who they claim to represents were being systematically murdered under their very watch and forced to be refugees and second citizens in their own homeland. No condemnations, no protests leave alone resignations.

The mass killings of Nuer or any other ethnic group was also a collapse of South Sudan national politics and politicians' conscience that could clearly condemned in the strongest term possible this huge setback in the South Sudan nation-building endeavor.

If money could buy humans conscience in the way we have seen in South Sudan political crisis than none of us is deemed to prospers, succeed and live secure in our country. Today we will sell Nuer; tomorrow Bari will be next and so on. Let us stand together for a better country for all.


## June 6, 2014
## In a Nutshell

When every South Sudanese is convinced and made felt at ease with the very systems of governance, fair distribution of resources and power sharing than the ills and bias that are pitting our tribes, clans and individual politicians shall be no more.

The strong calls for federalism as a just and suitable system of governance in South Sudan case were enforced and justified by what we have witnessed as a grave abuse of powers by the center in Juba or the central government in the current presidential system.

National resources and powers were and are still conceived by some as their clan's rightful properties given to them by so-called greedy concept that we have liberated this country and so we have all the rights to rob its banks, rape its girls and drives military tanks on the homes and families of its innocent citizens. Such a dangerous trend can never be left unanswered and unconfronted.

The clear and undisputed failure of what was perceived as national government, national army and most of so-called national institutions are well documented. Economically, 85% of national revenues are unaccounted for and most of it is uselessly spent within Juba through many gates and fake contracts that have made Yuri Museveni a stakeholder in our country affairs. While most if not all South Sudan peripheral territories are left marginalized and with a clear trends and indicators of development projects are all shifted to certain regions.

In terms of government and administrative institutions; nepotism, favoritism and tribalism make some what is supposed to be national government departments' looks like particular clans or tribes' villages. Where the head of department is a hyena and so are the entire employees, sadly.

Militarily and most of what are supposed to be national defense security organs are even worse. The doomed December 15th, 2013 has clearly proven how a single tribe or clan controlled army or security organ could be the most dangerous threat to the country national security and unity. In fact, our country failed even more that day when the supposed to be its national defense and the neutral shield of its national unity, integrity and stability has turned to be the killer of its very existence as a result of tribal politics and government. As such, the ethnic based killings, detention, rape, grave human rights abuse has come from those tribal dominated security organs and armies.

Those are just few of clear failures of the current system. It is only those who are manipulating it to their own benefits that can depend it. Those who became kings, millionaires and first class citizens overnight because of the very corrupt systems. This self-centered class is finding itself at risk of losing those privileges and hence fights back in multiple ways.

Let them not fool you that this whole thing is about Riek Machar. It is about this country, its system of governance, its resources and powers sharing. If we are not stupid enough to store another ugly war to be fought in future than let us seriously and willingly tackle these issues thoroughly and permanently.

Federalism as a governance system is not a recipe without some bias but so far it is the best in our case.

## June 11, 2014
## In a Nutshell

It will be a hit of stupidity to expect Mr. Kiir to dismantle his own presidency and his own pillars of power and support allies for the interest of the nation and country.

Under the international pressure and possible imminent internal collapse of his very regime, he is signing papers with Riek Machar in Addis Ababa that he immediately reputes and dishonors upon his arrival in Juba Airport and in the secret talks chambers with his Juba allies.

Mr. Salva has said it clear and in many ways and in different occasions that he is interested to end the conflict but not his presidency. He has to remain president during the transitional government and apparently the one after nominating himself and winning the proposed 2018 elections with 99.99% votes.

The world still sees him as the democratically elected and legitimate constitutional president of South Sudan and hence none of the IGAD countries heads of states will ever agree to topple a counterpart neither America or any other democracies will agree to that.

It is a fact that Mr. Salva has stains of thick bloods of his innocent people in his hands but also insisting in removing him by force does just add more bloods and possible complete disintegration of the whole South Sudan nation and state. The political wise should avoid that at all cost.

A peaceful exit to Mr. Salva is now handy; a roadmap strategy for transition to a different and better South Sudan is being worked out in Addis Ababa crowned by recent 60 days' deadline for formation of a transitional government. When the role of central government is accurately defined, its functions, it boundaries and limitations are entailed than justice and equality has at least rationally, been tackled.

The good news is that, the greater Equatoria has openly and courageously joined Dr. Riek Machar in the transition march for a better South Sudan. Federalism as a system of governance will assure fair distribution of powers and resources, powerful states and loose center that deals with national security and other national aspects.

As Dr. Machar said it before that a new government without a program is not the objective of his movement. What different a new blank government will make since presidential decrees were creating new governments and reshufflings ever since but it was more of the same, corruption, injustices, inequalities and power abuse.

This shouldn't be about people looking for new executive positions, political glory and power rather than a new system of governance, constitution, equal distribution of resources and power sharing in fact, a new South Sudan.

All that will never be easy to achieve. It is tricky, full of road blocks and political conspiracies. The political hyenas in Juba are sharpening their poisonous knives to murder Dr. Machar's inclusive approach to tackle the South Sudan problems once and for all. Dirty propaganda, misinformation and lies are already in political kitchens and ready for the long term offensive. Stays tuned, alerted and awaken.

Mr. Salva is moving to reaffirm himself, the opportunists are here to make him survives and the loser will definitely be South Sudan. They will attempt to divide us, confuse us and weaken us but let us stay strong and stand united for better change until the end. A new South Sudan is in the making and it is for all.


**June 21, 2014**
**In a Nutshell**

South Sudan president Mr. Salva Kiir and supporters should view the South Sudan problem as that of a failed company where a CEO or other executives in charge of adding values to the company and its shareholders are forced to quit or choose to resigns on their own to pave a way for a change that will bring a different leadership and direction to the company.

People who are in leadership positions whether in public administration or private sector are never there for show or fame rather than to lead people or companies to success, something Mr. Kiir and his many governments has failed to achieve during the last 9 years. Otherwise they (Kiir and supporters) need to give us the success indicators by figures, statistics and values of South Sudan stocks in the international market of success. I am afraid it is a big nil.

A quick review to what the leadership and administration of Mr. Kiir has achieved since 2005, before the independence and after, point to the fact that all falls below expectations. Given the huge financial resources allocated for his governments and the vast executive powers entrusted in him, he miserably felt short in stirring the country and the nation around to the direction of successful nation and state building and hence, his stocks in the political market and leadership are no more convincing.

If we are all for success of South Sudan as a nation and country, then that would mean we would agree on a competent leadership that will take us there to that success or promising land. Kiir has failed and hence Kiir is the problem. Mr. Kiir resignation or removable will pave a way for a different leadership and direction that might bring life again to this country dead body.

But here is where the problem lays. Mr. Kiir won't admit his clear failure leave alone that he would voluntarily resigns. His forceful removal may destroy the little connections and life left in the united body of South Sudan, the country and the nation. His supporters are not viewing his removal as a replacement of a failed leadership or leader rather than a removal of a whole tribe, clan and region. Given that, he chooses the Nuer and Riek Machar to hang on his little remnants of powers and to buy more days.

According to president Salva, it is a red line for any purposed transitional government without him as the president. But a new government with the same head and leadership has nothing new to add or deliver; it will be more of the same. The problem is not how many governments will be reshuffled as long as the head is still the same.

Accordingly, it is either war that may destroy the whole country or a workable political peaceful exit to Mr. Salva or one that might minimize his vast executive powers. Either way, Mr. Salva might need to admit that he has failed for a change to be possible or detaches himself from what made him failed, given the benefit of the doubt that he might be himself a victim of a pry or sabotage within his own regime.

In a nutshell, Mr. Kiir and supporters do not need to take or see this urgent need for a new leadership and change as a personal or tribal conspiracy. People are looking for electricity, clean water, adequate healthcare, good education system, food sufficiency, paved roads among many but above all security and more security to the ordinary South Sudanese in neighboring villages, Juba the capital and everywhere at any time within South Sudan.

## June 24, 2014

### In a Nutshell

Dr. Adwok Nyaba is still in house arrest. He just resigned from the then historical party SPLM before it was transformed into a tool of self-enrichment and tribal domination. Nothing could justify why an icon of true liberation drives and undisputed pillar of experience, education, truth and honesty could remain arrested after all his jailed comrades were all but released.

It is only the clear fears of the regime from what a great man in person of Dr. Adwok Nyaba could add to the calls of reforms and the unstoppable march of change to the current governance system that is being manipulated by a privileged few.

He was the first one to stand firm against the December 15th, 2013 fabricated coup. His accounts of events, truth and honesty has devastated the whole conspiracy and the expectations of those behind it and hence he has been singled out to "feels the heat" for standing bravely against the framed coup and its aftermath. Few of the kind like Gen. Mach Paul was stripped out from service and got fired the harsh truth of dictatorship.

Keeping Dr. Adwok Nyaba out of current political debate and negotiations is itself a planned isolation which is aimed at alienating a wealth of experience, education and true leadership that no doubt will stirs the whole process to the direction of needed reforms and changes.

Not every call for reforms and system fixes is an attempt of Dr. Riek

Machar to grab power from president Salva. The reality says otherwise, there is a serious failure that needs to be confronted and fixed; it will be of a good benefit for Juba to be honest to itself and to the general public of South Sudanese. Hence, preventing experienced leaders such as Dr. Adwok Nyaba to join the talks in Addis Ababa is itself a punishment to South Sudanese masses at large who are the end beneficiaries of such a debate. However, who could take the heat of Dr. Nyaba joining Dr. Riek Machar? Well, it is not likely something Juba of Kiir Mayardit can even ignore. at least from the very viewpoint of self-centered math of power.

As the old system is praying to stay intact, unchanged and playing with all cards to maintains the status quo, the new drive for change will have to draws new strategies and programs of action in the face of Juba unwillingness to compromise for a real deal that will bring a real desired change. It is the last hours of a dying horse that won't feel ashamed to still make you believe that it has the power to kick but in fact the reality says otherwise.

## June 26, 2014
## In a Nutshell

So the opposition is having a serious internal competition and power struggle over uncertain future and Addis Ababa could become another city for framed coup if not that it is not in South Sudan. That's not a surprise; all cards are being played by most of competing groups within the SPLM. Riek Machar may have regrets why he fought for the release of the would-be his rivals, oh, if he ever knew.

Credits go to Dr. Machar for fighting bravely to guarantee the release of the former political detainees and to the thousands of his forces who paid their precious lives to make that possible. Their release was then the first condition for any possible talks between Machar-Kiir, and what?

But what happened after the complete release of all detainees except Dr. Adwok Nyaba is a complete setback to what was expected. We did expect a united opposition front that would stand firmly behind Dr. Machar and the gallant forces that were fighting Salva Kiir since December 15th, 2013, irrespective of personal and political ambitions and rivalries. The case now is no longer personal rather it is about the destiny of South Sudan, the state and the nation, to be or not to be.

It is unfortunate that the fight over who should lead the SPLM in

Opposition has been taken to Addis Ababa and the prospects of political settlement are being wasted if not destroyed by this fierce internal competition on who will get what and who shouldn't follow who.

It seems that some groups think that a signed agreement between Riek and Kiir means the other groups will be either left-out or marginalized and here is the mother of all the hidden political conspiracies and the deals that are shaping new political realities. Juba is not negotiating seriously because it sees a fragile opposition, a one that is no opposition and a no government but still want a place on the negotiations table. How come?

Juba is reading the rift between the opposition keenly and wasting no time, money, promising future government and party rewards just to widen the gap and weakening of Riek Machar and hence the entire opposition if only they knew.

So who is negotiating who in Addis Ababa? It is a chaotic process and IGAD has to be blamed for allowing such a mess under the cover of inclusiveness. They should take the CPA of 2005 as a negotiations model.

There is a need for serious decisions from both SPLM in Opposition and the government so those who are playing in the middle shouldn't exploit the current mess. The opposition should line up under Riek Machar and those for government under Kiir. This should be the condition for the next round of talks.

The current negotiations structure of multiple parties is so confusing and will lead to nowhere. Government must come as a government with all its representation and so is the opposition. The roadmap and the negotiations agenda need to be clear and should reflects the needed change by opposition, in terms of issues and substance.


## June 29, 2014

### In a Nutshell

In a bid to provide an alternative leadership, the SPLM in Opposition led by Dr. Machar has appointed the heads of its national committees and structures. That's a good step forward in the formulation process of a political movement with a real mission and vision to transforms South Sudan, the nation and the country.

When we say transformation, we mean the visionary program(s) that will take South Sudan, the nation and country from the misery state where it is now to the best state of affairs where it should be according to the collective vision of the leadership and the people of South Sudan. It is the process of manifestation of people aspirations and expectations to better living standards, a better socio-economic and political realm.

Transformation is a daily process that's accurately planned, carefully scheduled and literally to be implemented as short or a long term programs. Its takes an ambitious, brave leadership, willing and determined to execute the transformation programs in order to achieve a new prosperous, stable country and nation.

The difference that count for any political organization to thrive for is the difference it makes in the lives standards of the people in term of service delivery, the physical infrastructures developments in the country and so on but above all how far or effective could its socio-economic and political programs go in creating a cohesive nation, peacefully co-existing and prospering. That's what creates prosperity. Without peace, nothing of what is called development will ever happen or will ever have a meaning.

What South Sudanese people really needs is not resources but a good manager/leader that will manage those resources efficiently and effectively and lead them to their dreams and it will be of great assets for the opposition leadership to address that in order to brand itself from the current leadership in Juba. The know-how will always deliver than the know- who.

South Sudan is planted in a region where its neighbors fear its success potential and it is also born to a world where interests are what governs the politics of international relations, so our leadership need to be cautious and play it right at anytime and anywhere, not everything that shines there is gold

Marginalization is the worst enemy to any country peace and stability. There is enough of everything in South Sudan but our greedy side can't see that and that's why we are fighting over nothing. Building a right country from start means an everlasting prosperity for everyone but being right itself is a source of enmity, internally and externally, stay aware.

**July 2, 2014**

**In a Nutshell**

Any future government of South Sudan should prioritize education as the most needed transformation substance and drive. A mass education revolution is needed throughout the entire South Sudan. Humans are the center of any desired change and educating them positively will have its impact in changing what is around them.

What is creating wars and corruption or all socio-economic and political bias and ills is the clear lack of practical and effective education that should have helped in engraving deep within the South Sudanese general character and personality the skills and the abilities of critical thinking, sound and logical reasoning in their daily quests for problem solving and life challenges.

An outsider, who physically sees South Sudanese from the very first time, will never know whether this dark skinned people have any differences whatsoever that could lead to such a disastrous war such as the one we have now. We seem from our physical appearance as one and particularly with the new generations barely had any of those traditional tribal marks used as identification in the older generations.

Yet we are so different in our conceptual worlds. What are setting us apart are the deadly and negative concepts we had for each other's. The mindset is so terrible to extend that it is a real threat to any future peaceful co-existence between our diverse communities. That's a weakness and not a sign of strength.

An effective education and cultural revolution that will erase those concepts and melts us into oneness and love and loyalty to our nation and country is needed and the most.

The substance we need into our quest of successful nation-state building might not be all political but good education and good national cultural orientation might do they do but of course this won't happen without the right political leadership.

Yes, there are those who climbed the higher degrees of education academically, yet they have shown poor trends in matters related to politics, social skills and reasoning. So not every highly educated in some field is as good as in others. Curriculum and type of institution we have attended do make the difference.

We need more effective educational institutions that will shape our national identity, embed in us the concepts of one nation and arms us with the critical thinking and abilities for reasoning until then, the realization of that South Sudan that we all dream about will be a mere illusion.

## In a Nutshell

## July 9th, 2015

### A Tale of Two Celebrations

July 9th is here, the day South Sudan has earned that hard-won independence, Unfortunately, the people who should be waving on the flag of independence proudly and joyfully in this day are either among the dead, the displaced, the exiled, the tortured and the imprisoned within walls of fears and terrors in their own country.

The anniversary of South Sudan independence this year is as sad as it never was an independence at all. God have mercy on the poor people of South Sudan If they manage to celebrate it this year within these heavy shadows of death, sorrow and lost than it is going to be another tale of two celebrations, the flag that Salva Kiir and Co. will be waving is not the same as those in UNIMISS or in many refuge lands will be waving, they look the same in colors but they stand for different values and principles, dictatorship vs. democracy and curfews vs. freedoms, respectively.

Independence means, we are no longer dependent to International aids, nor dependent to Uganda and UN protection. Independence means a free citizen who enjoys full rights and freedoms, can safely and securely travel and lives anywhere in his/her country, South Sudan.

Independence means no children going to bed hungry or dying young due to lack of adequate healthcare, joining army and streets due to lacks of schools and jobs.

Yet Mr. Kiir and Co. are still telling us all is normal, all under control and it is one of the best independence ever. oh God, maybe only that will make it so to Kiir and Co. is that the Nuer are no longer in Juba, they are either in UNMISS, Rebels Lines, dead or scattered around in refuge lands. Well, then, that Kiir's country independence not South Sudan independence and it is going down in history as one of sad reality this nation will ever held in its living memory.

Ethno-centrism is a sure destroyer to patriotism and nationalism and those who advocates for such factors of fragmentation are the real destructive elements of South Sudan house from within. If unity is power than whatever or whoever advocates for disunity and more fragmentation of South Sudan and its people is advocating for its weakness and its sure fall.

The legacy of our national hero/heroines and our collective national legacy as South Sudanese has never been in threat until the current tribal war ushered us officially into our narrow worlds of tribes and clans leaving South Sudan that house us all crumbling. If we have got to see things from the very narrow tribal lens, such as independence's heroes and heroines, then people like Dr. John Garang, William Nyoun Beny, Karbino Kuanien Bol and Samuel Abu John will account for nothing but mere tribal men rather than national heroes.

Yet it is a sad reality. I never have seen a nation on this earth who took tribalism to the extreme such as the one we have. Tribalists who have exceeded even Hitler false racism pride and yet they are complaining why racism is here. None of the lie or the sickness of superiority or inferiority of a race or tribe is even a new thing under the sun, but say what, the mentally sick may still finding some salvation there, surprisingly.

Fortunately, all the bias, the illusions and ignorant pride will definitely fade away, sooner or later. The reality that some still struggles to comprehends is that at the end of the day, we are one nation. The journey might be bitter, bloody and with all the sorts of humans' games and impunities but it is a sure arrival no doubt.

Kiir and Co. may need to tell us only one reason, why an orphan child, whose parents were slaughtered in that conspiracy coup aftermath, should celebrate the independence of South Sudan this year? They might need to tell us another reason why those orphaned children should be proud of the legacy of those deemed national heroes/heroines? We are ready to take your answers or be them reasons.

**July 15, 2014**
**In a Nutshell**

It is so ironic that the destructive elements of tribal superiority and inferiority complex are engraved deep within our African mind.

Yesterday we were suffering, crying and fighting collectively from the domination, religious and racial discrimination of northern Sudanese yet to find ourselves advocating for a superior tribes and other ones as inferior in the independent South Sudan.

Africa is going downward for reasons. It is not an out of sudden phenomenon or a destiny written from above but a simple man made state of affairs that either have to be overturned by the wise so this continent can have a meaningful progress or emphasized by the fools for this continent to stay in this bitter status quo.

While wise nations are seeing in unity more powers and more meaning and seeking more unions and coalitions to boosts their socio-economic and political existence and powers, Africa is celebrating more fragmentation and divides in the name of religions, tribes and clans and positioning itself to a more destructive path.

The superiority and inferiority complex within African mind has definitely something to do with colonial rule and domination, racial discrimination and tribal favoritism that long shaped the African mind frame during the reign of colonial rule and domination or how then could those colonists have ever prevailed and ruled without the infamous divide to rule strategy.

Africa has learned from there, unfortunately not the consequences but the same divide to rule policy and tactics yet to ignorantly apply it within its already fragile societies, this time, in the name of religions, tribes and clans, Sadly.

African social and political scientists and engineers are yet to answer whether they could overcome tribalism and all these social fragmentation elements and come up with a more effective social and political substance to melts their nations into a more cohesive larger forms, peaceful nations, and prosperous societies, economic and political powers. We can never stay in blaming the ordinary African man and question why he is acting and behaving against himself. Something is missing here and that's the task.

**July 17, 2014**

**In a Nutshell**

It will be a hit of complete ignorance if president Kiir, his tribal regime architects and policymakers thinks that they can conceal and bury deep their ill intents and tribal motives as the true reasons that are fueling this bloody civil war. The international community will never let the people of South Sudan to be slaughtered under its very watch.

An ethnic based government that is using state resources and foreign mercenaries for hire to fight an ethnic based opposition is the gravest threat and danger to South Sudan national security and its territorial integrity.

I wish Mr. Kiir can read the future of this nation and read it very well. After this bloody civil war, South Sudan will never be the same. It will be a great luck if its geographical territory will still be intact leave alone whether we will be still united as a nation and have the same cohesive peaceful social fabric before Kiir's war. The more bloodshed, the more we are slipping down to our total demise.

The nationally funded Juba SPLA faction has lost its neutrality since December 15th, 2013 and it is only in the world of propaganda that Kiir and supporters still calls it a national Army. The SPLA Juba faction is executing the war against the ethnic Nuer fighting for their survival and dignity and labeled unjustly as Rebels. It is waging an ethnic cleansing under the pretext of depending the constitution, nation and its properties. However, with all that, Juba will never win this war militarily and if it believes so then it has to redo the math correctly.

Sooner or later, Juba and its tribal armies can never run away with all the atrocities committed against its own people. The world will unearth every data and use every tech for just that. A better world cannot be achieved if such grave crimes against humanity can be let go unpunished. Otherwise the credibility of the international system is at stake.

The only way forward is either Kiir will have to voluntarily quit or a serious state restructuring and reforms to overhaul the system of governance, constitution, resources and powers sharing or there will be a day where the illusions of false powers, lies and cover-ups will be of no more. We are in it for the long haul, a matter of time indeed.

**July 20, 2014**

**In a Nutshell**

Somalia was a good example on how a tribal society may fails to govern itself, a clear fight of tribal egoism versus nationalism. Well it seems it is our turn as most of us South Sudanese are fighting over who should govern and how we view the government and hence it comes to what is the definition of the government and what are its constitutional responsibilities and duties toward the citizens and the country. Let us dwells there for a minute.

Is there any system of governance that's just, fair and sound? Does it serve the best interests of the whole country and the entire nation? Are there any checks and balances system that prevent it powers from being abused and exploited?

How the government is being selected, elected or chosen? Is it a fair, neutral and inclusive process of selection? Is it a government by people, for people and to people?

Who are the people who are supposed to run the government in term of age, health? Are they mentally and physically fit? Ethically and morally fit? What are their educational, professional qualifications and experiences, criminal backgrounds? What are their visions, programs of action, transformation and development agenda, short and long-term projects and programs? Could they deliver services, sustainable results and outcomes to the people and country?

Government money are public money, they are either local, states or nationally collected and generated through taxes or other public revenue means. How is public spending? What monitors public money, traces its flows and spending from point A to point Z? Any documentation, records and tacking system?

Government employees are public servants. How do we appoint government employees? What are the set qualifications and expectations? What measures are there to protect public money? Any clear laws and codes of conduct that guides the work of government employees?

What govern the government, prevent it from the abuse of power, audit its actions and is it accountable and to who?

Is there any independent institutions or media house that monitors and evaluate the performance of the said government?

Well, South Sudan problems are confined there, getting good and right answers might help break the cycle of confusion of where actually our problems do originate.

## July 23, 2014
## In a Nutshell

The only country that is so much blessed and gifted but destroying itself at will is South Sudan. Some countries would have made a true paradise on earth if given just quarter of what South Sudan do actually have.

Unfortunately, its leaders and the blind crowds are greedy fighting over 00.00001 of its resources and potential wealth. Poor countries like Uganda have already tested what it means to be poor and resources-condemned and hence they have no option but rule us through failed leaders in disguise.

Out of cowardice and impunity, Uganda has burnt our people alive through merciless use of cluster bombs, a banned weapon of mass destruction and a grave crime against humanity that should be condemned internationally. But this kill-for-hire African police has become the dirty fingers of neo-colonialism. So apparently getting away with it is a no surprise.

Uganda has been receiving the share of lion from our oil revenues since 2011. South Sudan is now the largest market importer and consumer to their low quality goods and commodities, the safe heaven destination for all the corrupt money. The first contractor of the many fake contracts and companies that are robbing and luring away all South Sudanese public money, All the Juba corrupts have at least bought luxurious mansions and villas there and living and spending lavishly while the ordinary South Sudanese lack even basic services'

Had we had any realistic development at all we proudly could have thanked Uganda by statistics and data graphs of the great projects they have built. Unfortunately, there is none, it is only the underdevelopment and more destruction that we are getting; they have to make themselves fit in, in a way or another.

So don't wonders anymore from Uganda sudden love to us and all the Don Joan acts of their president, he just found his lifetime jackpots in so much fertile corrupt Juba corridors. This won't stop until the whiskey sippers comes out clean and sober from their lost world. Well, hopefully they will collect some remnants of the already slaughtered South Sudan.

As for Gen. Salva, it never crossed our minds that a South Sudanese leader will ever hire foreign mercenaries to come and slaughters his own people in a purely internal conflict nor did we knew that the Buganda tribe of Uganda has apparently became closer to Dinka more than the Nuer of South Sudan. Unless the old man must have a calculator and a math of his own. It is sad chapter for the future of these two sisterly nations because neither will we ever forget what the Ugandans mercenaries have done to our people who were depending themselves against a brutal tribal dictator.

Accordingly, IGAD is a failure, with Uganda in it; it will never deliver any peaceful settlement to any East African conflict. In fact, Uganda and its allies will use every opportunity to prolong these conflicts. It is a bloody big investment and business and for SPLM/SPLA - IO, dealing with IGAD means always having plan B, trust is not an option

We do know that the region of East Africa need a peaceful South Sudan in order for it to prospers as well but not by Uganda selfish interests based approach. Uganda could have played a better and neutral role by not linking Ugandans short and long terms interests by a brutal dictatorship but by the constant mutual and physical interests between the two sisterly nations.

People of South Sudan have never thought to have any grudges towards their brothers in Uganda until the two dictators have decided to stays in power on their skulls and bones. Sadly. However, like it or not, South Sudan will definitely learn from this bloody experience and come out from it even stronger.

## July 25, 2014
## In a Nutshell

The arrogant thinking foundation is that truth and patriotism are never made and made only but in their tribal factories. Such a wrong foundation constitutes a real threat to any peaceful co-existence leave alone a viable democratic society, where ideas and concepts are freely debated, exchanged thought-out.

While it is a cheap attempt to promote self and tribe, it is also very counterproductive to their very claim as true liberators. True liberators don't end up into the same camp of colonialism. Unfortunately, they did. Not only that but with excellence too.

To pretend as a true liberator to just exclude other is cheap and to do that just to manipulate a public domain is even cheaper. These pretenders need to read and revise what true liberators really do and end up. I give them Nelson Mandela as a true world and African iconic and liberator to explore and read.

The professional professors from the "We Have Fought the War University" - "WHFTW" have graduated unqualified humans' resources that have ran and administered this country wrongly since 2005 and earned it the title of the first failed state in the world.

The whole process should have been designed, managed, implemented and monitored to have fruitful outcomes but what? It was never designed with a purpose of improving or developing this country, the whole public administration was an accommodation of family members, individual interests and money makers, a terrible hit of nepotism and hence we are now crumbling.

Employment is not a reward without specific duties and qualifications requirements. It is a time and space frame within the short and long terms process of country development. When it is occupied by the right person, a share and a portion of development is made and achieved. Given that, the big picture is that, the whole should also be right and sound.

But the opposite was what was quite happening in South Sudan case. Clans and tribes has owned ministries and government institutions in whole or in part and where the head of department is a hyena, the whole department employees will definitely be also hyenas and graduates of WHFTW university.

Government institutions became family business, source of enriching self, immediate and extended families and we wonder why people don't have to be corrupts and we ask where the ills are coming from. The problem is with us and within us, don't look any further.

Well, there will never be any meaningful progress and development in our country unless the misleading concepts are changed, social ills are corrected, public administration overhauled and restructured. Laws are made clear, just and enforced.

Universities and educational institutions should lead the transformation process, draft the right curriculum and substance that should improves the work of mind and its products. Media and press, cultural institutions should also do actively engage the public opinion for a better South Sudan.

Well, the higher office on land must take the lead and drive the nation and country. That means if Gen. Salva is not doing it let him let other to do it, we are no leaders-bankrupt nation and hence I know people goes deaf and into resistance when reforms are called for and particularly when the reforms are coming to slash someone income or position and this of course include Gen. Salva.


**July 27, 2014**
**In a Nutshell**

The quest for a good governance system is not to install a leader of this camp over a position of leader of that camp as some are preaching but it is for all South Sudanese welfare, peace and prosperity. The failure of the current decentralization system of governance is so evidenced and known even to the politically naïve and blind.

From 2005 to 2014, the ruling political elite of SPLM has manipulated and abused the decentralized system to the max. There is no type of corruption under the sun that Juba didn't exercised through that period and the result was a system gone awry, a country gone from worse to worst and a people gone to even poorer, dismayed and finally frustrated.

I am not denying the wrangling over power within the ruling party, that's a normal and healthy stream within a living political entity but I am not for the way they handled it, the way they set their conspiracy theories against each other's and the way they sorted out their ideologies and political differences. They didn't put the higher interests of the country and the nation first and above all those rivalries otherwise we could have avoided this deadly and destructive war. As skilled politicians, they could have handled those differences within the realm of SPLM and avoid sending them down to the public, military and security organs in a so much fragile tribally structured country. We could have been saved. But say what? It was the other way around.

If there was a working governance system, designed honestly to advance this country forward, maintain its peace and stability and to keep this nation united through justice and fairness, law and order in its many details and corridors, trust me, there would had been within that system what would have prevented power abuse, corruption and all the ills that has landed us to the title of the first failed state in the world. We can't stick on the same political structures of old Sudan; a new restructuring according to the new realities of an independent South Sudan is needed. Powers, wealth and resources must be channeled in a way that installs the sense of fairness, peace and equality in every South Sudanese citizen across the whole country

It is in our collective interest to be honest to address the governance system thoroughly and accurately. Our pure and sound objective is to create a great nation and a country where the South Sudanese who suffered a lot in the last 50 years lives in reality their dreams for peace, prosperity and stability. The Addis Ababa talks can achieve that without a referral to the blood waste in the senseless battle fields only that it requires a willing political leadership that weighs the higher interests of South Sudan. Remember, it is the blood of South Sudanese that is being drained in both sides.

The political leadership of this country must bring peace and stability to this nation at all the cost. You can't be a successful politician if you have failed to achieve the aspirations of your people in better living standards, peace, unity and prosperity. If they can't offer it then let them let the young take the lead and define a new brighter future for this beautiful nation and county.

## August 1, 2014
## In a Nutshell

The next round of peace talks in Addis Ababa may land us to hopes of final peace accord or to the bitter reality of returning to a full scale war. Given the defiance tone of the government and at the top of that is the latest conflicting statements from its head Gen. Salva Kiir and his Spokesperson Mr. Michael Lueth that there will be no more concessions given to SPLM/A -IO demands. However, I have no knowledge of any major concessions so far that the government has made to the SPLM/A -IO demands neither Mr. Salva has stepped down from power nor he accepted federalism as an alternative system of governance.

Peacemaking is not easy, it demands true leadership that put the higher interests of the country and the nation first and above all individual and selfish interests. For both sides of the SPLM, in government and opposition, sticking on the extreme end of their demands definitely means nothing else but the bloody war. Therefore, for peace to be possible, serious concessions and compromises are a must and since both are claiming to be for the interest of South Sudanese and country than one would question what would make it difficult on agreeing on what stand with the true interest of South Sudanese otherwise this whole process game is but cheap politics.

Mr. Salva and supporters won't agree on leaving the seat of power in Juba, even for the shine and the beautiful ring of being called president and even without executing of any meaningful performance and services towards the country and the nation. That's a fact the SPLM/A - IO should know and should be ready to bargain with but with realistic trade-offs. The sad and dirty reality of making peace is that you got to sit on the peace negotiations table even with those who have murdered your very loves ones. None of us is feeling at ease with accepting that bitter reality, it is truly challenging.

However, peace is for the interest of South Sudanese people, not the very murderers of Dec 15th, 2013. The murderers are in positions of command and control, leadership and decision-making and pushing the innocent South Sudanese youth to perish in the fields of the senseless internal war. If it was an external war, it will be a constitutional duty for every South Sudanese to defend this land and nation. It is not. It is an internal war between sections of one nation, the more we get deep into it the more the very cohesive social and national fabric that constitutes this nation is but being destroyed. It is in power of Mr. Salva to make peace and stability in this country, he should save South Sudan by at least agreeing to retire after finishing his term and not to run for reelection and to pave the way for the changes that will put to rest the conflicting issues of governance system, resources and power sharing...etc.

However, the worst case scenario that may befall the innocent South Sudanese is that Juba may have already concluded and made up its mind that going along with the approach of establishing a full brutal dictatorship and the security state is the only solution that would make Salva and his Co. rule for life and opt to control the resources of South Sudanese with its weapons suppliers and oil allies and hence pushing the armed opposition and resistance to a no choice reality but the option of military solution. In either way, the exit strategy from this war is a no easy one, it sure needs skilled, willing and determined leadership that put South Sudanese future and destiny above all.

In conclusion, Mr. Kiir is in a visit to the US to attend the first of its kind

African heads of states summit with the US leadership. Most of us are questioning the credibility of USA, the leader of the free world, democracy and human rights. America has always been with the people of South Sudan and it will always be and for that sake it must approach even the worst dictators. If you don't know what is in the mind of a dictator, then definitely you won't be able to change his perceptions and concepts. Leadership is a school of thought not guns. By being here, Mr. Kiir might learns that it is the leadership that counts at the end.

## August 4, 2014
## In a Nutshell

Interesting that the troubled Africa continent heads of states are traveling all the way the long distance between Africa and US (8,766 miles) just to meet and collaborate with the most powerful man in the world, US president Barak Obama. That's really nice but truly controversial too at the same joint.

Obama, the first African American president in US history for sure don't want to go down and finish his almost-over second term without any major legacy toward Africa and Africans. A legacy that people could refers to when he is finally no longer a president, that's cool, irrespective of whether it is a temporary facelift move or a real approach that will have its short and long term impact on the usual status quo of the manmade misery and isolation of the African continent.

Hopes of the poor Africans may raise for now, that the isolated and troubled continent finally has got a rare blessing represented by this huge invite of those leaders who, for worse or good, are deemed the ones who should shape the state of affairs of African continent and its poor people. It is good for Africa to be viewed as a place worth of attention but this time it shouldn't be as a raw resources destination but as a place belongs to humans rocked by manmade long civil wars, famine, acute diseases and all the ugliest and miserable situations and conditions have ever emerged and lived by humans on this planet.

Where to direct the blame of the misery and downfall of Africa? To the leaders in the capacity of heads of states or to the colonialism that has physically left 60 years ago but its residue has been living there ever since in shadows and pretexts of economic, cultural and political influences.

If the US and the rest of the western world decided over night to change their old and traditional perception about Africa and the Africans, the state of affairs of this battered continent could also change the other day in all socio-economic and political aspects. They have the high technology and the resources and the knowledge of how to deliver real results whenever they are willing but is there any true and genuine will to change Africa and value the Africans? That's the question.

Africa and Africans are worthy of attention of the world, they are worthy of cost-effective long-term investment of the US and the rest of Western world. Mr. Obama is a great man, a change promoter in a very conservative world that still view Africa as forest of trees and monkeys and only as a source of raw materials. We know how huge the challenge he is facing is but at least he has tried and still trying. The western technology could transform Africa to be one of the vital trade and economic markets to US if not the whole world. The love for good stuffs is something installed deep within Africans, so why not invest in that.

What would the 40+ African heads of states says to America about human rights in their respective states, democracy, tribal genocides, insecurity, terrorism, economics development and political stability. They shouldn't say this here while doing that there. It is time for change.

Obama could be remembered by many African generations to come by drafting a long lasting real cost-effective contract with Africa. He could coordinate with the congress to sign into law a long term cost-effective economic and political contract with Africa that will transforms Africa and Africans and make Africa one of the vital market for America trade and goods. The 1.111 billion Africans are not an easy number to ignore that even China is working tirelessly to win.

## August 7, 2014

## In a Nutshell

Just as they have proudly endured that freezing cold and snowy day of July 9th, 2011 to cast their votes in South Sudan referendum, traveling and risking everything just to say yes to independence of a country they have sacrificed so much for.

Today is another repeat of that glorious day as South Sudanese in North America traveled the many miles from across all the states, enduring sleepless nights and many other hardships and headed to Washington DC, the capital of the free world to protest the mass killings of ethnic Nuer on December 15th, 2013 as a result of the infamous framed and fabricated coup.

As he was announcing his self-made failed coup attempt, dressed in full military fatigue that bloody night of Dec 15th, 2013 was Gen. Salva Kiir the man that is so well dressed in western suit today and being showered by great hospitality in DC. What a world!

The aftermath of this fabricated coup was a systematic mass murdering of Nuer ethnic people, humiliation and grave human rights abuse. Those who managed to escape, ended up as a refugee in their own homeland at UNMISS compounds.

Few months later, the big lie of fabricated coup faltered like no other. The cost was, 10s thousands lives lost, three full states flattened and leveled to ground, 1+ million South Sudanese either internally or externally displaced and a country so divided across ethnic lines. What a win?
It is far from luxuries of Washington politicians and Juba alike to just come close to comprehend the magnitude of damage that has been done to our people, they both lack what can divert their luxurious souls and minds to even come close to it or imagine to live a fact of a woman raped in front of her husband before they killed him while she was watching with her young children and finally they burnt her with her young children alive. Why do you think these protesters never slept while Gen. Salva is sipping Whiskey in DC and talking luxury politics? It is because they know and they have lived every angle of the near death and after death of their people, the Nuer.

As we speak, the targeted ethnic killings of Nuer are continuing and happening in Maban County by a proxy militia armed, funded and directed by Juba intelligence of Gen. Salva. A scenario of the killer David Yay Yau, who murdered thousands of Bor Dinka, Fangak and Lou Nuer under command of Juba dirty intelligence.

The US, Museveni and Gen. Salva might need to clear the skies on what they have in common against the Nuer. As to you my people, the Nuer, I know you are firm, unshaken and will definitely win, not only for yourselves but for the entire South Sudan, for a better country and a better nation.

**August 12, 2014**
**In a Nutshell**

Gen. Salva Kiir has offered Dr. Riek Machar leader of SPLM-IO, the position of 2nd vice president and declined offering him a position of prime minister, suggested by Troika and IGAD mediators to quell the fire of 7th month civil war.

The case is not about a prime minister or vice president, however, a functioning prime minister is better than a symbolic president and if the president title has become what should bring the heaven down than Mr. Kiir could keep it at least for the rest of his term and a functioning prime minister should execute the much needed services and duties of the government. This will create a checks and balances in the system and a route for accountability.

Unfortunately, Kiir and team strategy revolves around the seat of power in Juba and the system that's sustaining and feeding it. Interests groups who are making millions if not billions out of it are not seeing a need for change. They don't see a necessity for subtracting the vast and huge executive powers that has made the president a king without accountability. They don't see a need for critical reforms for a system that is not delivering but more underdevelopment, corruption and power abuse. They want peace accords that don't change anything around Juba but only peace accords such as Yau Yau-Kiir that is pleasant to accept. Peace accords that are not a threat to the throne of the king in anyway imagined.

What will a 2nd vice president does that the current vice president is not doing? Isn't that an insult itself to the person of Dr. Machar and to all the waged efforts of peace? Isn't that a declaration of war as the only path for attaining the needed reforms and restructuring? The structure of this country and its nation doesn't need a second vice president. We are one nation without those major differences in race or religion that could promote such a way of thinking. It is unacceptable and it doesn't solve the core problem which is the governance system that being taken advantage of by a privileged few.

The quest for fixing and restructuring our new country is brought onto the surface by the new realities of an independent state which require a necessary restructuring to address the issue of governance system, resources and power sharing between all the people of South Sudan and not between Dinka and Nuer or Machar and Kiir.

Dr. Machar in his capacity now as a chairman of SPLM-IO doesn't represent only Nuer or a movement seeking a cheap accommodation with Mr. Kiir crumbling system.

Dr. Machar, represents a national movement that is seeking serious reforms and critically needed restructuring of the state of South Sudan in all its socio-economic and political aspects that will lays down under a strong foundation for stable peaceful and prosperous one nation. Gen. Salva needs to be honest to himself, to people of South Sudan and his own kids' future and destiny. He doesn't have to see this critical need for change from the angle of his fears and ego being played by the opportunists that it is him, his seat of power in Juba and his tribe, region and so on that they are the ones being meant by the calls for change.

Dr. Machar has affirmed more than once that an interim government should be an outcome of final peace agreement that represents the new reforms and the restructuring agreed upon. Such an interim government should be a facilitator of the road map to those reforms and restructuring. Acknowledging the destructive nature of the current war he has been trying to convince Juba, IGAD and the international community through negotiations and diplomacy that what this country need is not accommodating of his person in Kiir government but a serious overhaul of country systems for the short and long term interests of its people, regional stability and world peace in general.

We need change, not government positions. The people who are in opposition now were high ranking officials in Kiir administration system for the last 8 years; if such a system was adequate and set to deliver they shouldn't be now in opposition. Through these 8 years they have given the system the benefit of the doubt, subdued their own mental queries and moral substance while watching the abuse of powers to the extreme, corruption, nepotism and much more.

In conclusion, to stop this war, Juba in person of Gen. Kiir need to take a much needed bold decisions to fix the state of South Sudan. A stable peaceful and prosperous South Sudan is never a result of sudden magic but a hard work of true national leadership, honest one at most.

**August 15, 2014**

**In a Nutshell**

Some says it is unconstitutional to remove a democratically elected president from the seat of power in Juba.

Well folks, the same constitution should have subjected the so-called elected president long time ago to impeachment/removal from the higher office in the land for higher crimes and misdemeanors.

He has committed mass murdering the very people who elected him and that is never less unconstitutional. He has subjected the whole country to a deadly famine, one of the worst in the world since 80s and that is never less unconstitutional.

He has committed grave violation of his constitutional mandate and that is never less unconstitutional. If South Sudan was being ruled by constitution and democratic norms we couldn't have arrived to a one-man rule and there could be no way to a one clan rule.

What constitution do we have any way that we are hearing about now and not during the removal of elected governors, mass murdering of a whole ethnic group and the whole unconstitutional mess that has landed us to a bloody civil war and earned us the title of first failed state in the whole world? What constitution and what democracy are of that sort? Some people need to look around and learn how a constitutional democracy is truly functioning.

Peace is a serious bargain and series of realistic tradeoffs. Gen Salva need to make a realistic concessions and compromises on the peace table. I do believe that will give a room for opposition to considers serious tradeoffs for peace to prevail in our country otherwise let us be ready to who will make a win in the battlefields after all this nation and country is no more

**August 17, 2014**
**In a Nutshell**

Sometimes we have to think about the future, about our young people who represents a new promising face in the world for South Sudan. The old folks surely are held strongly to their old worlds of tribal pride and egocentric ideas. Don't get me wrong, I don't mean that our young people don't need to know where they come from and where they should be heading but what I mean here is how to use the self and history conscious context toward a better South Sudan, a united and prosperous one.

You can't be a true leader without thinking about the future of your country and the future of your people. The youth are the future and we want to know where do the young people falls within the very thought of our leaders, Leaders who thinks about future generations do plans and acts responsibly, thinks progressively and work productively. They know their words and acts will either destroy or build the precious lives of young people who represent the future of the country.

As a true leader, you got to lays down a better world for them kids and young people, they got to lives in better world and living standards better than what the olds folks are now struggling with, a better socio-economic and political standards.

These young people are the future, and what they live and experience now are also the very trends that make a bright or a gloomy future for this nation and country. What is leadership than without changing lives to better? The young and youth need to make sure they have a leader who will secure, build and achieve their futuristic goals. They can't be the ones victimizing themselves by just following and choosing blindly. The consequences are undoubtedly dire and certain.

The positive trends that we have seen from young people and the South Sudanese youth in Diaspora and back home indicates a promising future in all aspects of human activities. South Sudanese who are getting their PhDs in 20s, engineers and scientists professionals who have proven themselves in world class institutions, Icons of music, arts, modeling and more who are conquering the world and enriching its diversity.

When it comes to future making, give to Caesar what is to Caesar and what to God to God. Giving ourselves the benefit of the doubt, we certainly should start with there is no such a thing as the future will fall from the sky. Our leader's needs plan for the future, work together to build it, make the collective wise decisions to shape the future for a great country and nation through the young people. That's possible and within reach.

If anyone of us claims to be fighting for this country to have a bright future, then these claims definitely void the very reasons we are fighting this disastrous war that is destroying the very future we talking about. One of us must be lying and doing the opposite. It is easy to spot the liars. Watch them whether they are delivering, providing the services the country needs, opening new developmental projects every time and then, laying down their short and long term visions and programs for the country and nation. We got to be real and lives real outcomes from these leaders through accountability and monitoring otherwise we the people, are the problem, we do not need to play with our lives and the future to satisfy none.


**August 22, 2014**

## In a Nutshell

The Juba government is supposed to be a government of South Sudan, a national government for all South Sudanese with all their diverse tribal, religious and political backgrounds and accordingly being a minority nor majority should not entitle you to a lessen rights neither a much privilege than others. This should be the least standard where we could expect a healthy foundation for a better nation and country where justice, equality and liberty are the underpinning ingredients of our union and success and not quite the contrary.

South Sudan is a country fought for and liberated not on the bases of who was a majority or minority but it was fought based on South Sudanese nationality regardless of any differences. If that wasn't the case, liberation heroes like Lokornayang and Dr. Paul Anade othow who came from minority tribes couldn't even have thought of being pioneers of liberation.

However, with all the ironic and controversy of it, the Juba government which says it is representing the historical great party, the SPLM, is ruling and running the country as a private entity. Juba is shamefully deciding what tribe to have the bones and which one to enjoy the meat, which tribe to be chased away of the country or forced to the UN protection and which one to stay and be protected by the government. Which one to have the right to be president, and the one to be cheated to be the first vice president and the other to be forced to have no choice but to submissively accept the imaginary second.

It is Juba that decides who to occupy the key ministries and whom to be assigned the deputies. So don't be surprised if they tell you federalism is a failure and that there is nothing like a decentralization system as a right governance form. Ironically, what was Khartoum doing before the independence to the Southerners that is indifferent to the current Juba dictatorship? Read the independent and international media headlines and compare with what was going on several years ago when Khartoum was fighting us, we are a no match to Khartoum now, we are the worst, in term of media censorship, human rights abuse and security crackdown on freedoms.

What happened to SPLM patriotism in which we believed in for the last 30 years? How dare a SPLM co-founder and its mission and vision flag bearer simply came to have the very thought of finishing his people instead of liberating them? Do political differences and rivalries between the SPLM leaders justify a mass murdering of an ethnic group in which a certain leader belongs? How did they resist the allure of Khartoum money if they couldn't resist the booming money of their own oil?

Were the SPLM leaders trained? Were there strict principles, values and rules that guide the work and conduct of the members and in particular the leaders in sensitive positions? Is there any clear punishment and accountability procedures? I believe there were none otherwise we could have saved this country the innocent lives we have lost for the last six months. Don't all these questions indicate a serious vacuum in the substance and practice on which this promising country was being run by, a vacuum in the SPLM constitution, political substance, vision and mission?

If there were independent institutions that were working separately from the influence of the executive authority, the Dec 15th, 2013 Juba massacre could have been avoided and prevented, the corruption could have not passed through, the nepotism could have been stopped short and ashamed. But there was none. They were all presidents' men institutions, men that were appointed by the president and doing not necessarily what the president says and wants but it is still your responsibility Gen. Kiir. You can't let your car be driven by a reckless driver if you care about the consequences in the first place.

The status quo cannot persist. Change and reforms must be made for this country to be saved. Changes and reforms in the state political structure, governance system, changes in the political parties' substance and serious reforms in military and state security bodies. Change must be the norm until we have straightened this whole mess up and right.

**August 26, 2014**
**In a Nutshell**

I am just here to speculate; I am not for whether Dr. Riek the leader of SPLM/A-IO should sign the IGAD proposed peace document or whether he shouldn't. Neither am I here to tell you that Gen. Salva is honest or not in his offer of Prime Minister post and the federalism through the proposed transitional government.

I am here trying to speculate on the realities of peace or war on the ground that decides which option is more realistic, cost-effective and saves lives in the objective of Kiir must go. Yes, Kiir must go; most of us agree on that but how and when, it is where we do differ.

You have the military option, defeat Kiir/Uganda and Sudanese mercenaries militarily or you got to opt to mechanism process option that should led to "free and fair" elections where the people of South Sudan will decide to dump Kiir or keep him for another bloody year.

The choice definitely falls upon the armed opposition more than any other unarmed opposition whether they will accept the proposed peace or continue with the military option putting in mind the consequences and weighing the possibilities of winning in the battlefields or through ballots box is what should define their next move.

Dr. Riek and his crew should not be lured in as Rally Odinga of Kenya or the one in Zimbabwe MDC case, where everything at the end consolidated itself back to dictatorship, this need to be different and real transition. Either way, South Sudanese will need to learn how to make peace through brains and guts and not through destructive violence, it is them who are dying in both sides of an internal war.


**August 28, 2014**
**In a Nutshell**

A concerned friend asked me whether Dr. Riek Machar has done the right thing by not signing the proposed peace document by IGAD and my replied was strongly YES he did and he did so out of his sincere concerns on how a real and everlasting peace should be brought and negotiated. A shaky and non-inclusive peace that doesn't address the roots causes of this war is just another war being stored to be fought in future. We can't afford that, honestly this nation is tired of wars and we need this one to be the last, God willing.

Peace and war trends don't come from nowhere, they are definitely part of the human individual upbringing or nature and for that individual to be in a position of being a leader of a country and a nation, the impact is not anymore stands at scope of that individual personal damage when it comes to war or benefits in peace case, it is a collective nation-country effects and aftermath. Hence comes the importance of leadership decisions, ideas and behaviors. Dr. Riek has just done that.

But still we the general public are speculating whether this peaceful, highly educated man will truly decide to take his nation back to full scale war and mercilessly wage a destructive war in order to bring a one man down in Juba, that's a one challenge or will he with the same high caliber and peace loving mindset reconcile with the untold damage and loss of lives of his very people and accept to sign the document that is another terrible challenge. However, Dr. Machar still in a very critical historical spot here, whether he opts to sign the document or not, the decision of war or peace is still upon him, well, take it or leave it, that's what it means to be a leader.

We all acknowledge that the IGAD document is imposed and not a result of the two parties' negotiations. However, IGAD has given itself the right to impose what it sees as the least compromises and tradeoffs that can be accepted by both warring parties and its excuse here is that the warring parties are reaching nowhere in the last six month of face-to-face negotiations. It worth noting that IGAD has no mandate or power to remove Kiir militarily at least for now, neither Kiir is expected to give up power voluntarily but in fact he has shown readiness to fight and ascend to power until this country is no more.

The case of Dr. Riek is not a restoration of a lost job as some are preaching but a quest for serious reforms and restructuring of the state and its institutions and a work of professional is really needed here and in the context of current IGAD peace document. The CPA that delivered South Sudan was also an IGAD document and with that in mind, how the current one can be made trustworthy, authenticated and workable document is also possible. The objective here is to save this country and nation from a sure complete disintegration and collapse, more war brings us all to a point of no return. The opposition has a golden chance to work around the document, reduce the excessive executive powers of the president and channel them to the projected prime minister post and put Kiir in a corner where he is with fewer powers and a possibility of not winning the next projected elections.

Assurances of international community, UN and others are needed. Practical guarantees, realistic measures and monitoring can pave the way for a peaceful transition. All peace documents are work in progress; there are more that can be adds-on to the document to make it an inclusive and trustworthy. Otherwise get ready to remove one man militarily on the expenses of an innocent country and a nation, a scenario of Syria and Iraq in the soil of South Sudan and devastate a nation that has nothing to do with what Juba is all up to, an option that I don't recommend to the peaceful and highly educated Dr. Riek Machar that I know, sincerely.

**August 31, 2014**
**In a Nutshell**

The ordinary citizens who has no interest at all in chaotic type of politics in Africa should also be entitled to the right of protection, safety and peace. There is a need for a new definition of politics, its scope and its objectives in African states. African politicians have missed the point and are giving themselves the right to destroy everyone and the whole country in order to advance their own agenda. Politicians are no gods and hence are their visions, they are liable to fail until proven otherwise and accordingly they don't worth destroying the whole life.

Are African politicians above the law or considers they are the law itself? Is the destruction of public properties and murdering civilians a good cause or a crime punishable by law? Aren't there limits for what a politician and politics should be all about? Should politics be allowed to dictate the demise of the whole and interfere with public safety and national security when it is heading in destructive means and not peaceful and democratic tools?

Shouldn't the police and security organs be completely independent from politics? Aren't they for protection of every citizen and their properties regardless of any political background, ethnic or any discriminating ground at all? Is it right to victimize the whole in the name of politics? I think there should be a playground for politics, scope, objectives and limitations as well. There is a need to draw a line between crime and politics and there even a stronger need to brand criminals from true politicians with a good cause, the mentally sick from the sound minded.

Countries don't advance only by cheap talks but mainly by hard work in a peaceful environment, chaotic politics is doing the contrary and not every gossip monger is a politician or every gossip house a political party. Wake up Africa.

## September 1, 2014
## In a Nutshell

Kiir can be removed either by military victory or negotiated early elections. A call for early elections will definitely not remove Kiir immediately but until defeated in the said elections. The SPLM/A -IO need not to negotiate with Kiir if it is not ready to compromise with this option. If its ultimate goal is removal of Kiir from power without any compromises, then military victory over Kiir forces and allies is the only option realistic to that objective.

Military victory over Kiir and allies is not far achievable; it is within reach, costly, time and lives consuming but it worth it all. In my last previous in nutshell opinion I have argued the peaceful and highly educated Dr. Riek Machar not to opts for a destructive war in order to remove a one man from power in the expenses of all South Sudanese, I have also argued that opposition can turn that IGAD imposed document to a more sophisticated process to remove Kiir from power in a peaceful manner. How? This is what can be negotiated, detailed and initiated as process of removing Kiir from power even though such a process has no guarantees as well but it is also worth a try. Kenya and Zimbabwe are good example that didn't work but South Sudan circumstances might be different.

Otherwise, let the SPLM/A -IO pack and leave Addis Ababa and prepare itself for the fight in the bushes of South Sudan. It doesn't matter how costly and long it shall take as long as it is the only realistic choice left to bring the desired change. A new strategy to win over Kiir and allies is also needed; the capture/recapture of cities is not the goal. A strategy that ought to bring Kiir down should be better than that.

The decision is left over to SPLM/A-IO, they got to weigh the pros and cons of waging a lengthy war, the possibilities of victory, the consequences of a possible defeat and all that, you got to do the math and do it accurately. Having the big picture in mind, the suffering people, the displaced in UNMISS compounds, the hardy stricken famine populace and the million that toke refuge here and there, their lives and future is all at shattered roads.

Managing a war is a full time task, it is not only what occurs in the battlefields but it is mainly about the people you claim to be fighting for and how they will survive the long haul, and nothing can be left to a chance in a so ethnically driven war.

## September 5, 2014
## In a Nutshell

Still the great country that South Sudanese dreamed about and fought for is not the one Gen. Kiir is on top of it. Neither the march and the fight towards that dream will ever stop, there will be ups and downs in the process but victory is certain with the will of our people and the fact that we the Nilotic people never settled for injustice nor a rule of dictator is strongly evidenced.

The disappointing fact and the irony of it all is that the liberation revolution that we so much trusted and given all of what we have in the last 30 yrs. was stolen and shifted to the same point of departure to the bushes of South Sudan from Khartoum 30 years ago. The reasons are apparently the same, brutal dictatorship, socio-economic and political injustices, discrimination and marginalization of all sorts. In short, in the course of the 3 decades of bitter struggle, we came to the sad realization that we were fighting for our own sad demise, unfortunately.

ANC of South Africa was a true champion and inspiration of most African liberation movements that emerged in that time and so was the SPLM/A and the countless South Sudanese who left everything to join the liberation drive. The sacrifices during the decades of struggle were huge and unparalleled. However, until recently, the cause was so noble and worth it all and none of us have ever doubted that.

SPLM/A, how a national liberation movement could shamefully shrink in her national objectives and duties, nation-state building obligations and programs to just become a hub of greedy individual interests, tribal and sectional driven tool of domination and clowns of foreign greed and interests that is the hit of the lower-human in us.

How the liberation revolution and the men, who championed it, led it and sacrificed lives and everything went awry and strayed the direction and the cause of liberation is what is killing us the most. How the movement that was talking about liberation of all Sudan and Africa became the one eliminating its very people in the name of tribe and clans that is what is truly sickening

All indicators point to the bitter fact that this is not the country and the state about 3 million precious souls sacrificed the dear life for. From the then deformed Sudan, much sick society and a harsh socio- economic and political system to even a more fragile state, warring society, poverty and socio-economic political standards that are even harsher. Agree or not, that can never be a cause of people in their right minds and consciousness.

## September 15, 2014
## In a Nutshell

With its ceasefire monitors on the ground, the threats of sanctions on the warring parties are just a click away and an imposed peace proposal that has been widely criticized as impartial and pro- Kiir government, IGAD seem to has successfully neutralized the armed opposition while feeding them what Kiir only can eat.

How the SPLM/A in Opposition will free itself from this deadlocked and standstill situation is merely a matter of speculations and discussion. First there is not going to be a return to full scale war without freeing itself from whatever IGAD has put in place and the readiness to bear the looming consequences. Second, leaving negotiations venue and going back to war zones which you might just return to it again to find the same peace proposals proposed now is also impractical and might be counterproductive militarily and politically as well. Third, accepting the proposed IGAD document without serious work is even worse and might fire back at its leadership immediately from its victimized anger popular and military base.

Strategically, the SPLM/A in Opposition should not lose it temper now and rush to war, let its explore the remaining possibilities of fixing the IGAD document or bringing forth its drafted version of peace document in the next round of talks. Let it addresses in a more specific fashion the time and space limits of Gen. Kiir role, federalism and the rest of reforms. Thereafter, the SPLM/A IO might need to address the South Sudanese people and declare finally whether it is fed up with fruitless negotiations and is opting to military option.

With Juba moving at ease in the political corridors of IGAD behind the scene meetings, it is likely that whatever IGAD produces and proposes is a product of Kiir & friends carefully discussed and articulated towards Kiir longer stay in power and not necessarily South Sudanese people interests or SPLM/A-IO political gains.

Juba also has a role to play, if it decided to work positively, it can break the deadlocked political situation by moving closer to embrace the critical reforms and restructuring of South Sudanese state proposed by SPLM-IO. These are needed reforms to upright the systems underpinning the troubled nation and county of ours. It is only opportunists that throws stones at the reformists and not deliberately acknowledges the critical need for state restructuring just to protect their selfish interests.

The thousands of South Sudanese who joined the armed opposition, the millions and half who fled the country will not just return because of a fake calls for peace without realistic and permanent change in the state political and security structures. This is not about giving Dr. Riek Machar his seat back as Mr. Wani Igga is preaching and marketing it big these days, this is about a popular based change.

Accordingly, a shift in IGAD understanding to the root causes of the conflict will help in driving Kiir to embrace the reforms and sees the ever necessity of overhauling the state and its ailing institutions. Insisting that this is about Dr. Machar vying for a role in Kiir government is the worst crime against the South Sudanese people aspirations. IGAD shouldn't champion a quick political settlement between individual politicians that will not bring everlasting peace but instead it should initiate a process long peace and stability based on true reforms and restructuring of state and in which only everyone can be bought back to peace and unity.


**September 17, 2014 ·**
**In a Nutshell**

South Sudan is our country, all of us South Sudanese. Our martyrs from all walks of life and all diverse backgrounds has bravely fought and sacrificed the dear life just for this beautiful country to be independent and its great people to be free, lives in dignity, peace and honor.

Out of love to this great people and this beautiful country I have seen concerned citizens criticizing their leaders and leadership, institutions and systems underlying our very state and society and the general assumption is that, most of us if not all wants or dreams about a great society and country. Well, this doesn't mean we don't have few among us who out of malice and ill intents are internally working to add more salt on our nation wounds.

Well, that's how it is, imperfect world, we have to work on the good side and stay hopeful.

A great country and a great nation is all we dream about but how to achieve that is what we thought our leaders has in mind. However, we have discovered that the leaders to whom we placed our high hopes and trust has for reason or another strayed from the road map of our expectations and hopes, hence we abruptly out in disappointments, frustrations and fears and accordingly, the endless spiral of the blame game and pointing fingers has become the norm, sometimes with good intents and sometimes not.

However, all these cries and signs of criticism, frustrations and disappointments point to the fact that this nation is a great nation, its cries and its various ways of expressing itself tell it all, it reflects greatness of a nation with a great expectations and our leaders shouldn't have misunderstood it by seizing the nation freedoms, liberties and human rights abuses. In fact, they could use these indicators to transforms this nation to its best. I believe the key for good leadership is the deep and accurate understanding of whom being led.

The fact is that the people of South Sudan after all the lengthy struggle and the huge sacrifices they have paid for up to 50 years, haven't expected their leaders to be evils nor ignorant neither self-centered cliques. However, criticism and accountability are good trends of a nation and if our leaders really care and listen to what their people says they could have benefited a lot, they could have known what their nation truly expects from them and what they need do to achieve their dreams and aspirations. Leaders belong to people, chosen by people and should works for the people. South Sudanese leaders were once in history, the pioneers in feeling the very pulse of their suffering people, what happened?

Our leaders need to come down to the ordinary people, to those being led and to whom the leadership is all about and if they do really cares then I believe there never a disagreement or political conflict greater than the happiness, peace and prosperity of those being led.


**September 23, 2014 ·**

**In a Nutshell**

Just as we had the courage and resolve to endure the 50 years of bitter struggle, the loss of about three million dear and precious lives we might need to have the same courage again to save our country and nation from total collapse and complete disintegration. It is worth noting that some of this world countries' population don't even exceed three million but that was our recent lost between 1983- 2005, just imagine!

I have no answer how the community and the families of those who were murdered cowardly in this senseless war will finally reconcile with this deep lost and grave injustice done to them by once a man they elected or viewed as liberation war hero neither I have an answer to whether the man (Kiir) will relinquish power voluntarily or if he will be militarily ousted from power in the near future.

I only and truly doubt if South Sudan at the moment will be able to reconcile itself to be at peace, unity and prosperity again without an honest and genuine outsider help. I am sure that within battered members of this nation lives a true sorrow, mistrust and wanton to avenge as well as I know that some already have seized the opportunity to stretches their greedy selves along with their regional and international backers.

December 15th, 2013 is a terrible wound that will continue bleeding deep in our hearts and souls. South Sudanese need above average courage and resolve to overcome this deep wound. South Sudan at this very juncture needs its true and genuine regional and international friends to help bring her up from the deep sad ocean. I am afraid it won't be able to pick up herself by her own.

A lot of faith based work might need to be done in the long term process of healing and reconciliation. Hope and faith are only our redeemers, let us keep them alive. A brighter and stronger South Sudan may emerge tomorrow, hopefully.


**September 28, 2014 ·**
**In a Nutshell**

There you go again the fabricated coup still the corner stone of everything as Gen. Kiir tells the UN general assembly that whatever happened on December 15th, 2013 from the well calculated ethnic massacres in Juba to all death and destruction triggered by it was but an aftermath of foiled coup championed by the then his VP Dr. Riek Machar. Well, I knew it that there anything else Mr. President could tell the gathered world but to find someone else to blame for the country failure in which he is the president.

Mr. President and his supporters couldn't afford to drop the coup narrative and never will them. Simply because the series of grave crimes against humanity committed under the pretext of this infamous fabricated coup will definitely bring them to face the ultimate international justice. Crimes against humanity that range from deliberate plans of genocide to all the humans abuses and ethnic based atrocities committed since Dec 15th, 2013 up to the moment. However, Mr. president and supporters has forgot many dots in their narrative of this coup and hence whether Juba insists there is a coup or not it is likely not Juba narrative that will void or validate the case neither it is the one that will make them run away with all the heinous crimes committed under it. The international justice system will still get to the bottom of it at no Juba time or favor.

To refresh the memory of Mr. president and those who drafted the UN letter to him that the world nowadays is a small interconnected village and that the sequence of events that led to Dec 15th, 2013 are obvious and in fact they are well known to ever concerned member state of the UN leave alone the concerned human rights agencies or all the human rights watch dogs. The fact that there was never a coup that has been condemned by the world and that have been denied by many credible external sources and members states of the UN should have whispered something in the ears of Juba before they come to UN with the coup narrative but well at less if they have got ears for truth.

Mr. Machar has strongly denied he planned a coup, the SPLM former detainees were detained based on the fabricated coup and yet to be released later as lack of evidence that there was no coup. So why would this coup re-emerge again at the UN general assembly address? Undoubtedly, weighing accountability and the consequences of omitting the coup narrative versus going all the way with it to the UN, the president and supporters has preferred the later and to face the world with it, seriously.

On the other hand, Mr. President requested the UNMISS to review its new mandate and he also affirmed his commitment to sit, negotiate and compromise with the rebels. If this isn't for politics than Mr. President himself is one and who have done the coup against democracy and damaged the relations with UNMISS and in the same time asking why they have changed their mandate. The president UN address doesn't help the peace efforts; in fact, it just has taken the whole thing back to square one should the opposition fire back with the same madness as well.

**October 1, 2014**

**In a Nutshell**

It is a long road for South Sudan to be a healthy country and society as long as we have this sick leadership around. One's couldn't expect the people of South Sudan to be at war after only three years of their hard won independence. The 20+ years of civil war with North Sudan has already traumatized the South Sudanese beyond any doubts. It was a lengthy bitter suffering that has engraved mental and psychological scars that no conscious leadership that would choose at will to ignore, yet the peaceful people of South Sudan are set again on a terrible path of tribal hatred, vengeance and revenge by their own leaders. This is more than too much for a normal human being to bears and takes.

Anyone who can fly his/her simple imagination over the general situation of our people at UNMISS compounds, neighboring refugees camps and the whole picture of our people at home and in Diaspora will never fail to feel and live the deep frustration and agonies of all sorts that our people are enduring albeit you see the irony of some sick to the core leaders playing political cards that make you wonder where they truly came from, what give them this so much defiance and power while seeing their people dying day and night.

However, these should be good lessons to the people of South Sudan who always judges its leaders by covers. if they have ever learned from this, choosing and electing a leader by this time should be a careful and delicate process that must be used wisely, well at least if there is any opportunity or a system that would ensure such a process since what in the minds of Juba political elite is unpredictable given the fact that most East African dictators stayed for more than quarter a century in power and why such allure wouldn't entertain the guts of Wenna Mayardit and Co., stay awake in case you got surprised.

The people of South Sudan needs leaders who should work for its aspirations, higher interests of unity, peace and prosperity not leaders who come and proclaims themselves to be life-long rulers on the skulls and bones of the people they are ruling nor leaders who plays with all divisive cards in order to maintain power and political glory. The fact is, politics is a multi-layer's game as politicians themselves and with self-interest layer as the last to be shown and talked about, it is easy to pick up the likes of who are stabbing the very people on the back today, choose wisely.

**October 6, 2014**
**In a Nutshell**

A long lasting peace and stability in South Sudan are never easy to be achieved and maintained due to many intertwined factors that our leaders or political parties fails miserably to address or tend to ignore at will because they are either great windows for political exploitation or stored cards for political opportunism to be used later.

However, a stable and peaceful South Sudan is good for the innocent people of South Sudan but it is not to the internal and external beneficiaries of our conflict. A deal between Dr. Riek Machar and Gen. Salva Kiir is not seen as good for everyone as the rest may think and it is only the political naive that could think that a non-inclusive peace deal will reins everyone in. Third parties who any peace deal may fail to include are all prying in disguise and with their weapons ready waiting to kill every hope and window for peace whenever there is a potential one. Those third parties are also Juba's many tails and heads, using them as tools for political gains and tribal revenges.

Peace will be truly reached when Juba is ready and serious about it and hence it will stop sponsoring all the political and violence games that it is using to gains space and time. But here is a fundamental fact, Juba will never be serious if its core power and interests are threatening by any proposals or terms of any upcoming political settlement but in fact will continue to play here and there until it win politically or militarily. Such a game could be a dangerous bargain too that can jeopardy everything if the SPLM/A-IO has in the process came to a complete conclusion that Juba can't be trusted anymore. As long as Juba feels its core power and interests base is threatening, the game is on.

Whether he chooses to clink on power or honestly decided to rescue his people and country, Gen. Kiir has undeniable and a critical role to play. Should he decide, he can bring all his political spoilers back to their minds and sense and with Makuei Lueth and Gordon Buay in the forefront, these spoilers are not playing a game of their own but the King's himself and whenever the King says enough is enough, trust me all these spoilers in a no time should come to a halt.

Should he decide, that enough is enough; Gen. Kiir still can work honestly with Dr. Riek Machar, Dr. Lam Akol and all the political power players in our country to put our country again into path of peace, reconciliation, development and prosperity. Should he decide, the Uganda question and all the external players have no power over the sovereignty of our great country.

However, here are the questions and speculations, Does Mr. Kiir really own his decision making ability? Is he consistent and trustworthy in that? Is Kiir truly willing to step down voluntarily or is he willing to trade power in order for his country to reconcile? Should he run for re-election if Machar is given that same right? Will he agree to share his vast presidential power with the newly suggested prime minister? If no is the answer to most of these questions, then Kiir's game is on.

Given the current conflict of interest and mistrust between the two SPLM factions, the new Premier must by default be the chairman of SPLM/A-IO unless he declined, must have the right to stand for next elections and not necessarily should be subject to Kiir's approval nor he can't be removed by the president at any circumstances during the interim period. The post 2018 elections arrangements need also be addressed in the current peace negotiations. South Sudan arrival to true peace and stability is a long process in which every phase is a timing bomb that could explode anytime, should Gen. Kiir through his spoilers decide to do so. Hopefully not.


## October 6, 2014

## In a Nutshell

If you want victory, then one need not cool his fears with rosy illusions rather than one need lives the harsh realities on the ground and confronts the facts no matter how bitter or sad they might be. Your true enemies are the ones giving you the sense of false victory and keeping you happy and all smiles through lies not the ones telling you the real situation or the bitter realities surrounding you. Lies are like drugs, sooner or later all will fade away and you have to face the truth that you never wanted to confront.

If you lie on your own yard that's your problem but liars in powerful and leadership places are not dangerous and risky to themselves alone but to the whole fate of a country and a nation. Ironically, Liars in bright clothes of politicians are the ones also attracts the poor populace of Africa with false promises of development, construction, liberation and so on which sooner than later will just crumble on their heads. If we only knew that people were corrupts or that they will turns later to be dictators or worse than we couldn't have elected them but instead we could have opted to a better choice.

The thing is truth itself in African politics has become a stupidity and those who are asking or searching for it are seen or deemed as such, and accordingly the whole thing is all about big liars hiring other subordinate ones in a never ending cycle of lies. Hence the truth of life itself is lost in this terrible mess otherwise what would justify the thousands of lives murdered for no apparent reasons at all rather than that life itself in that corner of ours has become cheaper than nothing. In this new Africa, it is the lies backed by money not the poor truth that's shaping everything, that's the so called new smart Africans. These new breeds are burying Africa alive and with them in it altogether just for a bunch of few dollars.

So don't wonders anymore why we have ended this way in less than three years of our independence. It is simply because those who were supposed to be the founders and the framers of our nation and country foundation were never true to the core values of the liberation movement, they have abandoned the people who were supposed to be the sole objective of the liberation at any given time and space. They have gone to the world of false power, money and fame, stabbing their people on the back, unfortunately

## October 8, 2014
## In a Nutshell

South Sudan MPs should do the right thing by rejecting or seriously reviewing the proposed national security bill. The right thing is that the president is not above the law neither he should and hence the national security, police and all the armed law enforcement should swear obedience to country's constitution not necessarily the president who may use them to intimidate, jail and murder his political opponents and power rivals without any chance for fair investigations or trials.

The vast powers given to secret police and national security officers to arrest without warrant, with or without solid evidence but mere suspicions, grudges and malice which mostly will be politically or tribally or even personally motivated is a dangerous precedent and a gloomy future for everyone except Kiir himself. Such a bill if enacted, it is certainly that only Kiir himself will be safe in this country and not anyone else including the national security officers themselves, the MPs or the bill architects in disguise.

On the peace front it is absurd and irresponsible indeed that the government is suggesting the venue of peace negotiations to be taken to Kenya and the head of IGAD appointed mediators be replaced. What would that change? Will that subtract any demands for the suggested reforms or restructuring of our country and its government institutions, constitution and systems. It is not likely, it is just a waste of time and frustrated attempt to derail the peace efforts. What this government need is not a venue change but an entire change in heart and concept and with that only it will be able to bring peace and make itself fit to reconcile with its people before its neighbors.

As for the powers of the suggested Prime Minister (PM) position it shouldn't surprise anyone that the government will be reluctant to give any compromises or allocate some of the vast powers of Mr. Kiir to the suggested PM post. While the president should remain the head of the state and with PM as the head of government, many intertwined rights, duties and relations between the two has yet to be delicately and accurately sorted and worked out, given the current mistrust and conflict of interest, it is likely any failure to address those grey areas will result in jeopardizing the whole process.

A stable system of governance with real checks and balances is all what South Sudan need, it shouldn't be done for the sake of an individual interest but for this entire nation and country, its future generations, peace and prosperity. The fundamental fact is that, if we put everything right in this negotiations then we have done a great service to our country and nation and no one in coming generations should be subject to such a brutal war as the current one we are burning with, not in near or far future.

## October 16, 2014
## In a Nutshell

With regional and international players' eyes' prying on what could be the potential of this resource-rich new nation, the current internal conflict of South Sudan is a possibly to be one of worse African dilemma. The current tribal leadership of Gen. Kiir is a great liability working towards that direction, an agent of a new kind of colonialism.

The greatest interest of South Sudan is its people staying united and this is also where its peace, stability and prosperity lies. Any internal, regional or international power that contradicts with that cannot be described as patriot or friend. Mr. Kiir leadership has brought Uganda to help him survive the consequences of his own failed leadership, to help him kill his own people even through the use of cluster bombs and accordingly.

With Kiir regime dependent as it is, Uganda has found a fertile land to exploits to the maximum. Uganda and its South Sudanese Ugandans and international allies wish to see South Sudan a failed state, pitting the two major tribes against each and keeping that alive, why not, since it is the biggest the investment ever.

Uganda in its renewed military accord with the government of Kiir will continue to arms Kiir's Army to teeth while in the same time brokering a peace as an IGAD member. Where is the true interest of Uganda here if one may ask? The war itself is an internal one and has been known to the world as an ethnic based. What ground does IGAD members don't see to bring Uganda back from its greedy madness?

Mr. Machar is facing enormous challenges gaining any serious regional backer that could make Museveni rolls his greedy sleeves back. Sudan itself is not interested in either side of South Sudanese conflict to be a winner, it is in its interest for these old enemies to finishes themselves to death leave alone the Abyei issue and other unsettled borders disputes. Ethiopia has a neutral stand in most African politics that doesn't go further than her own prioritized internal interests.

Mr. Machar might need a more active regional policy in order to win for his movement a permanent ally should the war persists and peace efforts fails which is more likely than for him declaring Kiir a winner. Kiir himself has been working hard for the last three years not to have a serious regional enemy which is also another indicator that this war was not accidental but a planned one with Uganda at its core depth.

Internally, the recent targeting killing of Nuer ethnics in Malakal, a repeated scenario of Maban killings must not be taken slightly. Mr. Kiir first objective is to keep the greater Upper Nile divided in its leadership as well as its people and hence the recent kidnapping and cold blood killings in the name of Chollo vs. Nuer, does falls in that context. The political game of wenna Mayardit might not be an easy one for some to comprehend, it is tricky, the guy was a professional intelligence officer and if you know a bit of that world, you will know exactly how wenna Mayardit and his killing tools operates at large. Be Aware.

**October 21, 2014**
**In a Nutshell**

This has been always my personal assumption on Dr. Riek Machar, that the man has no intention or logical stand in his educational mind nor in his large intellectual capacity to see his people suffering due to a war he can stop or bring to halt and that he will do all that in his capacity, politically and diplomatically, to see South Sudan make it through this disastrous bloody conflict. I have always said in previous nutshell opinions that the math of making peace is not an easy one especially when you are the victim and your very people are the ones that has paid the utmost price of this whole madness. Thumbs up to Dr. Machar for defeating self and making South Sudan a winner.

I do feel and understand the voices of rejection of any peace or unification of the SPLM/A while Salva still president of South Sudan, I understand the feeling of injustice and anger in Nuer community and Greater Upper Nile region at large in particular, they are the ones who have paid so dearly in this whole madness for no apparent reasons of their own neither the outcomes of this war does frame any clear vision or foundation that those who have died didn't die in vain or did so for noble reasons.

I also understand those who are still determined on other side of the coin, the side of Mr. Salva, those who want the war to persist until the other region or tribe are no more, they are working to make things even worse as their regions haven't seen anything of this war at all while they are the victimizers, the perpetrators, the planners and presumed winners in this whole madness. Salva is still in his seat, they now constitute 90% of the government after Dec 15th, 2013, their region is hardly reached by this whole madness or its acute effects, and it is all Upper Nile lost.

Accordingly and upon this unbalanced math, some in the opposition says, this is not a math of peace and justice rather than a math of injustice, defeat and surrender and hence it is better to continue the fight until Salva Kiir and his regime are no more and hence if the push towards peace and unification of SPLM/A with Gen. Salva in leadership continue, defections are predicted within the SPLM/A-IO, the hardliners and the die-hards has it that they could even consider sidelining Dr. Riek Machar from the leadership if necessary.

I agree that the math of peace must be through justice and accountability. I also do believe that Dr. Machar just like anyone of us who doesn't want

South Sudan to slip down into abyss and disintegrate into more Somalization and more fragmentation is suppressing his own feelings and putting the interest of South Sudan and its people above all. His choices and decisions as I assume, are based on deep and accurate analysis, reading and forecasting of the future of both this nation and this country if the war persists. Given all these greedy internal, regional and international players involved in this conflict, weighing the costs, the consequences and the dire outcomes, South Sudan might need to be saved now and not tomorrow and I doubt that it is Juba who can do that.

Leadership is a huge responsibility, where you take the heat, blame and criticism even if you are doing the right thing. The fact is, there is no too many solutions to South Sudan crisis if we realistically narrowed them down, we will find exactly the same working solution that is possible as an exit to our current dilemma and hence, we may just need enough courage and honesty to tell ourselves, this is it. Cheating ourselves into illusions is never a good and useful option. However, the process mechanism must include all restructuring of the state and its institutions, accountability, justice for all the lives and properties lost, reconciliation and healing.

## October 25, 2014
## In a Nutshell

If they were wise enough, the SPLM/A leadership that was given credits and reputation for driving this nation and country to freedom and independence could have kept the power for itself unparalleled by any political rival, be it a political party or a politician outside the inner circle of SPLM/A powerful elite.

If they have chosen to be consistently faithful in executing the post-independence agenda of second phase of liberation which is the successful transformation of these diverse warring tribes and this just out of war poor country into stable, peaceful and prosperous nation and country respectively, they could have kept themselves in that glorious place of power and glory for decades if not centuries.

But how did the SPLM/A missed this golden chance and missed likewise the right road to successful nation and state building right from start? Did the ruling party have any clear vision and strategy of transformation and development, short or long term that was supposed to be executed, implemented to transform the country and nation into a viable state? Was the ruling party aware of the points of weakness and strength of our nation structure and how to use them to assist it in successful nation building? Some says the mission and vision of the party have died with the sudden and untimely departure of its founder and first leader Dr. John Garang, but whether this claim is true or not, isn't it right to say the vision and mission of a political party shouldn't be necessarily linked to individual life span more than it is the party long term programs of transformation at any time and space and hence it shouldn't go down with the departure of its leaders.

Whom to blame for the failed state and nation building, Gen. Salva Kiir or the collective SPLM leadership? Well, this or that, it is the SPLM that has failed as a ruling party collectively and I give them credit for accepting the responsibility of this current civil war and for all the innocent lives lost and destruction in the name of tribes and clans. Innocent people have died in their 10s thousands, all the Greater Upper Nile States are leveled to ashes, a million and more displaced internally, a million uprooted to foreign lands, hunger, diseases and famine are all finishing the ordinary South Sudanese on daily bases. What is the way forward, war until the Kiir and his regime is no more or peace and power sharing with Kiir?

How many lives and destruction will it cost to remove Kiir and Uganda from power? When removed from power(Kiir) it will be his turn to be a rebel and I wonder how many South Sudanese will be dead by then and what will be the shape of already poor South Sudan state and nation? You do the math and send your imagination a little bit further.

There is no easy way to bring South Sudan back to normalcy, peace and unity to its people once more time, but if we are wise enough, all of us, we will have to choose the one that's less costly and probably the right one that will bring us all back from this unnecessary madness. It is the SPLM that brought the whole house down to ashes and it is the SPLM that should bring and reconstruct it back, we don't have a choice. But SPLM must apologize to South Sudanese people first, it must repent, it must redeem and reposition itself to be a true champion of people aspirations. The South Sudanese people must be compensated, healed, reconciled and repositioned to a new brighter direction of peace, unity and prosperity.

**October 31, 2014**
**In a Nutshell**

The perception of some South Sudanese leaders towards Diaspora South Sudanese is fundamentally wrong and hurting the country really badly. Such perception and concepts culminated recently by VP Wani Igga statement about possibility of banning dual citizenship and accusing the Diaspora of lack of patriotism are another attempt to sidelines an important asset of skilled human resources the country could benefits from if it finds the friendly and understanding leadership.

I wish our leaders could have resend their minds back a little bit and recall how did the hundreds of thousands South Sudanese became refugees in foreign lands in the first place, I wish they could just imagine the bitter struggle the diasporas have endured to finally settled themselves in a highly demanding skilled and advanced societies of Western world, I wish they could honestly acknowledge the huge financial and political contribution the Diaspora has offered before South Sudan came to light as an independent country.

Just like the current dilemma, the mass exodus of South Sudanese to foreign lands has started with the conflict within the SPLM/A itself. After the tribal split of 1991 that has pitted the liberation movement against itself and the noble cause of South Sudanese people was strayed from its right direction, many have chosen refuge instead of taking part in inter-tribal fighting and self-destruction and in that regards, the South Sudanese were not only facing the Khartoum regime as the sole enemy but also the many tribal factions of SPLM/A , from SPLM/A - United to Nasir to Torit faction in which the then Major Wani Igga was a member of command .

No one in his/her mind can deny the huge contribution of South Sudanese Diaspora both in political lobbying, mobilization and support to the cause of our people nor its huge financial contribution in supporting our suffering refugees in east African countries and back home if it isn't for cheap politics consumption and greedy opportunism. Our constant constructive criticism to the leadership of the country is based on our love to our country and out of experiences and education we have saw and gained in the advanced societies we have adhered to, we don't say all we say is the absolute truth or that few of them are out of touch but those are our opinions and that's what democracy is all about.

All in all the Diaspora has always been seen as unpatriotic and a threat in the local jobs market and not an important asset that can be used for development and uplifting of the newly born country and as example, those who made it home just after independence to contribute with their much needed skills and education has faced enormous challenges finding jobs and integrating themselves back to society and the SPLM/A established system of we have fought the war and it is us who should lead and privileged.

However, South Sudan independence was not a result of military victory rather than a collective political mobilization campaign by all South Sudanese, home and aboard.

The Diasporas were always seen as opportunists or jobs grabbers and aliens in their owner country. Foreigners who didn't invest or saved a shilling inside the country were favored and hired instead. Such perceptions won't produce any good at all if we have to use everyone for development of this country. The land is vast, the riches are diverse and enormous, it is a hit of ignorance and greed to hate and marginalize anyone, clan or tribe but some are still deep into it, unfortunately.

The expectations were that, the leadership of the newly independent country will definitely render, attracts and use the various Diaspora skilled human resources in its development projects and capacity building rather than waging a war of jealously and selfish greed towards Diaspora and this is simply where things went wrong. I am not here saying everyone from Diaspora who went home right after independence were there to help the country rather than to milk the new cow in a corrupted manner but after all it is the government that must ensures that the cow is being milked right by anyone and not only Diaspora.

Nothing but love between the Diaspora and South Sudan and those who fall short about getting deep on understanding that they should look around and quell their own very reasons on why they would deny such a great country the benefits of its Diaspora skilled and educated sons and daughters. While it is bad and damaging to the country, it is not a surprise at all because if it wasn't selfishness and greed of the few, this fire that is burning us now won't start at first place, let us be honest.


## November 7, 2014
## In a Nutshell

It is only the lack of a spacious political mind in our politicians that make them quickly opts to violence and war as an option for solving political differences. The current disaster in South Sudan might have been created by people at their peak of temper, anger, influence of Alcohol or ego-centric mentality. Whoever decided to disarm the elements of Nuer in presidential guards in that doom day surely lacks the ability of seeing the consequences of such a dangerous decision and which have set the whole country into flames and turned everything upside down in no time.

The consequences of such a drastic decision are now over 10,000 human's soul lost, over two million displaced either internally or externally and three states destroyed to ashes, mistrust that might takes decades if not century to be reversed. In contrary, people now wouldn't be spending time and efforts in fixing what can be avoided by putting responsible people in sensitive decision making places.

The consequences and damage done by such drastic and wrong decisions of those in power can never be avoided and hence it is imperative to consider the wellness and qualifications of those who should occupy those powerful places that can change a destiny of a nation in a split second. Wellness of powerful people like presidents, prime ministers, defense, police, intelligence chiefs respectively, Judges and particularly those in security organs which should be regarded as the most sensitive positions that need to be held by people at their utmost sobriety, maturity, mental wellness and integrity, professionalism, nationalism and all of the self-disciplined values and standards.

Such important and vital standards If not put into consideration, the troubles for South Sudan will not end with this current conflict but you should expect more unless the criteria and methodology of selection of who should be in charge of those powerful places is accurately and timely changed. However, acute nepotism is one of our main problem and sure obstacle of purifying the body of our leadership, government and institutions, it is not necessary what you know but who you know in every government department appointment or employment, this need to change for the sake of nation safety, peace and long term development. If you can't hire a failed relative as a manager in your private company than why in public administration?

One thing for sure is that a doctor who performs a life and death surgery operation while 90% under the influence of Alcohol will send at no time the victim into his/her early grave without any doubt likewise so is the president, judge, police officer and every employee big or small. A safety and peace-wise and keen government with vision and interest of keeping its own country and people in peace and harmony shouldn't at any circumstances tolerate such risky behaviors no matter who or what.

It has become a culture for South Sudanese to usually tolerate life threatening behaviors and actions, underestimates early signs and warnings that would develops through time into deadly conflicts and acute problems in future and later continuingly dwells in endless blame games and helpless outcries. We can do better; prevention is better than cure as the saying goes.

This negative culture need to be changed if we care about our collective safety, peace and stability. I have no doubt that we have brought with us the culture of fighting over positions and titles in governments with or without qualifications from old Sudan even though it is the nature of humans to compete but this one of a kind is not healthy and doesn't serve any good at all. It is destructive in many ways. In fact, it was a methodology used by Northerners in old Sudan to divide the ranks of South Sudanese under the divide to rule policy. As an independent country and free nation, this negative culture should change because putting this country in order requires from us as a nation to face the facts and the realities and that's by putting ourselves in order first before we build an orderly country.

## November 9, 2014
## In a Nutshell

According to Dr. Machar and Gen. Kiir the prospects of peace and striking a final power sharing deal are real and possibly near. The two rival leaders must have finally came to the much needed compromises in their recent face-to-face meetings in Addis Ababa for peace to be possible for their devastated country and suffering people. Caught between soul searching and a realization of sure gloomy future of this country should the war continue and the much regional and international pressure and threats of sanctions that are closing in to the very assets of the two leaders themselves this time and around and which include but not limited to freezing assets, travel ban, Arms embargo among many. The more defiance and violations to IGAD and international community measures and recent resolutions, the harsh and the ugliest are the sanctions down the hell.

The East African regional bloc IGAD has given the two leaders 15 days to go and consult their constituencies and military commanders. However, Mr. Machar whether truly agreed to the terms of the deal or not, has a nearly impossible mission to achieve and faces true challenges within his own camp, the SPLM-IO. Democratic as he is Mr. Machar by nature has nothing to hide to the also victimized democratic Nuer community, the backbone of his movement, SPLM-IO, whether opting for peace or war, Machar need to presents the details of the deal, the prospects for peace, what in it for the SPLM-IO, the country restructuring, the possibilities of winning this war militarily, the challenges that faces his movement if he refuses to abide by the IGAD resolutions and the looming UN and international sanctions. What justice and accountability the deal will be doing to the victimized Nuer community, Greater Upper Nile State in general, reconstruction and compensation of lost lives and properties; those are just few among many anticipated expectations and changes the deal must have to settle.

If he truly agrees, the 15 days' consultation mission for Dr. Machar is like walking in a field full of mines to convince and persuade his mainly Nuer supporters and commanders of the SPLM-IO who have firmly and repeatedly rejected and violated many deals on the line of their ultimate demand of Kiir must go, resign or be removed through military means as the only exit to this bloody conflict. It is also a test for whether Mr. Machar truly controls his army and movement and whether he is truly being regarded as the commander-in-chief in which everyone that claims to be under his movement must abide by what he says and order. The consultation mission is also an open risk to invite political and military fractioning of the SPLM-IO should they failed to reconcile the many competing voices of peace and war from within.

However, the magic in the deal would be how the it addresses the injustice done to the Nuer community on Dec 15th, 2013, if removal of Kiir means more blood and destruction than what would Mr. Kiir do to the victimized Nuer community that amount the many thousands of lives of their loved ones lost in order for him to be forgiven and reconciled with? The bitterness of the lost and the grave feeling of injustice is obviously larger than any deal less than Kiir exit but this is a real world, we have to be realistic in our approaches if plan A didn't work, than how about plan B? Remember, a similar question might also be addressed to Mr. Machar regarding the lives of their community's members lost in this war.

The other important aspects of the deal are how it does address the powers of the new prime minister allocated to SPLM-IO versus that of Kiir's president post, restructuring of the state and its institutions. A one government with two conflicting heads is not what can take this country to a safe shore rather than a government that all its functions of powers works smoothly towards advancing this country and delivering services to its poor citizens. Hence, the aim here shouldn't be who has much more aggressive executive powers to undermine who or abuse what rather than a delicate power sharing between all that prevent power abuse and corruption in a check and balances system that truly works. It is the professionalism and political skills of Dr. Machar, Gen. Kiir, and Gen. Igga that might successfully bring this country back to normalcy and peace, they might need to act as true leaders and not game players.

Apart from this deal, any possible peace deals that ignore the other players such as greater Equatoria, SPLM- G10, other armed groups or political parties with aims to be included in any power sharing is also incomplete and might as well crumble. Such an incomplete deal does open a window for more negative political play and pockets of military offensive that might setup the whole process. Gen. Johnson Olouny might be fighting on side of government in the hope that a similar autonomous Chollo administration such of that of the Murle David's Yau Yau of Greater Pibor be granted. Hence, the Chollo grievances might need also to be addressed, I think they deserve to be who they want to be in their own ancestral territories but my wish is that this shouldn't be by bloody letting with their blood brothers, the Nuer or Dinka. It is worth noting that the would-be spoilers and threats of any peace deal are many, few among many are the small armed groups, the propagandists of lies and misinformation and those with interests and ambitions that don't thrive but by keeping this war aflame.

This conflict has changed many platforms and metaphors of what we have inherited from old Sudan. Neither Gen. Kiir nor Dr. Machar can stress that their SPLA factions are by any standards still constitutes national armies. The SPLA-Juba which is fighting under umbrella of national Army doesn't deserve that title at all, with the entire well documented ethnic atrocities and tribal profiling in its current chain of command structure. Therefore, a new national army that will be the safeguard of this nation must be rebuild, reshaped and educated in way that it be a true national army at any given time and space, unshaken by any possible ethnic politics or divisions, this applies to all security organs as well.

The Uganda military withdrawal must be a priority; however, it is not likely that it will take place too soon until Gen Kiir sees no threat to his throne. South Sudan need to roll back the foreign military and political role in its own affairs, it is undermining our very sovereignty, keeping our internal problems alive and widen to feed from and invest huge in it and with that in mind, a thriving and an endless business of troubles is what is in store for South Sudan, which patriots will ever accept that among the ones that are making noise about patriotism? Something must be wrong with our definition of what patriotism means.

## November 11, 2014
## In a Nutshell

At this critical juncture in the history of our country and at this point in the lifetime of each of us, we South Sudanese from all different walks of life might need an extraordinary courage and resolve in order to face the bitter facts of our current crisis and decide how the future of our country could be rather than we accept to be driven by the wind of political events and end up in uncertain state.

The current crisis in our country has divided us in every way possible and pitted families against each other but mostly it has finally categorized us into two major opposing groups; the advocates of war as a solution to this crisis and who sees the ultimate exit to the current crisis in a military and violent destruction to either Kiir or Riek's camp respectively, regardless of the bitter consequences and dire outcomes and in which the sure possibility of total disintegration of our country and its complete failure as state on the map of the world and nations is but certain.

The second category are the advocates of the peaceful solution as an exit to this bloody internal war. This group argue compromises and concessions from each of the two rival leaders, seeing no near or possible military victory to any side and seeing in the continuation of war more loss of lives and more drastic consequences where after, the possibility of harmonized nation and South Sudan as a country is but slim.

Either way, war or peace as an exit to this crisis, courage and bravery is needed. Those who want to make peace, they will need the courage to admit their crimes, apologize, accept accountability and justice, redeem and change in a whole new path that will help them reconcile with their victims. On the other hand, the victims will also need courage to accept the perpetrators apology, be ready to sincerely and everlastingly forgive, reconcile and open a new chapter in a way that will build new relationship and brighter future with the then their enemies.

When it comes to the advocates of war, they might need the courage to wage a lengthy campaign of bloods and skulls in order to reach uncertain victory on other rival. But before they opt to this destructive option, they might need to do a true math and realistic forecasting on possibility of winning this war through military means, putting in mind, all the surrounding factors, internally, regionally and internationally and of course those of short and long term cost and consequences of this war. Remember, in this war, the fuel and supplies of this internal fire are people that have no direct connection with the true causes of this conflict and hence the war also may create new enemies rather than Salva Kiir or Riek Machar because those who will lost their loved ones, will avenge in a cycle of no ending without regards to where the war has started.

In my opinion, the removal of Salva Kiir or destruction of SPLM-IO are all but truly costly through military means and therefore. South Sudanese must choose wisdom over arrogance, defiance and egotism. Neither does the courage to build have any ground of comparison with the courage to destroy because in the former a new opportunities of peaceful coexistence, forgiveness and reconciliation are always there, in the later, a new wound will be created, new enemies will be made, lost nor will misery accumulate as never before. In short, a long lasting peace will heal them all, a long lasting war will destroy them all. However, it all rest on the skills of our politicians and leaders and their willingness to save their county and nation. If they have what it takes to rebuild the house again and heal the nation than lucky are we otherwise let us be ready for the long haul, hopefully not.

## November 13, 2014
## In a Nutshell

The main objectives of fabricated coup of Dec 15, 2013 has been achieved. The state sponsored revenge on 1991 Bor massacre has been executed successfully, and the Nuer has been taught a hard lesson, they have been mass murdered in their thousands and the rest are between internally displaced or externally in the refuge lands. Riek Machar is no longer a possible successor to the president and demoted to whatever he may accept, a powerless prime minister or second useless vice president. The kings of fabricated coup, wherever their hideouts might be, must be somewhere in Juba or else, proudly laughing with a devilish boggling minds, the victory of humans' evil.

In future, a state sponsored or a rebel sponsored Dec 15, 2013 revenge might occur, why not? If 1991 massacre could be avenged why not Juba massacre? Isn't it the cycle of no ending revenges the so-called leaders of this nation has chosen as a way forward? Who is expected to be the dominator of such a society? Who is expected to accept and trust a final reconciliation if the last reconciliation between Dr. Riek Machar and Dr. Garang now appeared to be a temporary tactic, a temporary lies and arrangement yet to be destroyed and void at all cost in Dec 15, 2013. Who Salva and Kuol Manyang and the rest of Salva Junta are fooling here, themselves or the nation?

I wouldn't recommend for peace with gang of SPLM/A - Juba at whatever expenses and cost, if it is not for the sake of young children and the rest of innocent South Sudanese, who have nothing to do with the dangerous thought of those who have been ruling the SPLM/A as a liberation movement, and hence as a political party that's ruling South Sudan now. I could have opted for a long lasting war that should turned South Sudan to ruins until the ego-centric mentality and the arrogance of the few lost souls has been corrected. Simply and fundamentally, I don't believe in any racial or tribal superiority of any human upon another human, the virus that is destroying the world today including South Sudan.

But again here comes the question, should South Sudan and South Sudanese be subjected to war and victimized just for a heinous evil of the few who used the liberation slogan just to do the opposite, who after independence, have toke over the power of the country and nation just to advance the sick pride of their own and selfish greed of their very corrupted souls. South Sudanese state of affairs today is no better, in fact it has degraded to the worst in all aspects. All the aspirations for liberty, freedoms, dignity and a better living standards has been jeopardized by greed and arrogance of few corrupted souls. What a shameful lost

The 98.99%-win vote of referendum for the independence sure wasn't made by a single or two tribes, it reflects the will of all South Sudanese from all their diverse tribes, small and big, neither it reflects a will of fractured political party in the name of SPLM-Juba, SPLM-IO and SPLM-DC nor a will of ethnically divided SPLA. Shouldn't someone that claim himself as a national leader reflects a bit deeper on this nearly 100% figure high turnout for separation from Sudan.

Again, peace with Salva Junta and his group is not a genuine peace, it is not a just peace, but it is a deal that can be accepted to save South Sudan, it is a deal that can be temporarily signed in a hope for a better South Sudan. We must be aware of what in the minds of Salva Junta, it is even dangerous than you might have thought and hence, the two armies of the SPLA-Juba and SPLA-IO must be kept separate in any possible peace deal and as long as Salva Junta are still around, the SPLA-Juba that committed the Juba massacre can never again be trusted with the lives of our people. When a new national and truly patriotic leadership is in place, a new national army and other security organs must be recruited, educated on what a national security and army can truly be and do.

We only choose peace, only in a hope that the next generations of South Sudanese might opt to a better thinking, a better self that will breed a better country and a better nation. South Sudan has a great potential, when unleashed, I have no single doubt that it will be the best of the best. However, to unleash the potential of South Sudan, one must know what is in the minds of its neighboring countries and the international powers of greed, one must know how a country can be made a failure even if it is rich with resources and one must know South Sudan can't make it to the top when it is internally broken and divided and hence one must know that every single tribe, small or big in South Sudan does count in that process, these are pillars of good leadership and governance that the Salva Junta and their think tanks have no courage to accept or even come across. Let us hope for the best

**November 20, 2014**
**In a Nutshell**

**Pagak, the Expectations, Part 1**

What is expected from the SPLM-IO conference in Pagak due on November 24th, 2014? Even though it is being eyed as a meeting for consultations between the political leadership, top military commanders, and the various grassroots supporters, youth, women and others in regard to the last IGAD brokered power sharing and peace proposals, the Pagak conference is also expected to bring more in term of organizational structure and dynamics to SPLM-IO both politically and militarily.

It is not an easy predict whether the SPLM-IO will either opt for peace or war, but all options are on table, defending mostly of what they think about the outcomes of the 10 month long negotiations and whether they can compromise on their basic demand of president Kiir must relinquish power or whether they believe Juba will truly honor all that has been agreed upon. However, should they opt for peace and sign an agreement with SPLM-Juba; they must put in place true measures and guarantees that will assure the implementation of all agreements with a distinct scope and timeframe. Justice and accountability should be an integral part of any peace deal that is expected to last, it is the villages, families and loved ones of the ordinary South Sudanese who have paid the high price for this conflict brought forth by failed politicians and therefore, the lives of these villagers must be restored, healed, compensated. Justice must be served.

The urgent need for peace in this country can never be underestimated and war as an option has its drastic consequences, but in South Sudan case, it is never unlikely. All the factors that can make a U-turn to war are all but there. Even when a peace deal is signed, the whole environment will for some time be volatile and a timing bomb that can explodes anytime. This war has created deep psychological wounds, trauma and misery as a result of loss of loved ones and properties destruction and hence the mechanism in which the peace deal will be implemented need more clarity and formal structure and to avoid inclusion of grey areas that could confuse for conflict, anytime and anywhere. The regional body IGAD, UN Security Council and international community has already made it clear, that violations will not be tolerated and the consequences are clear and available. But this is South Sudan, where defiance and arrogance are the norm not the exception, so stay awake.

If it is not for cheap political consumption, then both warring SPLM/A factions knows that there is no such a thing as a non-executive prime minister or president, but there ought to be executive powers to both, the magic is who should take what and how they will be made to work in a checks and balances. This should be viewed mostly in a good way, in a way how the president and the prime minister could have a smooth formal working relationship, where powers and duties are all but delegated to serve the nation and the country better and where a working and effective government that truly deliver should be the end result and not a government that is in conflict within itself and that definitely will take the country back to square one.

In conclusion, apart from the consultative notion of the conference regarding the latest deal of power sharing brokered by the regional body IGAD and the prospects of peace and possibilities of military solution to the South Sudanese current conflict, the SPLM-IO, if it decided to be an independent political movement with a different name, has a rare opportunity to apply itself as the only viable political movement with a chance to transforms South Sudan into a democratic, stable federal state. This also will effectively enhance democracy in the country, the SPLM-Juba, with its decayed leadership and authoritarian notion, need a competing rival with the same magnitude but paralleled different political substance and direction in order for it to reconsider reviving itself or choose political extinction.

**November 21, 2014**

**In a Nutshell**

**Pagak, the Expectations, Part 2**

No doubt that all eyes are on the SPLM-IO conference in Pagak due on November 24th, 2014. The expected outcomes of this important conference are decisive and will decide on the question of war or peace in South Sudan but much also will be revealed. This is the opportunity where the political leadership of the SPLM-IO is expected to tell it all to its top military commanders, civil society organizations or its popular support base, women, youth, church leaders and others.

The political leadership is expected to brief everyone on the progress that has been made on the negotiations table for the last 10 month particularly on issues relevant to the country constitution, federalism as a governance system, power sharing, restructuring of the country and its various institutions but most importantly on the question of Kiir must go or whether the movement, considering in mind the massive internal voices for peace, the dire consequences of war as an option, the pressure and the threats of sanctions by regional body IGAD, UNSC and the rest of international community, is expected to grant Salva Kiir a temporary stay (projected as 30 months) until elections and what if Kiir is willing or not to run again for another term.

We surely know that a negotiated peace and peaceful solution to this deadly conflict is a series of bargains, tradeoffs and compromises from each side of SPLM/A warring factions. Each one must give up something in order to make peace possible or get something in return. However, if the biggest and riskiest bargain on the side of SPLM-IO is granting Kiir a temporarily stay under all various circumstances for the projected 30 months until elections than what are the steps taken to redeem the lost and injustice of December 15, 2013 in terms of justice and accountability? Steps that can convince the angry victimized masses and make them feel justice is done or at least it is on the way. There must be realistic measures and assurances that what has been agreed upon must not later be dishonored apart from keeping the armies of the two SPLA factions separate until later, there is a need of a clear implementation matrix with clear scope and timeframes under IGAD, UN and International community witness, monitoring and support.

But on a realistic note, war is also most likely at any moment, should the spoilers be left loose to undermine any potential peace deal, should Juba insist in its arrogance and defiance, should the SPLM-IO insist that Kiir must be removed militarily, should Museveni act reluctantly on its army withdrawal and fear of losing its vast bloody revenue as war come to halt, should other armed or political group(s) feels like they have been left out from any possible power sharing deal. War is most likely to persist should the IGAD, UN and international not actively engage in the long term process until South Sudan is able to stand on its own and that might take decades to be achieved but it is worth it at the end.

Any political party that lacks inclusive vision and solution to the question of transformation of South Sudan is also deemed to fail. Pagak conference is also a great opportunity to the SPLM-IO to demonstrate a capable national leadership with an inclusive vision and agenda. It is an opportunity to enhance its competitive political advantage on what make it better than SPLM-Juba in term of good leadership, good governance and nation-state building transformation. South Sudan is a great and blessed country and what truly lack are political leadership and political party with a keen will and substance to see through the great potential of this country and its nation. People should see South Sudan first before they can even know what tribe are they from.

South Sudan dilemma has been always a question of competent leadership not lacks of resources. If there was any good in the cultural aspects of politics of old Sudan than Sudan itself wouldn't be permanently a country in conflict neither the South Sudan will ever opt to secession and hence we can't live in our new independent country with the same poisonous substance and in the same time we expect to be better. Our political culture must change into one that builds not one that destroy, into a one that unite not one that divide. Politicians and intellectuals must do a better job for South Sudan to be a better country if not the best and this can be done in Pagak if Juba has become another bloody prison for democracy. Let us hope for the best.

## November 23, 2014
## In a Nutshell

It is likely that each one of us as South Sudanese could have been pulled to a better position and attitude and in much love and loyalty with our country when our politicians and leaders irrespective of their political parties and affiliations focuses mostly not on what divides us but on what unites us and works for betterment and development of South Sudan in whole. That proves that whatever the current of state of affairs of our nation is not but a true reflection of the state of a divided and wrangling political leadership and as well as the fact that public opinion can be shaped and directed towards great things or the opposite, it is merely not a work of chance.

In fact, what have setback our high expectations and hopes as we celebrate our hard-won independence in 2011 is that from the first day as a new independent state and nation we didn't find the great leader or leadership that could truly lead a much packed nation with hopes and aspirations, energetic and willing to create for herself the long denied dreams of better life, better living standards, and enjoys its new gained freedoms and liberties.

Our leadership failed to feel the pulse of the nation, failed to join, use and drive the much packed nation and wrong from start they have chosen to engage in their own fight of power struggle, corruption and selfishness. Whatever happened next was merely a result of a government and political leadership living in another world leaving the country and nation struggles with lack of services, insecurity, tribal and territorial disputes and hence day by day, the frustrated nation started to see a gloomy and uncertain future and has chosen instead to resort to quick shortcuts to get what it is being denied from through crime, corruption and violence in a bid to try to achieve to themselves what the leadership failed to promise or deliver.

There is no doubt that for this country to come back again to normalcy, its political leadership need unity and a new substance and resolve that must come from their acknowledgment of their grave past failure and that nothing else that contributed for the collective failure of the nation-state building process but the miserable failure of the political leadership in pulling everything and everyone into the right direction from the very first day of independence. Dwelling in the blame games really doesn't help and who is who role in this miserable mess has proven to be fruitless and a waste of time. The question is who is able to bring accountability, saneness and righteousness to the powerful, lost and much corrupted political leadership?

Popular role in bringing accountability, correction and punishment to the political and executive leadership has proven to be not effective if not working at all. The parliament or the legislature branch of government is another inefficient institution that the executive has successfully invaded and voided its independency and the same apply to the judiciary. People in legislature and judiciary positions should be elected by their popular base and not appointed by president in order for them to be independent and hence refers to public as their only source of legitimacy and accountability but it is quite the contrary right now in South Sudan case. It is likely that it is the president and his immediate security and intelligence agents that are ruling the country and hence putting everyone in line of what they want through terror, intimidations and murder.

The SPLM/A with all its political and military factions be it SPLM-Juba, SPLM-IO, SPLM-G10 and SPLM DC has much more soul searching to do and reflects back on the core values, objectives and principles the liberation movement was founded upon. We the people need true liberation this time from poverty, diseases, illiteracy, corruption and all forms of negative tribalism, nepotism and favoritism and we believe there is no coming together for this nation to make it through while its political leadership is still divided and lost.

In this regard, I think the various SPLM factions have a historical choice to make, either they have to go for a complete merger of their factions under new values and principles or opt for a complete divorce and names change. There shouldn't be fear of being oneself because it is never the name that make what you are rather than what you stand for. It seems to me that the name of SPLM has been robbed from what it was actually intended for and hence it either have to choose between a revival revolution and political extinction.

## November 30, 2014
## In a Nutshell

Our good resolve will always unearth the real strategy behind this war, the tribal men in disguise who are executing it behind the scene wherever they might be, their malicious intents and plans whatever pretexts and cover-ups they are using for the time being. Now, with the start of dry season, it is a good time to know whether the whole IGAD process that was carefully exaggerated until this time with fruitless outcomes was just a tactic of buying time, while the Uganda, the main Juba ally was supplying the Salva junta with all weaponry to teeth.

Accordingly, chances of political solution are being over shadowed by a military one and this apparently is being enforced by the fact that the Salva Junta thinks that its tribal army is now well equipped and have a better military competitive advantage over a shaky poorly equipped rebels who has no strong political backer or military supplier. Additionally, Mr. Kiir and his defense minister Kuol Manyang want to resolve the question and the challenge of Nuer threat once and for all and by any cost and hence, any political solution that gives the Nuer a window of recovery and regrouping should be denied at all cost. Well, if this is an achievable task than the question is who after the Nuer has been defeated and finished will have the courage ever to challenge the rule of one tribe in Juba?

But is it really a one tribe rule or a tribe being used to advance and sustain a failed leadership of Mr. Mayardit? I will go for the later since all the dictators comes by the names of their tribes and race until they reveal that it is the other way around neither it is a new phenomenon in Africa politics that when the political leadership fails, the resort has always been the tribe and tribal politics, Salva and his Junta are no exceptions nor fools. However, time will reveal a lot of awful plans being cooked in the kitchen of our bad tribal leaders, each tribe and individual in our victimized nation will have to come in understanding and consciousness in the right time. However, in aftermath of all these divisive plans, chances are that we might not have a country called South Sudan as a result, hopefully not.

I have hopes that the SPLM/A-IO will be a true leadership alternative and that it will strengthens and evolves with time until it become a true national movement that is not about the victimized Nuer only but about a new South Sudan where all South Sudanese are truly free and dignified. Juba and Uganda will not militarily defeat the SPM/A-IO even though if they acquire weapons of cluster bombs and other weapons of mass destruction. Towns will be captured and recaptured, villages will be burnt to ashes, ethnic based grave atrocities will be committed and civil populations will be uprooted and displaced but this won't bring defeat to rebellion with at least 100,000 manpower.

If the current peace efforts fail and chances for political settlement become nil, then this dry season will test the credibility of everyone and in particular the IGAD whole role. It could mean an end of a game and start of the worst but let us also stay hopeful that the Salva Junta may do an accurate reading and forecasting to realities on the ground as well as the future.

There is nothing that is up to Juba alone to decide and impose even if they acquire the most powerful military might. The proposal of two armies is here to stay simply because the SPLA Juba that committed the Juba massacre can't never be trusted with the lives of our people again and until a new true national patriotic leadership is in place, a new national army and other national security organs shall be recruited, trained and educated on what a true national army can be and do. We have said it before and we will always stand by that.

All in all, it is the oppressors who should be redeemed not the oppressed, and Juba this time and around should know it is upon the ruins of South Sudan that we all should make the decision of peace and war and not its ego-centric tribal mentality. South Sudan destiny cannot be left to a few corrupted souls to decide neither on a one tribe rule that is using the pretext of sovereignty and constitutional protection to bring the rest to submission and servitude of a tribal dictatorship.

**December 1, 2014**
**In a Nutshell**

The future of South Sudanese nation should not be let haunted by the past grudges of its leaders and hence whatever happened between Late Colonel Samuel Gai Tut and Late Dr. John Garang in 1980s shouldn't be what judges the destiny of this nation nor what is between Salva, Kuol Manyang, Makuei Lueth against Dr. Riek Machar in regards to 1991 crisis shouldn't be what condemned the state of South Sudan and its future generations to death by endless tribal wars.

Unlike Makuei Lueth, defense Minister Kuol Manyang was the least talkative in this current tribal war until recently when his controversial remarks about those who refuses to join the tribal war in which he stated that those who refuses to be recruited or fight as part of his army must be ready to be women and must be ready for their hair to be plated and wear a skirt.

Apart from the fact that it is problematic towards women, the statement in itself stand as a clear prove that Kuol like his boss Salva both have a clear lack of leadership skills that also should consider their national stand as leaders of diverse nation where women constitute 60% of its populace. Manyang should send his mind a bit into the world around him where women are presidents, defense ministers and active combat and military operations commanders. The best example to him should be captain Nyapouch of SPLM-IO who has shown a rare bravery in this imposed war. The world today is not the world where women were regarded as inferiors and incapable of what men do. However, this should not surprise you either simply because the Salva-Manyang leadership mess has proved behind any reasonable doubt why the ship called South Sudan piloted by the two is still stranded in troubled waters with no clear safe shore to land.

Second to none but Kiir himself, Mr. Manyang, is a fundamental architect of this revenge war against Riek Machar along with several others behind the scene even though he is the least to publicly appears and make statements but in fact the most effective and efficient mastermind in the whole mess. The December 15th, 2013 massacre occurred just weeks away after he assumed his new position as a national defense minister. During the SPLM Political Bureau crisis that brought this war, he was first and the most vocal supporter of Mr. Kiir dictatorship tendencies beside Luis Lobong of Eastern Equatoria

During his tenure as a governor of Jonglei state, the largest and most populated state in South Sudan and home of many veterans of liberation war including himself and late Gai Tut, Late Garang de Mabior among many, Kuol leadership to the state was honestly a pure disaster. Whether was it part of the master plan against the Nuer or a mere leadership failure, the majority Lou Nuer was pitted against the minority Murle in a tribal war that almost led to genocide. It is worth noting that the Lou Nuer section of Nuer tribe was also the first to be forcefully disarmed in 2006 shortly after the CPA was signed. The disarmament has left the Lou Nuer the weakest and the vulnerable ethnic majority in Jonglei state.

With all that in mind, this war may seem to many as accidental rather than to believe that it is a calculated and planned conspiracy and that the Salva-Manyang and of course the rest of the crew, the intellectual think tanks, the elders authority and the military, intelligence and security support base are all but deep in it. Details of the conspiracy will sure surface by time and for those who have keen minds to read you won't likely not be surprised that the mission of the then movement we regarded as a liberation tool, the SPLM/A is now shrinking shamefully to only serve Pan-Mayar-dit, the head of state and Pan- Manyang-dit, the head of the tribal army. However as independent as we are, it is likely that this country will be just a field of endless tribal wars.

I have no personal issue with Gen. Kuol and with all due respect my criticism to him is purely based on that he is in a position of national leader and a politician and from my firm belief that, the grudges of 80s and 90s between our leaders shouldn't be the ones that failing the future generations. It is a constant reality that we either have to heeds to what the great leader Dr. Martin Luther King said before that "we must learn how to live together as brothers or perish together as fools". We can save lives and our country by being wise enough in both of our tribal ends.

All in all, public opinion and mindset is always shaped by behaviors and attitudes of the leadership and as such our leaders cannot deny that they have failed to erase the hostile mindset created by the past neither they have healed the nation from the wounds of 80s and 90s divisive wars but in fact they have revived every single grudge and used them for political gains and survival. Ironically enough, from 1982 to 2014 and after 32 years of Garang vs. Gai that the Salva-Manyang vs. Riek Machar is still hunting the lives of South Sudanese in thousands and still counting. This should stop if we are to have a nation and a country.

## December 3, 2014
## In a Nutshell

Politics to some in South Sudan is assumed to be an evil business that apparently involves most devilish ways and techniques of bringing your rival to defeat. Some thinks that defaming and defamation and all sorts of character assassinations are part of any effective political and rivalry campaign that rivals should wages against each other's. The fierce competition for public opinion control is likely off limits and knows no boundaries of good principles and values of good politics. Well, if there is any such a thing as principled politics as the majority seems to believe that politics is a dirty game and hence must be waged and played as such.

However, in a society where the good, the bad and the ugly seem to be all in equal footing and hardly have any effective systems of distilling the good from the bad of its leaders, politicians or administrators alike, it is likely that who wins is never the right guy but the one with most effective tools of propaganda, lies, misinformation to the control of mostly illiterate public opinion.

You got to hear all sorts of information anyway, wait and analyze them before you judge or take action of any kind but those are not techniques and skills that everyone is good at and particularly in a society where literacy is as low as 27%. This has proven to be a root problem of most South Sudanese political and bloody conflicts where political elite with better educational backgrounds has exploited and manipulated the illiterate rural population in political adventures and bloody conflicts of their own and where these innocent people have nothing to comprehend or gain.

Only through efficient education and mass communications revolution a politically-wise society can be attained, an informed society that could accurately pick the meat from the bones within the accumulated political mess and intense stream of political propaganda, misinformation and chaos. With efficient education, people will tend to make better choices and may choose the right that come from others than the wrong of their own; they may weigh reasoning and logic over arrogance and defiance.

Most problems of South Sudan can be reduced through more effective and efficient mass education and communications. Any future leadership of this country may need to set a long term educational plan to the entire nation without any marginalization, design a working education system with good end results in mind and hit the most isolated rural areas where illiteracy is living the most. These were first things first that our leaders supposed to have done after the signing of CPA and right after the independence. We could have been saved from the evils of our own.

Education and efficient mass communications will strengthen our tribal society weakness, heals its social bias and help sustain our unity and the upper interests of the nation and country. Education will help creates an informed society that can protects itself from manipulation and exploitation of political hyenas. Moral and financial and all types of corruption will be reduced, good and healthy practices will be encouraged, tribal mindset will also be reduced and shifted towards a more nation oriented mindset.

Good and efficient education system will help creates a society that practices good politics to protects itself from being dehumanized and being destroyed from within by bias of hearsays, gossips and destruction of good values. It is through effective education that we surely will unearth the best out of us as individuals and nation as well and in return, this will sure create a better and peaceful South Sudan.


## December 8, 2014
## In a Nutshell

Any discriminatory leadership no matter what tribe it originates from is not good for South Sudan and is surely not the one this country and nation need. Those who truly want to fix South Sudan will need to be above themselves, their tribes and their selfish interests. Those who are mingling around to just replace tribal kingdom with just another one with only difference in the name of tribe are also doomed to fail and will surely end just like Mr. Salva tribal regime.

If the SPLM-IO failed to heed the call as the only hope for South Sudanese people, then, things might take a while before we can find the kind of leadership that will take South Sudan to the needed safe shore. We might need a new breed of generation, with a new mindset, more nation-oriented, and that sees the true potential of South Sudan and not the selfish individualism or the low-shallow tribal and clannish interests. We also know that such a generation can never be a work of chance or will come out of nowhere but must be a work of truly willing patriotic leadership. Undoubtedly enough that if the SPLM under the leadership of Mr. Kiir and as the ruling party did have any vision and mission from the first day of our independence, such a generation could have been recruited, taught and oriented in such a noble direction but say what

The troubles with South Sudan are deeply engraved within a tribal society that thinks and breath tribally, a society where tribal ego and prejudice are what drive nearly everyone and where also its politicians have found a fertile land to exploit to the max. The constant truth and reality is that, there is no face for any future good leadership for South Sudan but the one that ought to be truly good enough. Until now, I am afraid that I didn't find anyone who don't think and act in the name of his/her clan. It is for our general salvation, that we may need to abandon the way we think and do things. Too much focus on tribe more than the nation and the country, too much focus on a bitter past more than we can work for a brighter future and breed a better educated, healthy and united future generations, we have to think about solutions not more complication of the problems or the constant whining and dwelling in the blame games.

There is no such a thing as an ideal or perfect society but at least the human dream of reaching such a noble cause is still not impossible, at least a society with less bias and social ills. The problem is not the society but those who claims to be the leaders of the society. Modern society are shaped, oriented and positioned by their leaders and hence what is important here is what substance do such leaders possess, morally and intellectually that constituted their drive to fulfill their people dreams. How do they envision the transformation of their country and nation, from point A to point Z. Do they have what it takes to transform a nation and a country such as leadership skills and others? Any bunch of people with common interests could form a political group or party but the remaining question will always be; where do their interests meets with the common interests of the nation? What sort of head is driving that body? Those are the questions and what make the difference.

We are fragmented nation and the fragmentation thinking of our society has no distinctive end or noble destination but more fragmentation, divisions and weakness. People will start from their tribes and then all the way downward to their clans, sub-clans, section and sub-section until their nuclear family unit. Hence, and in the light of the crisscrossed and intertwined interests it is likely that such a society can't never attain a nationhood stage of development unless luckily it has great selfless leaders and intellectuals that bravely take the lead to shape a nation-mindset, something that South Sudan has missed in its current troubled leadership and intellectuals.

Mr. Salva has stabbed himself from the back and damaged his liberation legacy simply when he has chosen not to confront the facts of his leadership failure and instead he plunged the country into a tribal war and divisions for him to survive. It is going to be a similar case for any tribal based political group that is cheating itself in context of ruling South Sudan diverse nation and hence such a group may need to reposition itself to a more nation oriented political strategy and philosophy. You can't replace a tribal marginalization or manipulation with the same stuffs of former regime but you got to be different, totally different.

In conclusion, there are greater goals and objectives the people of this country can embraces and devote their wasted energy, efforts and time to achieve. It is the leadership folks that can take a nation to Mars and in the other way around, it is also the leadership that can make a nation just a bunch of food beggars. Which way do we choose? It is all up to us, let us examines the ways and means we chooses our leaders and leadership

## December 14, 2014
## In a Nutshell

The Pagak Conference of SPLM/A-IO was exceptionally successful, well organized and it came with great resolutions that if implemented, will reposition this country onto the right direction and change the lives of its people for better. But no matter whether you feed them gold or logic, the Kiir camp will always vomits the same, arrogance and more arrogance. Juba government is not the kind of leadership that considers or recognizes neither the importance of peace nor the higher interests of South Sudan and its victimized nation. As long as the Pagak conference resolutions bears the signature of Dr. Riek Machar, the man they consider their arch enemy and constant nightmare, rest assured, they will always find ways and means to deny and play around with it. They are the same people that are enjoying the independent South Sudan now that came as a fruit of the very idea of self-determination who the man, Dr. Riek Machar, came with when the Kiir camp was lost so deep in the ocean of big lie called united secular Sudan and instead of honoring the man, they are just trashing and chasing him out of the county.

You don't have to expect the beneficiaries of a failed Juba leadership to embrace the successful, outcomes and resolutions of SPLM-IO conference in Pagak simply because the arrogance and defiance has always been the norm to those who have been in control of SPLM/A as a liberation movement and now as the ruling political party that brought us to this sure drastic end. These people will always stick to the wrong road and the wrong structure of state that emboldens part of the nation in riches and marginalizing the other parts in misery and poverty. They want to keep the status quo system as long as it is guarding their interests and securing their grief control of power. They are not here for a healthy South Sudan for all, a one that is united, prosperous and peaceful for the next generations.

But wait don't panic yet because the SPLM/A –IO reserves to itself a plan B while giving the Juba the chance to rethink its irresponsible stand in various issues concerning the country's governance system and restructuring of its ailing institutions. Juba has a rare chance to seize and work with SPLM/A – IO in a series of workable tradeoffs here and there based on Pagak Conference and the outcomes of peace negotiations. There is a great substance in what the Pagak conference recommended in its final communiqué. It has recommended many working solutions to where most of the problems of South Sudan lays and most if not all the roots cause of our problems were addressed accurately and that ranges from governance to the socio-economic and political programs, restructuring of the state and in particular the recruitment of a new South Sudan Army and the various security organs in term of manpower and substance.

It is correct and right that if we need a country with a foundation and a maintained sound direction, the civil administration should be far from politics and most importantly should be recruited based on qualifications, merits and the know-how and not through nepotism and the know- who. This is the true body of any functioning country and where any possible political failures will be sustained by a working non- political civil administration. Politics is not everything as we think in South Sudan.

Well, Bravo SPLM/A –IO for a more national approach in addressing South Sudanese origin of problems and for great proposal of keeping ethnicity out of politics and civil administration. However, the thing is not that Kiir and his support base don't know that what the SPLM-IO is recommending is the right formula of cure of South Sudan problems but it is that it touches the very core center of their powers and means of controlling the state and its resources. This is truly ironic to come from people who claim they have fought Khartoum for 23 years to free the people of South Sudan but ironically enough since we departed Sudan about 4 years ago, nothing seems to be reflecting such a claim.

All in all, any political entity that knows the history of people of South Sudan may benefit from that knowledge and correct its path before it is too late. The people of South Sudan will never surrender to whatever they think is wrong and unjust, hence and far from arrogance and defiance, both SPLM/A factions can tradeoff working solutions here and there to fulfill the dreams of their people. Choosing to bury our heads deep into the sand of arrogance and defiance is not good for our country and nation.

## December 15, 2014
## In a Nutshell

December will never be the same again in the rest of our lifetime and neither in the lifetime of our children, its celebratory mode has been stolen and poisoned forever by the one we assumed once as our national government and army. On Dec 15th, 2013, a day when our lives were turned upside down and the precious lives of our loved ones were abruptly cut short. December used to be the only unique month that brings the whole together, the families, the nation and the Christian world at large. It is the month Jesus Christ was born, a month of special happiness and a gateway that usher for a whole lot New Year with rejuvenated hopes and wishes.

In the then beautiful Malakal town of South Sudan and like the rest of this beautiful country and nation in those days of 70s, 80s, 90s even when the Sudan civil war was ravaging and aflame, anyone of my peers and childhood friends would never miss to remember how we all waits for the month of December of each year not just only to celebrate and get together in joy and happiness but also to renew oneself physically and spiritually as well.

The celebrations preparatory mode of Christmas in South Sudan in those days is something uniquely magnificent and a whole lot joyful as it turns everything around beautiful and new. The decoration fever in every household and the whole town was something notable, houses are painted colorfully and beautifully new, sweet candies, cookies, cakes and refreshing drinks are made in their different beautiful shapes and colorful taste and in short everything in the house must be turned around, clean and neat for Charismas celebrations. The preparations for the Christmas actually starts earlier from October and on and as children and youth in those days it is never that we celebrate with the same clothes of last year, if affordable, we must have a new of everything, from clothes to shoes to watches and everything that come between and hence you have to make sure that the tailors have your clothes tailored and ready before December or at least before the Christmas eve.

After our hard-won independence, it was our great expectations that the month of December will just add more beauty and joy to itself, simply because we would celebrate in peace and far from war this time and around and more to that, we would celebrate as free and dignified people in our own land and among our families, relatives and friends something we have never fully enjoyed for the last 23 years. This has been a unique trend and tradition for us in Diaspora and those who have been scattered around the whole world and separated from families for decades. December was always a month you waited for as you work hard for it to save money all around the year to be able to pay a reunion visit with the family, the people and the land we dearly love.

Unfortunately, things are never as we have wished and as we have lived before and December now has become a month of mourning and a month of sad memoirs. Each year on 15th of December we will still look for answers on why and what those thousands of innocent souls murdered mercilessly have ever done to the ones they thought as their leaders and their guarding army. On the 15th of each December, while we mourn and commemorates those lost precious souls, we will also be looking for clues on how the guns that were meant to protect the citizens of this country were turned into the ones that terrorizes and kills them without a crime of their own.

December 15, 2013 was a culmination of the evil acts of people who have been planning willfully to rob this country and its nation from their new gained powers and freedoms, it will always be the peak of envy, evil and pry from the shadowy devils and from people who have recruited their armies and friends of evil to just steal the lives and the resources of this nation in a bright daylight, unashamed and mercilessly. However, the December dilemma has started earlier as we may think, it is in a fact an evil trend that the government of this country under the leadership of Kiir Mayardit has sought as a necessary mean and philosophy to survive on.

On December 5th, 2012, one of best mind and intellectual whose writings we joyfully anticipate every morning and whose writings were like a guiding compass to the many ills of the new born state and to the struggling leadership of this country. Isaiah Abraham or Isaiah Ding Abraham Chan Awuol, a leading critic voice and brave pen in the war against corruption and our failed leadership was dragged and murdered brutally in front of his house by agents belonging to the country government of the day. On December 9th, 2012, around 100 of innocent and peaceful protestors were mass murdered and injured in Wau town. They were simply exercising their democratic right and protesting the relocation of their county headquarters to another location.

Those are just few among many atrocities committed against the people of South Sudan by their own government. Things are never the same again not only on the month of December alone but in any time and space as long as Juba regime still believes in terror, intimidations and murders of its own citizens as a means to install itself and sustain its dictatorship rule.

The sad part yet is that justice to those innocents and many more are never served and their killers are still walking among us proudly and thirsty for more blood of the like innocents. There is no independent arm of justice and accountability in this country since the government who is supposes to be the justice arm is now the criminal itself. The whole justice system in the body of judiciary branch of government is dysfunctional and has been overridden by the executive branch and since then most of the state institutions are but mere accomplice in the crimes against citizens, there is none that is working independently and that for sure includes the legislature. It is unfortunately, a horrible done deal.

All in all, and as we commemorate the victims of December 15th, 2013 and as the civil war enter its second year without justice or peace in sight let us renew our commitment to overhaul the way things are done in our country, it is our collective responsibility to put things right and reposition our country on the right track and if you think in your comfort zone that the crimes of the regime haven't reach you yet, it is obviously a matter of time not a matter of you being indifferent. May the Almighty grants peace to the souls of all the innocents and upon South Sudan, the nation and the country, we shall prevail.

## December 22, 2014
## In a Nutshell

As Christmas approaches, the only wish to the people of South Sudan is peace and more development, simply because all the things and objectives people are fighting for can't be realized but within a peaceful and a stable country. This country need true leaders who must make it enjoys a long-term managed peace while all the underpinning programs of transformation and development are being secured, implemented and positioned onto the right direction. The question is whether there are any short or long-term transformation and development projects that were initiated and are currently being funded or under implementation.

It been about 4 years now since South Sudan independence and if there were any long-term developmental programs initiated from the very first year of independence then at least by now they could be yearning fruits and changing lives for better. If we are expecting a modern South Sudan, then the foundation of such a country have to be build first before we can't enjoy a modern and advanced lifestyle and stuffs and join the rest of the world in the march of civilization and modernity. However, the thing is, we are robbing our country oil money and live comfortably in foreign lands trying to match a lifestyle that is not related to our poor country by any realistic means. That isn't right thing to do, we may need to rethink our ways and habits as independent nation and let see if they are truly cost-effective and does pay-off at the end of the day, after all, it is not easy to emerge as successful country and particularly when you are an African country rocked with all elements of weakness and born to a world that fears strong African countries and nations, you got to think thoroughly and work efficiently twice than your rivals.

Right from start, South Sudan with its vast oil resources could have started with the major projects that are the development movers. Projects that could have stirred all the rest of the process attributes on the right track and this wasn't difficult to achieve at all, given the standard of technology today and South Sudan petrodollars, the whole process could have been a lot easy. It could have been a matter of good long-term contracts with the technology-advanced countries of the world to transform everything in a relatively short timeframe. The Arabs Gulf countries successful transformation from empty deserts to a booming oasis of development, modernity and civilization are the best example on what petrodollars can do. We can do a lot far better because we have more extra resources apart from oil, much smaller in population size and a vast fertile agriculture land, what more do we need? But come on, something is playing with our heads and making us completely blinds of seeing our true wealth and potential, that's our collective dilemma. Get off it.

In my simple opinion I think the major projects that can move the development and life forward in South Sudan are simply the electricity power plants, clean running water infrastructure, paved roads, highways and bridges that connect all the country, adequate healthcare system, communications and information infrastructure and above all an education system that trains the current generation to copes with the requirements of such a transformation and that educates the next generations to be of different level of education, positive mindset and nation-oriented cultural substance. But wait, this is not it, the role of political leadership in the development is the most major factor and if not addressed accurately, such a transformation process wouldn't happen at all, simply because without a willing, focused and competent leadership that leads the way, determined in the right direction and while implementing and securing the transformation process, such a process will be still a dream far reachable.

However, the transformation and development of South Sudan should be our collective fight and I think if there was any right fight within the SPLM as the ruling political party, it should be this fight apart from their many fights of interests, power and wealth. This right political fight between what is good for this country and what isn't could have started long time ago and not in 2013 and it could have been handled politically not militarily and managed wisely to breed an efficient political party with a transformation agenda. The right thing for South Sudanese people at the end of the day is for them to gather and groups on what is right or against what is wrong and not on tribal and clans' lines; this is the true drive and conscience of a healthy society.

But now and with the frustration brought forth by the current war, it seems the talk now is about saving South Sudan from vanishing as a state and nation on the map rather than ways and means of developing it. We have chosen as a nation to go down the lower side of humans' world rather than being brave enough to create a place for ourselves on the developed world spectrum, that is not a good choice and what puzzles me the most is how the leadership of this country has avoided by all costs a foreign war that is more likely justified than going all the way in an internal war that is tearing its nation and country apart, still not a good choice and up to this point, still the problem of South Sudan is not about resources or physical capabilities as a state but the human factor displayed in the type of leadership leading this nation. Merry Christmas.


**December 23, 2014**
**In a Nutshell**

In this Christmas, our minds and hearts are with those South Sudanese who lost their lives, the IDPs in UN protection compounds and those scattered and forced out of the country to the far refuge lands and of course those in frontlines. It is yet another sad Christmas that they will have to celebrate in those dire conditions far from their homes and families with sorrow, worry and   feeling of hopes of when this nightmare will finally hit the finish line.

This is not my first time to see the tale of two cities of human making, the booming city while people lives, mingles and dances happily like no other and in total contrast to the city of the sorrow, poverty, and agony while the only gateway to a brighter world is hope and more hope. Those South Sudanese in UN protection sites and refugees' camps symbolizes the city of sorrow by any reasonable meaning, yet, it is likely that their being there is finally have been given a solid justification by the mockery political elite.

Well, this is not even a new phenomenon, back in the days when Sudan civil war was ravaging and aflame, a similar tale of two cities was common to the eyes to see and the contrast the war engraved in Sudanese people lives was so obvious and appalling and accordingly, the have and have-nots, were so distant in everything and were of no match by any standards. The tales of two cities whether from political or socio-economic dimension has been always a side or a direct product of many political or religious ideological wars and systems and this isn't a surprise at all in the history of our troubled world but to see it again repeated by the very people who were the city of sorrow in former Sudan and more to that by the ones who claimed to be in position of leadership of a liberation revolution than this is for sure, what puzzles everyone.

After independence of South Sudan it was my belief that every South Sudanese irrespective of whatever background they originate from will not have to be subjected to be a second class citizen again neither denied any right of enjoying the hard-won freedoms and liberty and honestly I haven't think of a mind that will likely comes forth and make another tale of two cities in South Sudan, categorizing its nation again into; the city of sorrow and the city of happiness, simply because, we were all second class citizens in our former country and we have seen and lives what it truly mean but more importantly because the two millions precious lives we lost to the war of liberation haven't die for that and haven't expect their children one day to celebrate Christmas in UN protection sites, neither in bitterness of the refuge lands because of their own leadership and leaders.

I recall that before we headed to the referendum polls in 2011, the echoes of the late Dr. John Garang following words "When time comes to vote at referendum, it is your golden chance to determine your fate. Would you like to be second class citizens in your own country? It is absolutely your choice.". His words were strongly and repeatedly resonating in our minds and hearts and victoriously enough, we did it with 98.99 votes in favor of separation and out of knowledge of what being a second class citizen means.

Well things have changed ever since and in short, we are in war and in path of destruction now, how, when and why we have arrived to this bitter juncture is generally known to everyone. However, human's actions are reversible, it is not impossible to fall in wrongdoings nor unlikely to do mistakes, but the ability to correct, repent, improve and reverse the course whenever you have discovered things aren't going the right direction is one of the God greatest given gift to His children. The war that has divided our country into the city of sorrow and the city of happiness is reversible; it is a man-made disaster that can be put to rest with courage and resolve. This is our land and the land of our forefathers and war cannot be the way foreword neither the mean to resolve our internal and nation disputes, dialogue will always be the only way for a peaceful co-existence as usual as it was in the time of our forefathers who have kept our land and nation intact and indivisible.

I still believe all the issues that are the cause of this war can be addressed and resolved in peaceful manner and the leadership of this country has all the powers to make South Sudan a country we all cherish and love. It is our collective responsibility to see our children lives in a world free of war and enjoys the fruits of peace and freedom and as a matter of fact, none of us in these generations of wars haven't seen, directly or indirectly, the bitter consequences of war and If we all claim to be patriots and doing what South Sudan deserves, than there will be no need for war simply because whatever good for South Sudan is good for our common good but not necessarily whatever good for one individual or particular group is good for the common good of South Sudan and its entire nation. Therefore, it is in our collective interest to arrange our house in an orderly manner that prevent any sort of manipulation of power or marginalization of some in term of power sharing and resources distribution, rights and privileges as well as duties toward the society and the state. We can sit and debate, collaborate in peaceful environment to tackle all those issues in good faith and free will and arrive to South Sudan that we will all dream about.

Well there is no magical formula in this very moment and the creation of a peaceful, prosperous and stable South Sudan is a process in the making, we can't jump neither we can't run from the bitter realities on the ground but we got to face them with courage and resolve. This is possible unless the whole process of negotiations and debate is merely a cheap politics that is being waged by people whom interests aren't related to the core needs of South Sudan and its nation.

In this Christmas, may we promise ourselves not to deny another generation of young South Sudanese children not to go uneducated, malnourished and hungry, may we remember the pillars of Christianity of Love, peace and forgiveness, and may we thrive to live the values and example of Christ. Think about it and envision it, it is like no other. Peace to you all and Merry Christmas.

**December 31, 2014**
**In a Nutshell**

A new year is just around the corner, couple hours only and the year 2014 will be a history, whether sad or happy was it, it is a personal opinion and reflection more than it is collectively general, but as most years, the ups and downs, the additions and subtracts are never a consistent or constant stream, that's life.

Optimism and hope are the fundamental and essential ingredients that drives life forward and out of experience, we all have witnessed in a way or another and at some point of our lifetime a serious moment of distress, failure or lost but with hope and determination, we have overcome many life ordeals and have raised again and again. Let us hope that the 2015 will be a good year for everyone, a year of great yearning and positive changes at personal and general level as well.

Let us hope that peace will return to South Sudan, even though it seems like a miracle is needed for that hope to materialized. Let us hopes that a sudden change happens in the minds and hearts of architects of wars and the advocates of violence as a solution to human differences and disputes, let us hope they will choose peace, a just and sustainable peace, simply because peace is the mother of the all good things that life is all about and without peace in this country and of course around it, regionally and internationally, the hopes and the dreams of a good 2015 for the majority of South Sudanese will be still a hit of illusion.

All indicators points to a hardly unpredictable year to South Sudan and its suffering nation, there is a military buildup, there is a setback in peace efforts and a widening distance between the warring parties in this current civil war. Each party believes that victory is certain upon another, that compromises and concessions are but a sign of weakness or defeat and most dangerously, Uganda has finally annexed Juba as one of its ruled territory and I doubt now that even Kiir himself has an ability to tell Mr. Museveni to pack and go.

It is not clear what IGAD will do next at this deadlocked juncture of the two separate armies and the saga of executives powers to a never functioning president or they would be functioning prime minister. Logically, if I was in the position of Mr. Kiir as president and at this age, I would agree to delegate important executive powers to the prime minister, the one who want to carry out the reforms, architects the changes and that plans the overhauling of the decayed systems and to bring this country back to normalcy and performance. But says what, those whose interests are at stake by this suggestion surely has the ears of Mr. Kiir and has for sure, the last words that impedes South Sudan in continuous chaos.

There is no way around that South Sudan as a state will truly function without a genuine peace deal between the two warring parties, not in socio-economic or political dimensions or on the regional and international functions. If the two parties insist on the military solution in this dry season as it already indicates, a more shrinking state deep down the worse is the expected outcome with more additional 100s of thousands South Sudanese between dead or displaced, God forbids. The war is becoming increasingly a war of international and regional interests, fought by South Sudanese and in their own land where weapons will continuously pour in and the conflict will be kept aflame by all means possible until the very social fabric that forms and unites South Sudan as a one entity and as a one nation is seriously damaged and at worst, is no more.

Defiantly, Gen. Kiir is choosing war over peace and will held his own 2015 elections, may be around Juba and Kuajok, win it with 99.99% votes, however and apart from giving himself a form of illegitimate legitimacy of another 5 years' term, there is no other objective for such an incomplete and unconstitutional elections. However, this won't stop the war but the message from Kiir is clear, I am not stepping down, not now and not in the near future whatever maybe the cost. The opposition camp is also not backtracking, their demand of Kiir must go is intact, the die-hards has it and Mr. Machar has no magic of peace without his base, he will have to join the fight and win. Kiir has a chance to save the little he has through IGAD peace process, now and not tomorrow otherwise a war of no winner is about to add more lives lost and destruction in the long run. Well, apart from politics, Happy New Year.

# CHAPTER 3

## 2015 ARTICLES

**April 9, 2015**

**In a Nutshell**

The Confusion and Dilemma of Greater Upper Nile Region.

What is happening in Cholloland? Is it the time to massacre the Chollo people after the Nuer? Well, in my opinion, Johnson Olouny is honest in his quest of securing and liberating the Chollo land, he is neither with Nuer nor with Dinka but he wants them both out from Cholloland and territories. His strategy and alliance with Salva is to get the Nuer out first using the Dinka but if this phase is a success, he will be puzzled by how he will drive the Dinka out of Malakal. Hopefully it shouldn't be the opposite. The Nuer hasn't claimed Malakal as theirs unlike Dinka who have declared that clearly and in many cases.

The Nuer has been controlling the seat of power in Malakal not because it is theirs but because it is the capital of the Upper Nile State in which they are the majority. This may have printed a sad image of domination and marginalization in our Chollo brothers' minds and hearts something that is preventing the unity of greater Upper Nile and giving Salva Kiir a solid ground to exploit and hence pitting Upper Nile against itself. The War has started in Upper Nile, and it been destroying its people and its infrastructures as well for the last 15 months. Upper Nile is the field of war, its cities, represented by Malakal, Bentiu, Nasir and Bor are merely ghost towns, and most of its people are between the dead, the displaced or the uprooted to the far refuge lands. Ironically, still its politician's sons and daughters are in disarray and begging Salva Kiir for more destruction of their own region and people in return for false promises and useless positions.

It is Kiir who has promised Olouny like he did to David Yau Yau on how he will give him the control and power of Upper Nile State should he fight along his side against Riek Machar and the Nuer. Well, general Olouny has been doing his job very well, securing Malakal for his own reasons and not necessarily Salva's until last week when his second in command was ambushed and killed mercilessly. Now that has opened Olouny's eyes and his army about the hidden strategy of Mr. Salva and his supporters' base in Upper Nile. Salva Kiir has brought Greater Upper Nile to its demise, Nuer are fighting Dinka, Chollo are fighting Nuer, Dinka are fighting Chollo, Murle are fighting Nuer, Nuer are fighting Annuak and the cycle of tribal violence continue. However, don't expect Mayardit to send a high delegation being led by Wani Igga to come and solve the problems of Upper Nile region. The man never contradicts himself in such cases.

Kiir has incited tribalism among the people of South Sudan in order for him to rule and it is destroying the social fabric of this nation, bringing this country to a sure collapse unless reversed. The SPLM-IO has provided federalism as a solution, proposed the 21 states to ensure all are represented within their rightful and ancestral territories. The Nuer are going back to their original states leaving Chollo with their own rightful Malakal, Pashuda and all their ancestral territories and so is every ethnic group will be represented in their own land. The SPLM-IO must not let the Chollo people down even though some of their politicians are still confused and back stabbing the movement for reforms and restructuring of South Sudan on new bases. Johnson Olouny is fighting for Chollo people but someone needs to assure him where his true allies are before he himself is victimized as well.

It is high time the Greater Upper Nile realizes what Kiir has in mind for its people and future. It is the time we see the divisive politics of Mr. Kiir not because we are tribalists like him but it is important to know the devilish politics that's being cooked in tribal palaces in Juba in order to protect the innocent people of Upper Nile and South Sudan as whole.

## April 22, 2015

## In a Nutshell

Gen. Kiir still believes South Sudan won't disintegrate or collapse, well he might have chosen at will to bury his head in the deep sand or have chosen to avoid reading all the indicators and realities on the ground pointing towards that miserable end. South Sudan is slowly but surely sinking and its Captain is in an absolute state of denial. Mr. Kiir needs to know he is running a country where its collapse affects the destiny of all South Sudanese and not a business entity of his own.

I don't blame him either since he is neither the first nor the last dictator who will cling to power until his last breath and until his country and nation is no more. However, the metaphors and maps of his power base are changing and so is the war and the economic performance of the country leave alone the question whether South Sudan is still truly functioning as a viable and sovereign state in the regional and international functions.

Riek Machar will be doing a great favor to Kiir if he signs any peace agreement any time soon. Strategically, it is not Reik Machar and his movement or powers that are shrinking and fading but Kiir's powers that are truly in constant decrease and going down the sure fall since the inception of this current political crisis. The longer the war rages, the more his powers diminishes even further and his regime lies and plans comes to light. The problem with Kiir is that he is not aware of the fact that being a head of state is something and being a rebel is completely a different thing otherwise he could have hurried to stop the bleed and fix what is broken. No country can fully function economically or politically while more than half of its army has rebelled, its economic resources and outlets are malfunctioned and shut down.

Mr. Machar is advancing and his suggested systems and reforms are proving to be the right formula that is needed to fix South Sudan and to assure an equal and fair distribution of resources and power sharing yet he still being politically bullied off. I haven't figure it out yet how Mr. Kiir will restore his credibility back and neither I know how he will bring together again the warring South Sudan tribes in his name nor a country he so divided along tribal lines. How the trust within this battered nation will again be rebuilt, how the wounds of losing loved ones, personal properties and the sad effects of the ongoing untold suffering will be healed by the same man who made them possible in a way or another. Someone else may have a better chance of bringing this country back to life. It is a time for new leadership

## April 22, 2015

### In a Nutshell

The tribal extremists have something in common. Each one in his/her narrow world and shallow thinking strongly justifies the inhuman deeds and words committed against the innocents. They also fail as always in identifying their soul targets and the best ways to get down with them. Otherwise, the innocents shouldn't be the ones paying the price for this madness of the few.

I have seen the spokesperson of government of South Sudan, minister of misinformation Makuei Lueth one of the brutal tribal extremist that has helped breeds the extremism ideology in this about to collapse nation. He is by all accounts unfit to hold a national seat and should be made to resign at least if the government he represents has any remaining credibility and popular conscience. If parts do make the whole, then any acts of disintegrating the parts to destroy the whole should be condemned and fought against. This is what our tribalist minister is excellently doing, disintegrating South Sudan.

One does wonders that whether what this sorry minister says and does has any relation with the so-called national government in Juba. I don't know whether he speaks for a national government or his tribe or in particular his clan.

If so, then Makuei Lueth is the spokesperson of the genocidal network, disguised under umbrella of national government. Hence, every branch of this government is a function that serves one of these tasks, the planning, execution, cover-up and misinformation of the ongoing ethnic killings. They are using the national resources and capabilities of South Sudan state to executes tribal agenda, personal envy and a campaign of mass murdering, uprooting of the very South Sudanese people. It is systematic, well planned ethnic based killing, rape and uprooting of certain section of the nation, namely the Nuer.

Ethnic killings! Well, Juba has started it on Dec. 15th, 2013 against the Nuer ethnic group to cleverly divert the real reasons behind the political crisis that caused this war and to engage the poor people of South Sudan in killing each other rather than Kiir regime instead. It is unfortunate, that it succeeded. Anything that comes after Juba massacre, is but pure revenge and counter revenge.

In a society where tribal pride is high, politicians always tends to use their tribes to cover-up for their personal and political failures, shortcomings and selfish narrow interests. Manipulating the tribal ego, they, the politicians, end up pitting the primitive's tribes against each other's and this is what Kiir and his team in Juba have done. Well, no doubt now that the wining evils are celebrating behind the scene while the poor South Sudanese are finishing themselves.

First, it was Nuer revenge against the cold blood murdering of their loved ones, rape of their women, and humiliation of everything they have pride of. Now, the Dinka has followed the suite in counter revenge and the cycle continues in a more extreme fashion, brutal killings, rape, humiliation and total destruction. What was the regime in Juba expecting really if not this?

In a quest for a balance in the game of blame and accountability, the United Nation is trying to condemns all of these brutal killings and all human rights abuses. That's their job. Who started it or who acted in revenge is not theirs.

In such cases, revenge is always traced back to who started the acts of murder, rape and all brutal humans' abuses. It is Juba who started it and it is the same Juba who is igniting its flames, here and there, in a well calculated game behind the scene. The goal is to divert the direction of the war from South Sudanese vs. failed Kiir regime to South Sudanese tribes against each other. All this, is for the sake of Kiir to stays in power and his regime to survive.

Astonishingly and without a least degree of shame and in the midst of this shameful bloody game, Juba still saying it is a people government. Comes on, which people?

In real world, if you hit a car and made the car hit other cars, it will be still your fault. Juba, can never be innocent in this, in fact, it is the mother of all this misery and it should be made to pay twice, its faults and its victim's faults. That's justice.

Well, anyone who still don't get it because his/her immediate environment is saying otherwise, South Sudan has already collapsed and is going down further on the complete disintegration, Kiir will not give up powers in Juba nor Machar will give up resistance in the bush. To avoid this catastrophic cycle, someone should win or both shall come to a compromise.

However, the tribal feud is widening, the rate of death is climbing higher and higher and the tribalist mindset is even deep down into the extreme hatred. Congrats wenna Lueth-dit, keep the fire of tribal hatred aflame and cultivates the dead bodies, as many as you want. It must be the residue of communism that guides that brutal mind of yours, no doubt.

**April 23, 2015**

**In a Nutshell**

The Greater Upper Nile (GUN) region has gone from bad to worse, its social and economic fabric is already in disarray and merely destroyed. Its political and intellectual elite and leaders are far from touching base. Mrs. Nyandeng De Mabior, Adok Nyaba, Riek Machar and Lam Akol can't just play politics without a strategy or fight a war without direction. Salva Kiir has kept the Bhar Al-Gazal region at least in some kind of union and untouched by this war so far and so is Wani Igga of Greater Equatoria. Greater Upper Nile once a leader of south in all fronts, now a center of chaos that is deteriorating every single day, what is the future of GUN?

Upper Nile can't afford looking at itself in context of tribes, doing tribal politics that harm its collective will, political and economic power, that's definitely an outsider wish, an approach that makes Salva Kiir and Malong Awan giggles big with mockery laugh. To draw a new direction for GUN region, its politicians and intellectuals must touch base and draw a direction for their actions and policies that direct their region towards a meaningful destiny rather than leaving it to outsiders to determined its fate. That fate will not be in favor of any stakeholder of GUN Region.

There is no national approach to save neither GUN nor a national leader in Juba that's concerned with the level of destruction and loss of lives out there. Kiir has declared it a war zone, and managed to exploit its tribes' differences and political rivalry to install his policy of divide to rule and hence pitting the Dinka against the Nuer, Nuer against Dinka and Dinka against Chollo and so on.

But all troubles and political turmoil in Greater Upper Nile can't be blamed to Mr. Kiir rather than to weakness of Upper Nile elite base and poor coordination of GUN politicians and intellectuals. They could do better if they weren't concerned only about their tribes and immediate interests promised to be fulfilled by Kiir from Juba at the expenses of their own region and people. Should we say the peaceful co-existence between Chollo-Nuer-Dinka in GUN is almost over, why and to whose benefit?

A political union in GUN could hasten bringing a political settlement to the civil war. When greater Upper Nile region acts as a one political entity it is likely that more national gains will be secured as well as great local interests. People may need to know where their feet are before flying their heads high everywhere. Well, I know it is never easy for politicians to come to union point. Kiir is still a distributor of power, positions and wealth and for any region to be safe and in political union is merely up-to how Kiir uses that power. In absence of any resistance from our patriot politicians we will never know where we are going to land. Hopefully the opposite

## May 7, 2015

## In a Nutshell

With every presidential decree and every new SPLA-Juba recruits' graduation, Kiir and Paul Awan are on the gradual march to consolidate their firm grip on South Sudan's power pillars both at military and political fronts. A long term plan like one that enabled Omer Al-Bashier of Sudan to arrive to his 30 years' ultimate power in Sudan with his only few trusted men and everyone who has a recall on how the Omer Al-Bashier junta came to power in 1989 will realize that not those who brought Omer Al-Bashier to power are still around him and that for sure include the mastermind and architect of the whole 1989 coup, namely Dr. Hassan Al-Turabi. However, East Africa in particular and Africa in general has many bad role models who have ruled for more than three decades and that inspire Kiir to rule for life and do everything in that context.

Political Power has its layers, those that in the far distance, those in middle and those that are close trustees and the true movers of everything or let us say those who has the ears of Kiir in South Sudan case. Mr. Kiir and Mr. Awan and in the process of enabling their expected lengthy and long rule are coming to clear the hurdles in their way and hence it is likely that those who pose potential threats and would-be power challengers in the short or long-term timeframe and in both political and military institutions will be eliminated in a conspiracy or another. Gen. Bior Asud, a man who has his own contribution in the liberation war and who has kept himself out of this Kiir and Junta tribal war and been silent since then is now under a malicious attack and a target of well calculated conspiracy. They called it a financial transaction case. However, what raises one's eyes brows is that how a $30 million contract service could ever bypass a financial system that is all setup and packed with Kiir and Awan close loyalists? We know for sure of the many fake contracts of Kiir inner circle that has robbed this country of its valuable resources and crumbled its poor economy but could Bior Asud be that fool not to know that the system is Kiir and Awan owned and in which for sure he is not one of it or at least not that close. Not likely.

At least you have to be one of those insiders of the Juba corrupt system to pursue such a foolish endeavor shamelessly and fearlessly. Well, it seems the conspiracy itself is the one proved itself to be foolish, shallow in both design and reasoning and its planners were no better at all. But that doesn't matter to them. What matter is that they are removing powerful figures and those would-be threats from both military and political establishments. Someone must be doing the thinking and planning part for Kiir and Awan and now the question is who thinks and plans for Kiir and Awan? I have to leave it to the readers to speculate on that. However, Kiir for sure is the one who implement the terms and recommendations of the masterminds in disguise through the presidential decrees and Mr. Awan through recruiting of the private army and of course the notorious national security services through cracking down on political opponents. The implementation is ongoing so expect more presidential decrees, political conspiracies, Kiir's national security kidnapping and disappearances without a trace

Gen. Bior Ajang case is a political motivated conspiracy; the allegations do not hold waters. But anyway, what does really holds waters in Juba of Kiir and Awan? Neither in the case of former acting governor of Aweil, Kuel Aquer Kuel nor in the case of Gen. Mach Paul the former Military Intelligence Boss but ironically enough it is a case of power consolidation in both military and political institutions and hence expects other to join the list, sooner or later. Welcome to Kiir-Awan era.


**May 1, 2015**

**In a Nutshell**

It will be a hit of illusion for a social or political organization or even a business entity to make it through to success without unity of its team, objectives, and mission. Out of knowledge and experience, those on the top echelon of such an organization must ensure that the body of such an entity is united, sound and has the abilities and capabilities to execute the mission and objective of the organization to success.

Organizations that eats itself from within in a way or another cannot blame but themselves for giving advantage to others to succeed. Weakening one's own competitive advantage at will is the greatest ignorance and harm an individual or organization can cause to self. Yet our beloved country South Sudan has one of the most effective divisive, harmful and self-destructive ways and techniques that we have known so far. They are enshrined within a social culture, a political philosophy and a mindset that were inherited from both North Sudan and Anglo-Saxon divide to rule policy. It seems it will take a while and great deal of troubles and lots of lives before we reach a stable character of our own as a nation, a country and a society.

We could be lucky enough if we have leaders of their own class of high wisdom, knowledge and guidance that could have had diagnosed at early stages of these social and cultural characteristic ills that are the causes of our problems today. However, the reality is the complete opposite. Neither our leaders nor the intellectuals seem to be any different and hence there is no different between head and tail, no direction to this nation and country. We are all tribally and mentally sick and good leadership bankrupt. But at least the sick need to acknowledge first that he or she is sick to find the right cure and treatment. Well in our case that is not likely because our ego-centric collective character is far from coming down to this and hence we have chosen the collective Hell. Unfortunately,

In the name of politics, the devil is doing a great harm to South Sudan. Our society is infested with massive divisive and harmful elements that have done a great deal of damage, divisions through propaganda and lies. Gossips become the norm, defamation and character assassination is the new politics. Well I thought politics was for a high purpose and a good politician is the one with principled politics. Unity, Peace, Security, and Development of a nation and country should be regarded as good principles that the good politicians are all about.

Our leaders may need to step back, regain the goodwill and faith to lead their people. They can't live in the same standards of the ordinary man when it comes to wisdom, knowledge and good governance. They must be different. They should be the shepherd and the compass of the ship otherwise the drowning of the ship is high likely or are we already deep under the sea? Hopefully not.

**May 13, 2015**

**In a Nutshell**

**Bentiu will outlive Salva Kiir**

Despite the enormous destruction and the untold suffering, Bentiu will outlive Gen. Salva Kiir, Gen. Paul Malong and Gen. Kuol Manyang and thirty years from now it's today malnourished and battered children will never forgive nor forget none of these brutal generals. How their mothers were raped, killed and subjected to this brutal violence and untold suffering and confined for more than a bitter year in over water-flooded UNMISS camps where poisonous mosquitoes make their lives another nightmare.

Thirty years from now, Bentiu children will remembers the sad ordeal of their Bentiu elders who were chased away to the snakes and beast swamps riddled where only fear, hunger, disease and hopelessness are what they know. Surviving on the tree leaves and wild fruits and living the moment when you don't know when and where the aggressors could emerge from nowhere. To be killed by an external enemy is something but to be killed by your own is another. Not in our fresh memory that even the enemy of yesterday, Khartoum that we have fought for 50 years and received our independence from haven't done to Bentiu or any other South Sudanese town what the SPLA-Juba have done. Destroying cities and burning them to ashes like they are never part of South Sudan map, killing its people and subjecting them to the utmost suffering as they are never part of South Sudan house of nationalities. What could justify such a hatred, such a violence and such brutality in what the SSTV calls shamelessly "One Country, One Nation"

The damage is already done my people, engraved within these children minds and hearts. These would-be the men of tomorrow and future of this country and realistically let us tell ourselves the truth, in thirty years from now, whether these today's kids will ever remember Salva Kiir, Paul Malong and Kuol Manyang as in any other form rather than pure killers of their mothers, who raped their young sisters, destroyers of their future aspirations, homes and the whole cities of state of Bentiu. Their lives have been turned upside down, hopes and dreams are no more and ironically it is by the SPLA-Juba, Sudan's People Liberation Army. A liberation Army, I repeat. But what a liberation Army by any standards?

The message of Juba in destroying Bentiu and making it the scene of the worst atrocities ever through the course of this war could be summed-up in three assumptions. Apart from it being the rich hub of the cursed oil, it is fundamentally where Dr. Riek Machar comes from and hence destroying it and its people is an enjoyable trend to the Juba aggressors.

Bentiu is strategic economically but now it has been brought to zero-sum economic value, none of its oil fields or refinery is functioning. However, what is fundamental about Bentiu is its historical and cultural value as the heart and origin of the Nuer people, its destruction to the tribalists has for sure a devilish joy.

Bentiu is the gate of this war to Warrap and the rest of Bhar-El-Gazhal. A total control of the SPLM/A-IO to the Liech state territories make the war transferable to the hometown of Kiir and Awan. So they are keeping SPLM/A-IO pre-occupied and at defensive position. Destroying Bentiu and then later Lou Nuer, mark the end of SPLM/A-IO major supporters, so they think. Those who are still confused of Kiir-Awan strategy won't blame any but themselves.

The bravery and firmness of Bentiu Nuer people in depending their historical city is admired in the greatest meaning. They have been fighting with SPLA-Juba, Sudan Mercenaries, Ugandan Hire-to-Kill army, and the Kiir's Nuer Militia but despite all that, they have been there fighting all these military woes with a rare resilience and bravery for the last 17 months. Bravo Bentiu Liech. You should never and never give in. Victory is near and certain.

However, the SPLM/A-IO might need a new military strategy to save and depend Bentiu despite the fact that the capture and recapture of cities isn't the ultimate objective of this rebellion but paralyzing the regime economically and politically in whatever advances the objective of the total regime change and the Kiir- Awan dictatorship collapse and that will lead to the sure rebirth of South Sudan for all South Sudanese, democratic and united. The war has reached a point of no return and it is worthless not to finish the mission. Our people have paid the highest price, the precious and valuable and nothing should stop their march, nothing at all.

## May 16, 2015

### In a Nutshell

How do we celebrate May 16th? When May 16th has become privately owned, tribally and selectively celebrated and when the government of South Sudan became Kiir & Awan Company Inc. Shamelessly, Our Martyrs are being dishonored every day with every tribal presidential decree that appoints a new member of a tribal government. With every tribal presidential decree that profiles our country tribally. Our Martyrs haven't died for a tribal country or a tribal government. Unfortunately, with every biased presidential decree, Gen. Kiir dishonors our Martyrs and the true cause they fought for.

The simple men and women who came from all diverse tribes of South Sudan and from all walks of life, the simple and ordinary men and women whose love and loyalty for this country and its good people made them to give their valuable and precious lives for the hijacked independence. Never have they died for a tribal country or a tribal government or a tribal Army.

Martyrs whose today sisters, mothers, fathers are subjected to all sort of grave atrocities, killing, rape, hunger, diseases and uprooting from the land their brothers, uncles, nieces and fathers died for. Martyrs whose villages are burned to ashes, leveled and destroyed to the ground. What a dishonor and what a way of giving back to those who have given the most precious and the most valuable, LIFE, for the independence of this country and the freedom of its people.

Martyrs whose families have been scattered around in UN camps and far in refuge lands, martyrs whose sons and daughters are aging in exile afar from the land their fathers died for. But behold and never give up. The truth is there, shining like never before, our Martyrs haven't died in vain. The South Sudanese revolution was right and just. It wasn't a wrong revolution neither it was a one without a cause. Unfortunately, it has been stolen by the greedy and the liars, hijacked by the corrupts and opportunists in a bright daylight and the South Sudanese people must unite and be strong to take it back from the thieves and lairs disguised in the skin of liberators and patriots.

The memory is still fresh and can't ever be distorted by any greedy liar in Juba or elsewhere. Those who found a new qualification and a degree called "We have fought for this war and we are here to rule this country" and "we have liberated you" and we are the "Liberators" and so on of all the reasoning and justifications of the corrupts, incompetents and thieves. Simply and firmly, Which South Sudanese family didn't have a Martyr within its immediate or extended family ranks and file until these thieves and hijackers want to tell us and write us a fake history and distorted version of South Sudan liberation war?

The history is still there, fresh as never before. How those South Sudanese who went to bush between 1983 until the CPA was signed went there to liberate themselves from Khartoum domination, religious and racial discrimination, socio-economic and political injustice and marginalization. They were all one tribe called Jubin or South Sudanese, all from their diverse tribes' small and big and all different walks of life. They left to the harsh bushes of South Sudan united in purpose and objective until they have there in the bushes they discovered new masters and new ugly domination and injustice in the name of tribe and you don't have to ask why people keep defecting back and forth, all is clear, just send your imagination to the Tribal Empire.

To be a nationalist and a tribalist at heart is a non-working combo. You can't play them both forever. Sooner or later, the reality must appear as we have seen now. There is for sure a time South Sudanese people will know and discovers the truth, sooner or later and take their country back and in case the luxuries of power and wealth have made you forgot, let us reminds you again and again that lies are short lived.

## June 2, 2015

## In a Nutshell

Only the suffering people of South Sudan, the true victims of Kiir's war can truly value the vital role Mr. Toby Lanzer, the UN relief coordinator has played during the 17th month old South Sudan genocidal war. For the victims of this war, Toby Lanzer, is the food, the security, the shelter, the medicine and all that saves ones' life from a sure death. Mr. Kiir should be so much thankful and appreciative to Mr. Lanzer instead of expelling him.

This is a man who has saved millions of people of South Sudanese when their leaders were busy butchering and killing them, chasing them away from their homes, starving them to death and leaving them vulnerable to the diseases and dangers in the wild bushes of South Sudan. Kiir should be thankful to Toby Lanzer who has successfully coordinated one of the most effective and massive relief efforts the world has witnessed in recent history. Efforts that without, both South Sudan and Kiir regime by now could have been a gone case. Since the start of this war, billions of dollars in relief and humanitarian assistance has been poured in to save South Sudanese people. Toby Lanzer was sleepless rallying the world to save the severe malnourished South Sudanese children and women when the president of the country was busy spending billions hiring mercenaries and buying heavy weapons to murder the very same people he claims to lead.

But here we go again and just as we as South Sudanese will never learn from our terrible past, someone is repeating the scenario of Khartoum politics and actions against UN during the North vs. South war, when the UN was siding with Khartoum's war victims, the same South Sudanese in this case and where Kiir himself was a second in command of SPLM/A, the national liberation movement turned today to a tribal empowerment movement.

10 years, is the relative time in which Mr. Kiir has gone from a rebel to a president of a country, a relative time indeed that can't erase the bitter and the sad part of yesterday even though the power and glory in J1 is so abundance. Today the views and actions of Mr. Kiir as president against the same UN and in comparison to his past as a rebel are no less than double standards and contradictory stance for a man who has claimed to be a

liberator and had spent half of his life fighting for justice, liberty and prosperity as the SPLM/A's coat of arms declare clearly. Toby Lanzer's role has saved South Sudan but say what? Again Kiir and his decision making consultants has shown that they are out of touch with what is truly the situation of the people of this country.

The recent atrocities of Kiir's army in Bentiu and Malakal in which the international community has documented all sort of heinous crimes; rape, abduction, killing of children, torching and burning whole villages to ashes shouldn't make Kiir and his support base gone wild. They should just admit the truth and fix what is wrong with their tribal militias named wrongly as South Sudan National Army. There is no national army that its mission is to kill, rape and abduct the very people they should be defending. No national army that will burn to ashes villages within the national territories of South Sudan they claim to defend.

The truth of the atrocities is out and will always be, expelling Toby Lanzer or not, this won't change the mandate of UN or the responsibilities of International community towards the people of South Sudan. South Sudanese leaders won't change the world but all they need is to change themselves to be better leaders for their own country and people. Technology has made the world just a small village today and not possible for dictators to hide their atrocities anymore. Kiir and Co. should blame it to technology not Toby Lanzer.

## June 4, 2015

### In a Nutshell

How the South Sudanese civil war will be put to rest is a puzzle in itself. Neither the South Sudanese nor the international community has an accurate predicted answer on this complex question. The war definitely is hurting Kiir's regime economically and politically but how long will it take to defeat him militarily and what is likely to happen before the opposition forces could achieve its final victory is a matter of critical speculation. The economic collapse of South Sudan doesn't literally mean the end of Salva regime. Remember, this is a tribal –based regime and it will stay as such as long as it is the only air that gives it the means for survival and protection.

If Juba fall today to the opposition forces, it is likely that there is not going to be a smooth transition of power that will finally bring stability and peace to South Sudan and its people. It is likely that a new bloody chapter of tribal blood bath will be what will take place. The socio-political structure of this nation is so shaky and tribally based to the extent that it is a fertile hub to those tribal politicians to manipulate and exploit. We are not yet to call a spade a spade in our politics, we side with our tribal politicians whether they are wrong or corrupt and this is strongly evident in this current war. This means crowning a new leader on political humiliation of another from a different tribe brings but more tribal genocides.

At the moment, the hawks of war and the die-hard supporters of both camps are living in the joy of capture and recapture of cities and the allure of battlefields of how many soldiers has been killed and how many heavy weapons has been captured but I bet that any of them has a clear say on whether they will make a clear-cut victory on the other side anytime soon. Well if not, then such a war is a waste of lives and resources and a destruction of the country we both share. Alternative thinking and approach should be given a chance. A political settlement will save us lives and total collective collapse of our country and nation.

But is political settlement likely with Gen. Salva Kiir in power and as president? I believe the majority of the opposition don't even want to hear such a thing neither its leadership want to jeopardize its credibility by even suggesting such a risky approach. A political tradeoff between the two warring parties is what should work. Well, whether this war will bring a productive outcome or not, some want to fight Gen. Salva to avenge the injustices and massacres of their loved ones murdered by the regime and even though that's also a cycle of more death and loses that is even increasing the agony and suffering of the victims but at least it is not a surrender or a give in to Gen. Salva.

Mr. Salva is already in heated seat, he has been weakened and his power is shrinking on daily basis. He is losing the international community, his government and army are increasingly becoming tribal and the latter is committing appalling ethnic based grave atrocities and this encouraging dissertation and defection from his government and army as well. Economically, he is almost done, dollar prices are sky-rocketing and the inflation is just climbing higher. Any political settlement this time will be a rescue to his regime and not the other way around.

G10 or the former political detainees and their ongoing initiative of bringing a halt to war through the SPLM reunification is but an attempt to save the little political wet they still have. That's a rescue to them first and to Mr. Salva more than it is a rescue to South Sudan and its people. Salva and after all the destruction, loss of lives and the enormous mistrust and tribal divide he created, is in this case being crowned by G10 again and like nothing have ever happen. On the other hand, I have no idea by what face they will suggest to Dr. Machar, Dr. Nyaba and the rest of the opposition crew the possible revocation of their dismissal and re-instatement of each to his former position in both SPLM party and the government by Salva Kiir, the president and sadly how Mr. Salva will revoke and re-instate the lives of South Sudanese lost during the 18 month bloody war or how their burned to ashes villages will be build, mental and psychological wounds be re-instated back to normalcy.

Dr. Machar and his colleagues in SPLM/A-IO are likely to reject the G10 proposal or accept it with conditions of reforms and restructuring of the state but what next? If the SPLM/A-IO rejected the proposal, it is likely that G10 will join Salva faction and it is possible that a political move will follow shortly by appointing a Nuer vice president other than Dr. Machar by Salva to weaken and divide the opposition backed by Nuer majority.

However, Dr. Riek Machar has the army and the political movement that is hurting Salve's regime economically and politically and as long as he plays with the war card, the nightmare, economic and political decline of Salva regime won't be saved by G10-SPLM-Juba reunification. But the concern is what political and military gains Gen. Salva will add by bringing in G10 group. It is likely that a combined strategy that will isolate, weaken and divide SPLM/A-IO from within will be pursued by the new coalition. However, if G10 group play it on side of reforms and restructuring of state, a political settlement is more likely to occur. Let us see what G10 will say about the suggested reforms and restructuring of the state and its deformed institutions or whether they are joining Juba empty handed and just saving their political destiny.


## June 24, 2015

### In a Nutshell

Don't be surprised of Cde Pagan Amum reinstatement because this is what the Arusha reunification agreement has recommended and there is more to follow in the coming days. The Arusha thing actually started earlier with the revocation of dismissal of all the SPLM members of political Bureau dismissed in the course of this political turmoil by Gen. Kiir and that include of course the reinstatement of Dr. Riek Machar as the deputy chairman of SPLM.

However, the G10 or the former political detainees, whom Riek Machar and the Nuer fought bravely and paid so dearly for their release in the first days of this madness war, refused from the day one of their release to give

Riek Machar the political and military boost he needed most in order for his movement to have a national image and a national echo that could attract most of South Sudanese if not all to his case against Gen. Salva Kiir. That was so deadly a denial to success. That denial alone has helped the war to be conducted, viewed and so far regarded as a Dinka - Nuer war rather than a South Sudanese uprising against the failed leadership of Mr. Kiir.

Another narrative is that Kiir himself was smart and clever enough. He has released the former detainees with effective conditions and restrictions that were still engulfing their movement and decisions. Their financial assets and properties rights were freeze and could be completely seized if they have shown any active political activities against Kiir or joined Mr. Machar in a direct way and hence the G10 stayed out of the game, at least pretended to be dumb or active indirectly and behind the curtains.

We all agree that an internal power struggle within the SPLM party was mishandled and let out from the party political corridors and parameters to the fragile- tribally composed army, security services and the public and hence came the slaughters and the massacres of innocents in the name of tribes,1991 and Riek Machar.

In the light of that, the road map to peace as per Arusha and IGAD, is that, unite these politically shattered SPLM party and which the war was a result of its divide and this shall bring the warring tribes back to unity whether in the many opposing armies, security organs, and the divided nation. There is a total rejection to Arusha by the opposition supporters and by the majority of South Sudanese. That's because the current SPLM/A is no longer the liberation days' SPLM/A but a bloody corrupted one in South Sudanese's minds now.

Therefore, a re-unification of the SPLM that caused all this suffering is not the case now. The case is beyond the SPLM, it is a national demand for reforms and restructuring, accountability, a new face and direction for South Sudan. The case can be summed-up in is these pending following questions, who for the God's sake will re-instate the thousands of the lives of precious souls lost, whole villages and three states leveled down to ground, who will bring healing to the mentally and psychologically traumatized nation. Those are the pending questions

I think there is a need for an official statement about the position of SPLM/A-IO that declare clearly whether that they are not part of Arusha and that what happened today is not part of an inclusive process. Predictions are that the SPLM/A-IO may split to those for Arusha and those who aren't but it will be for the best interest of the movement to abide by any decision of the leadership. A new political era is in the making, a one that need courage from the leaders and the nation alike. Where does Mr. Machar stand? What is his new strategy regarding the unfolding political situation, any official statement from the SPLM/A-IO?

**June 20, 2015**

**In a Nutshell**

How to avoid going down at an end of the presidential term limits? You either have to amend the constitution and extend the presidential term limits or plunge the country into a political crisis that will enable you to declare a state of emergency, postpone elections and keep the country at war until all your political opponents are no more and until all your political objectives and personal interests are achieved. The Dec 15th, 2013 political turmoil that brought us to this deadly war in South Sudan is not a work of chance by all indicators.

However, enough has been said about the conspiracy of Dec.15th, 2013 and I am not on a repeat but rather to explore whether the latest political events do instill any hopes and expectations of a final peace agreement between the two warring parties and of course with the inclusion of the rest of stakeholders. My guts are telling me that a close doors and intensive political consultations amid international pressure is currently ongoing to narrow the gaps and differences between our political leaders and warring parties regarding the latest IGAD's power sharing proposal.

There is no military victory or solution in this war in the near future and those who are insisting on taking it further have also to read the tribal structure of South Sudan that frame the underpinning political foundation of our tribally-structured nation. Mr. Machar will need to win the Dinka's public opinion in order for him to be a substitute good leader than Salva Kiir and to form the federal democratic, united and prosperous South Sudan he does envision. Salva Kiir may go but the Dinka people are not going anywhere just like the Nuer, the Bari, the Chollo and the rest of 64 tribes people of South Sudan. For Mr. Machar, that's a hard political reality that is not less than Salva Kiir winning the Nuer's public opinion back after the Dec 15th, 2013 Juba massacre and all the grave atrocities committed in its aftermath.

In context of what is achievable and what is not, what is realizable and what is not, a political compromise must arise between all the political stakeholders and in particular the warring parties. Our leaders must demonstrate the needed political will, abilities and skills that provide political solutions to nations problems rather than the blame games and fishing in dirty political waters. Lack of solutions to South Sudan's political problems are due to a political poverty of our politicians but not because we have political problems that can't be solved or impossible to solve.

Bringing South Sudan back to normalcy, peace and stability is not an easy task either but if our leaders from both camps are putting the welfare of their people first, the dreams and the hopes of future generations, nothing is hard to them that cannot be tackled and resolved. Putting this country back to what it should be and to where it should be heading as a stable, peaceful and united democracy is a shared responsibility of all South Sudanese and in particular if a final peace deal is realized.

## June 25, 2015

### In a Nutshell

I wish we all know why the old man and his son have decided to carry the Donkey instead of them being carried by the Donkey in that famous old story. Political decisions regarding critical matters such as war and peace can't ever be made by a divided political public street. That won't ever happen. War and peace related decisions must be made by those leaders who have the destiny of the people and country at hand and based on the higher interests of both two. The old folks in Africa do need to consider the future of the continent and its young generations. Leaders do step down voluntarily to save countries from collapse and to change the course of events towards a meaningful end. Africa can't still be run with the same style or seen with the same lens of 1940s and 50s.

South Sudan case is no different. There is no single doubt that the SPLM as a political party does need a new blood and style of leadership, the one that can be said as truly transformational and unitary in real sense and with a solid long-term nation-state building vision. Now that the SPLM is in disarray and divided, we can't deny the fact that as South Sudanese people, we are also divided nation and confused as hell.

Ironically, most if not all of us don't know that we all belong to the SPLM in a way or another, either to the SPLM-IO faction, Juba or G10, Cobra or DC and just to mention few among many SPLMs and that all the gates of the SPLM/A are still being controlled by the same tribal politicians who have been there for three decades or more. Recycling the same ideas and approaches no matter whether they have worked or not because if they did, our situation won't be the same or in fact, the worst. However, none of us is telling this old generation to retire the political life and let their grandkids in the age of Obama and Cameron to take over and maybe a new fresh ideas and new style of working political leadership may inject a new fresh wave into the country and its socio-economic and political life.

We thank them for their tireless efforts in delivering this country from Khartoum's domination even though they ended their mission miserably reflected in this deadly war. However, they need to retire the political life for the sake of the country and the new generations. Even old computers don't perform well as new ones neither their RAM memory are still in the same capacity nor performance as Moore's law has predicted right decades ago. For instant, Kenya and Rwanda has witnessed a new fresh ideas and direction brought by their relatively young leaders and both countries are now witnessing a socio-economic and political transformation in a uniquely rapid rate and Rwanda's economy is said to be one of fastest growing economies in the world. This is because of leaders that are talking about vision of 2020, 2050 not setbacks of 1991 or 1983.

With all due respect, these old men need to retire the political life because their non-working ideas and never settled political grudges also will retire with them and pave the way for South Sudan to have new blood and embrace new ideas that are connected with the world current state of affairs and futuristic trends. The old style of Saddiq Al-Mahdi and Mohamed Osman Al-Margini kind of leadership where you need a blessing from the two traditional Sudanese leaders to have a position in government or the party can't work in 21th century's South Sudan if we do seriously mean the talk of development and transformation and not a sort of political manipulation.

Change is the law not the exception and it should be accepted smoothly as long as it is within the context of country and nation's higher interests. Now that the young and would-be tomorrow political leaders are also poisoned and got involved in this never ending cycle of old folks' grudges and political feuds, chances are that they will likely pick up the same old style of leadership that is not delivering a thing and end-up in the same cycle of violence, poverty and sectarianism, I wish not.

## June 30, 2015

### In a Nutshell

In the wake of South Sudan Independence fourth anniversary, the South Sudanese nation still at large an orphaned nation without a caring government and leaders who should take care of its wellbeing, betterment of its living standards, security and the dreams of living in peace, unity and prosperity. Thanks to the United Nations for being there for this nation from day one of our struggle with Khartoum's successive regimes before the independence up to these days of our self-destructive war and as a matter of fact 2/3 of this nation is now under UN food assistance. Thanks to the nature that has blessed this country with a good fertile land, river Nile and all the natural resources that without, this nation without a caring government and leaders could have a tough ordeal on earth.

Traditionally, cultivating the land and looking upon one's herds of cattle and all other domestic animals was the traditional survival way of our good people since time immemorial. If you ever lived there among our good people in their villages and saw with your eyes how they love the way they live their simple lives in their villages you will know that government's help and interference is the last thing they ever thought about.

Unfortunately, amidst this tribal war, who any longer cultivate crops and look after his cattle when most of the country and in particular the greater Upper Nile region became a battlefield and with these innocent villagers being the first victims of the untold violence and all sort of terror. Their villages are either burned to ashes, cattle stolen and crops destroyed and the villagers themselves if lucky enough and their lives spared by the violence, they are either internally displaced to UN protection sites, uprooted to the far refuge lands or they have joined the opposition army or the government's. They must be in a miserable state, disconnected from their farms, cattle and most importantly the simple peaceful traditional life they never imagine to depart.

Ironically enough, still the claim that governments were formed to look upon their people, to plan, enact and administer the policies and actions that should improve, enhance and protect the lives of its people. Still the claims that leaders are chosen or happened to be there to lead their people to a better life, raise their living standards, harmonize them to live in peace and build the nation and country that all dreams about. Where is that from our government and leaders?

Something must be wrong with our government and leadership style otherwise this shouldn't be the situation of people who have endured so much in their struggle to gain their independence and freedom. Something must be wrong with our ways of thinking and living. Something must not be functioning in our governance, socio-economic and political systems. What we inherited from Khartoum must be again redefined and restructured according to the new realities of an independent state and free nation. We must be on our own, stand on our feet with the substance and structure that will make us prospers in union and peace.

## July 3, 2015

## In a Nutshell

Rumors has it that the two warring SPLM/A factions are about to ink a final peace deal on July 7th, 2015 and in which the world and regional dignitaries are invited and that include of course president Obama who will be in tour visit to East Africa region and particular, Ethiopia and Kenya.

Whether these rumors have some truth in it or they are just mere lies spread by propagandists from here and there, the fact is, we cannot deny that there have been in recent few weeks, intensive consultations; face-to-face meetings between Kiir and Machar amid remarkable international pressure and efforts aimed to bring a possible breakthrough on the most deadlocked issues. On the other hand, I have predicted in my previous (In a nutshell) as well how the political game in South Sudan might change, how its outcomes may unfold with the G10 –SPLM/A-Juba merger under the Arusha process.

Sadly, peace in South Sudan will be realized when interests of our politicians are first realized and not necessarily our country or nation's higher interests. However, the possibly to re-unite SPLM/A as a party if it ever learned anything during this crisis, they should re-unite not to get back into business as usual but to repent and apologize to the people of South Sudan even though the magnitude of the crimes and lost caused by their political rift can't never be fully compensated or erased.

Therefore, for the possibly re-united SPLM/A should it be the case in the few coming weeks, the best way to repent and apologize to the battered people of South Sudan is an apology that can be translated into actions and not rosy words without any meaningful manifestations on the ground. A true transformation agenda for the nation and country might reduce the bitterness and hopelessness throughout the nation even though it will take years to eradicate the effects of this destructive war both on humans and physical infrastructure dimensions.

Accordingly, the SPLM/A-IO if it is opting for the possible peace deal, then it must connect and associate it with its agenda of constitutional reforms, governance system, restructuring of the state and its institutions as well as the demand for two separate armies until a new national army has been established but most importantly the demand for accountability and justice to victims of war. The grave war crimes committed during this war can't be left apprehended.

Predictions have it that the SPLM/A-IO my split upon such a possible peace deal that keep Salva Kiir as the head of the state. Well, that's likely but any mature political movement who has given its leaders a mandate to fight the war as well as to negotiate a political settlement should throw its full support behind its leadership and here the reasons; first, the leadership for sure may not have opted for such a decision unless it have reached it after careful consultations within its ranks, weighing and analyzing all the cons and pros and it implications in short and long run.

Second, SPLM-IO as a political movement has no gains to make by alienating itself from the political process in South Sudan and give Kiir's SPLM a green card to enhance its political advantage on SPLM-IO's expense. The SPLM-IO must stay engaged and active with all South Sudanese political forces and civil organizations in order to acknowledge its vision and programs of actions and find a common collective ground for change.

Our hard-liners from here and there might need to review their stands and re-invent themselves based on the possibilities and realities on the ground. Insisting on false strategy a thousand times doesn't make it any right. Whether, the rumors of July 7th peace deal are true or not, I trust the leadership of the SPLM/A-IO that it will never let the people of South Sudan down and that it will negotiate and engage the regime of Salva Kiir until a better South Sudan is realized.


**July 9, 2015**

**In a Nutshell**

Today is South Sudan's Independence fourth anniversary and the question of the moment is whether we are truly independent or are we even more dependent to others. The current state of affairs does emphasize the later. For instance, Uganda is occupying our decision-making apparatus and our leadership decisions are no longer independent neither we can claim that our sovereignty as an independent country and nation is still sound and intact. Museveni is now part of this country whether you like it or not and what is between Kiir and Museveni is bigger than you think and will still shape how things will look like in this country as long as the two dictators are still around.

But what sort of anniversary when 2/3 of South Sudanese are under United Nation's food and relief assistance program in which about 2.5 million are either refugees in neighboring countries or internally displaced to UN protection sites and the rest who are managing to live insecurely in Juba and elsewhere where the current civil war haven't reached yet. They are struggling to survive the shortage of food supplies, insecurity, and lack of adequate healthcare services amid skyrocketing inflation, high commodities prices and with South Sudanese pound at its lowest rate ever versus US dollar. These few among many indicators reflects a grim reality that our independence which we have won with huge sacrifices is still a bright name far away from any real manifestations on the ground.

It is with no doubt that the controversial legitimacy of Mr. Kiir has ended yesterday even if it is considered to have popularly ended since Dec 15th, 2013. The day he decided to betray his own constituents. Today the King of Juba and his parliament has inaugurated the dictatorship officially with another three more years to be repeated or increased at the end of every term and under a different pretext. To summed it up, Kiir is not going anywhere anytime soon.

However, the unfolding political situation is even grimmer; the merger between G10 and SPLM-Juba is a plus to Kiir and the status quo but a minus to the efforts of change and reforms most South Sudanese were expecting but not necessarily a minus to Mr. Machar's SPLM/A-IO. The new coalition as long as it is under the direction of Mr. Kiir will unite itself against Riek Machar's SPLM-IO to gradually weaken him and finally resort to destroy his movement if they could. The Juba coalition will adopt a strategy of extending unfaithful peace olive branch ever time and then to Machar while holding it back in the same time and whenever it seems to be finally inked. I doubt if the new coalition of Juba-SPLM has a sincere will to welcome Machar among its ranks.

As for Dr. Machar and his colleagues in SPLM-IO the best strategy is to continue the resistance and fight their way to force Salva Kiir to quit or force him to at least accept the reforms, restructuring of the state and the terms and conditions of separate armies among other. SPLM/A-IO might experience some setbacks in forms of political and military figures defections but if it stayed the course, Juba will prove itself again and again that it is no fit place to defect to, and all the defectors or returnees will surely regret their decisions otherwise the SPLM/A-IO might find itself accepting a political settlement and peace deal less than what Juba is offering today.

Well, it is just another tasteless independence anniversary coming in a time when most people of this country are mourning their loved ones being killed in this current civil war and with no hopes for peace in sight. Peace this time and around seem so difficult to attain because a possibility of Machar and Kiir working together again in the same party and government is truly in doubt and it seem that the two men have narrowed their options to either a full victory of one against the other or the likelihood of both quitting the political arena for a possible new political era in South Sudan. However, in the world of politics and politicians nothing that seem impossible when it comes to retaining power and hence expect surprises.

## July 15, 2015

### In a Nutshell

To be honest, I have nothing against you Cde. Pagan Amum but how you will function effectively and stays clean in Kiir's SPLM is what puzzling me. Honestly, there is no way Cde Amum that you can operate in a rotten-to-core system but either to be fully part of it or act as a tool to let pass of all but all types of corruption without a NO and which is a repeat of the same from 2005 to 2013.

However, I understand you as a smart man. First you regained your job and the rest that you know. Now you can let your eyes sleep saying you didn't see the dinosaurs passing by or the heads of innocent South Sudanese being hanged or cut off in your watch or nearby you. You can now dance with the current and the wind of Kingdom-dit and when they slap you on the left, turns the right one 77 times or pretend to be a conscience-dead or indeed be a real one ((your interests and money will be rolling of course no problem)) nothing more or less but even with that too these folks will never trust you.

Maybe you and the rest think a magical change shall happen but I do believe the settings of after Kiir era are already arranged too. Trust me, they haven't left anything for chance Cde Pagan Amum otherwise Dr. Riek Machar and Gen. Johnson Olouny won't be still fighting Kiir as we speak. But I wish you every good Luck and when you successfully transformed the SPLM from Self and Tribal Empowerment Movement to a South Sudanese's National Transformation Movement, me and the rest shall join you.

I doubt that Cde Pagan Amum. As long as Kiir is still the ceiling of that

SPLM's house in Juba, none is going to jump above to make the right change. The door that they have let you out in December is the same door they are letting you in today and nothing have ever changed since then or maybe they have whispered privately in your ears that " we have changed". If so, please let us know too in case we are missing out Cde Pagan Amum.

## July 17, 2015

### In a Nutshell

My in-a-nutshell the day before was based on how our Cde Pagan Amum can't ever operate effectively neither stays clean in the already rotten-to-core Kiir's leadership at both party and government level and that as long as Kiir is still the ceiling of that SPLM's house all the good attempts for a better change will be revoked and not necessarily by Kiir himself but by all the misleading bunch of advisors and interest groups surrounding him.

After untimely death of Dr. Garang, I haven't lost hope that much that the vision of liberation and transformation of South Sudan will be kept intact and carried on by a few faithful loyalists to the national cause of all South Sudanese. Cde Pagan Amum was and still in the forefront of those few comrades that I entrusted to accomplish the unfinished mission. I regard Cde Pagan Amum to may have known Dr. John Garang well at heart and at political philosophy second to none but the lifetime partner, his widow Rebecca Nyandeng Mabior. I wasn't surprised at all during the nights and days of Juba massacres to see Mama Rebecca de Mabior to be the first declaring on the BBC to the world that there were mass killings targeting the members of Nuer ethnicity in those December of 2013 doomsdays.

It is easy to read who truly Dr. Garang was from the behaviors and actions of the closest person to his thoughts and life, his wife. If Garang was about the revenge of 1991 Bor massacre then December 15, 2013, was the golden chance for his widow to go on it fully to avenge it. Garang may have played with all the cards within and without the SPLM just to keep the strategy of liberation alive and let it achieve its objective and hence he was a subject to misunderstanding, misjudgment and misinterpretation of the purpose of his actions. The objective of liberating the darkest people on earth within a complex systems of regional and international politics, interests and ideologies wasn't an easy task at all, Dr. Garang did have what it takes and have played it and very well at an extensive knowledge of how the international system works.

Those who know Cde Pagan Amum, will not differ with me that the man has what it takes to carry on the vision. He might not be John Garang but at most he is a faithful loyalist to the pure vision of the SPLM and would like and work to transform South Sudan to be one of the best countries in the world. The conspirators who have failed Kiir politically and murdered his legacy as well under his very watch have started by setting him up against Cde Pagan Amum. Well Kiir might be in a path of re-inventing himself but I am afraid it is too late and beefing up security in Juba nowadays due to the expected cabinet reshuffle may have to do with that. He might finally realize and about to let go all opportunists, money and blood suckers that has crippled him and made him the Kiir of today.

If the SPLM vision and mission has to be revived and repositioned onto the right direction and the true cause of the people of South Sudan, then Cde Kiir has a lot of work and thinking to do. He simply may know by now who is truly damaging him and who is not. Pagan Amum will not be effective under the same surroundings of money and blood-suckers who has failed the party, the government and the state. Kiir need to side with him, listen to him and give him the mandate to fix the party and the whole house if at least a new dawn has to emerge in South Sudan.

When it comes to effective thoughts and solutions that can bring our current political crisis to halt, Cde Pagan Amum is a no joke but it is up to Kiir if he wants him to fix the mess or just use him to continue with the same business of failure as usual.

## July 22, 2015

### In a Nutshell

Before we randomly hit South or North let us try to narrow down the possible solutions to this civil war and then judge the actions taken or will be taken in the course of the coming days by the main leaders, Dr. Riek and Gen. Salva. First of all, a military solution to this conflict is not possible. Second, a political compromise that brings everyone in and incorporates the reforms and restructuring of the state and its dysfunctional institutions, an inclusive, fair and balanced power sharing is the way out.

The longer the war persists, the longer the suffering of our people (not the Facebookers thou) but the people in the hell of the war zone, refugees' camps, UN's PoC sites. The war is also a profitable business to some regional and international powers that want South Sudan to fail and disintegrate. War spending alone is incurring a skyrocketing national debt every day and the social fabric of this country is getting destroyed in a threatening manner to future generations' well-being. There is an international pressure on both leaders and we are no isolated island. The hardliners in SPLM-IO and SPLM-Juba want the war to stay on not because it is the solution, but it is becoming a joy and a pride. In Juba, interest groups and blood business are making huge profits and keeping their positions through flaming the war which they fear losing if peace arrives.

SPLM-IO is a political organization that must change and adapt itself to developments in the political arena in order to survive and stay active in the socio-economic and political transformation of this country. There is no viable goal seeing Salva consolidating 3/4 of political groups and support (G10) while doing nothing. Salva is coming to use this 75% against the 25%. In this likely scenario; Another Nuer rival might pick up the position of VP and let Salva use it against SPLM-IO (with the majority of Nuer supporters) this is problematic to the community to say the least. There is no certainty that the SPLM-IO will keep the same momentum of support and effectiveness in the long run due to internal and external factors. A political movement is a living entity that must evolves with time and the reality of the situation on the ground in order to stay politically alive and effective.

Dr. Riek has weighed the cons and pros in the possible political compromise, he has been reluctant because he doesn't trust Salva Kiir and his group plus a deal that keep the main problem intact and untouched (Salva in this case) is not what he can sale to the very victims of the same Salva. But leadership is leadership, peace is made with the enemies and not with friends and at the end of the day it is Salva or his representatives that SPLM-IO must sit down with even after 20 years of war to settle for peace or political deal. General Gadet and Gathoth are known to be in the line of opposing any deal while Salva in power, they are backed with supporters in US and elsewhere who are playing the effective role in all aspects. No one in fact within the SPLM/A-IO does want Mr. Salva to stay in power. However, removing him through military means has proved not possible given the presence of Uganda and other support groups or at least has a far more consequences to the state and nation of South Sudan in the foreseeable future d hence a political compromise between the political forces the country is seen as the only alternative.

Mr. Machar is a brave leader and he has the interest of his people at heart, given the realities and the circumstances on the ground and based on sound analysis on the future trends, he might opt to sign the deal in August and hence a change in both political and military within the SPLM-IO is a must and beefing up security for the leadership and within the army is also a must. Propagandists, conspirators and the confused are up nights and days with phone calls and media war to blow-off anything. But here what most don't know, a war within the Nuer community brings everyone including Gordon Buay to the worst they haven't imagined yet.

The situation with Gen. Salva Kiir is no different; Malong, Kuol, Igga and many more whose political ambitions are in the line with this possible deal are also obstacles plus the tribalist and interests-based hardliners. However, both leaders must demonstrate the courage and bravery to make a paradigm shift in this bitter situation South Sudan is in its helms.


## July 25, 2015

### In a Nutshell

Political or social organizations that have no tendency to keep their unity and cohesion under any circumstances are not likely to attain any political or economic power whatsoever. Shaky societies or political organizations that fall in disarray, confusion and disunity whenever faced with a test of division from within are nowhere to be found among the powerful organizations or nations of the Earth.

Anyone who has interest for the SPLM/A-IO to win should be convinced at heart that the only way for victory be it militarily or politically is for the movement to stays united, intact and focused on the already set higher goals of the nation of South Sudan and not necessarily individuals or groups' interests. At any revolutionary or political movement, there is no way to avoid differences in ideas, political thoughts or ideologies and in fact this is where its strength originates from if carefully channeled to enrich the substance and the drive of the movement.

However, the possibility of some differences, disputes and rivalry getting away of control is also likely and real sometimes and in that context, only how the leadership and the other structures of the organization deals with such internal disputes and differences. In that regard, sound mechanism for conflicts and disputes resolution must exist within the organization structure in order to avoid escalation and development of those differences into real threats to the very unity and objectives of the said organization.

I might be wrong but my observations are that we have three groups within the SPLM/A-IO. A group that is fighting to remove Gen. Salva, the head of the regime that has murdered their loved ones and this group has set itself not to accept a political compromise or peace deal whatsoever as long as Gen. Kiir is still in power and the president. This group is likely to stand against the leadership whenever they decided to opt for a political compromise with Juba and with Gen. Salva as the head of the state.

The second group shares the common ground with the first group which is fighting to remove Gen. Salva and overhaul the system to establish the Federal Republic of South Sudan. However, given the realities on the ground, Uganda military presence, the tribal nature of the war and its implications on South Sudan national security, social fabric, well-being of future generations and as a result of carefully weighing the cons and pros of war, its political and social trends on the long run, they are ready to strike a strategic political compromise with conditions; the separate armies must be kept until the terms of agreement are all implemented, accountability and compensation of the innocents victims of this provoked war, introduction of serious and real constitutional and institutional reforms, governance system, and security sector among others are all but completed.

The third group consists of those who reacted in solidarity upon Juba massacres but later opted to keep political align to Juba as their immediate interests are connected with Juba in a way or another. They are embedded within the SPLM/A-IO, they are in disguise doing harm and damage and some are not necessarily doing so. They are pulling the movement down through activities of ill-advisory, spying, confusion, sabotage, encouragement of internal divisions among others. They are against SPLM/A-IO making any political gains through opposing and confusing any policies that enhance its strategy and direction in both political and military grounds while in the same time building a secret alliance with Juba that should be the substitute if they successfully failed the SPLM/A-IO. They are the enemy from within. However, they need not be chased away but instead an approach of caution should be applied. You never know when a chameleon will permanently change his color of skin and settle.

Undoubtedly, we do believe that the leadership of SPLM/A-IO has what it takes to lead the movement to the desired victory either politically or military. If the leadership is opting for a political compromise with Juba while Kiir is still a president, we believe this isn't done for any individual interest rather for the interest of the entire movement, the people, and South Sudan as a country.

True supporters of SPLM/A-IO must believe in their leadership's actions and policies and channel their grievances through the structures of the movement. SPLM/A-IO is in needs of our collective support the most in the upcoming days just like the first days of our struggle. I bet the leadership is aware of all the concerns we are all about and if we have to realize real political gains in this struggle, our unity behind the leadership should not be a matter of question.


**July 28, 2015**

## In a Nutshell

Let us give thanks to president Obama but most if not all the governance systems in Africa are too deformed to be reformed given the fact that who else has the power to champion and enact the reforms rather than the same presidents that has disabled institutions, suppressed the popular masses and are obstructing the constitutions and violating the laws of the land in order for them to stay in power indefinitely and enrich themselves and their cohorts with public funds.

Obama shouldn't waste his time lecturing African presidents because it is not that these presidents don't know these self-evident facts but because greed, lust for wealth and power has made them deaf and blinds to the very logics and principles that they have bought the votes of their deceived constituents in an apparent one-way ticket up to seat of power and never the other way around. Whatever you said today Mr. President is true and those are the missing ingredients in the never realized Africa's development dream. These African kings in disguise have heard you and heard you well but what they have heard is not there in their heads anymore because they have heard it with their right ears and unfortunately it got out with their left ears and before you Air Force One haven't takeoff from Africa.

Mr. President, Africa has no democratic presidents but Kings in disguise. A democratic president like your person would be elected and serve the first term with great efforts and achievements in order to be re-elected once more in the second and final term. I like the way you put it today at your African Union Address that even though you are pretty good president and would be re-elected for another term should you run. But that can't ever happen in the United States because of the law and the law is the law and when it come to the age, you still young unlike us in-age- of grandpas' presidents who have stayed for nearly forty years in power and have seen their grandchildren ageing before their eyes while tightly holding on that chair giving nothing but troubles and more of the same.

When it come to the achievements, you have given this country much more than any US president, a legacy and performance that would make your people re-elect you for the third term if it wasn't for the law and the law is the law, I quote you again. All these goodies and strength doesn't make you above the law. I wish our African presidents, Oops, our African Kings, have got what you mean and not again to stage fake coupes, amend the constitutions or plunge their nations into tribal and political chaos and civil wars in order to stay in power for life. That's not an effective system of governance that generate new ideas, new characters, new energy, not a system that gives young people hopes and dreams, a deadlocked system that doesn't aspires the young to be leaders of tomorrow, good leaders of tomorrow.

Young Africans are crossing rivers, oceans and seas, drawing in thousands, escaping the most resources rich continent on earth, risking it all just for an opportunity of being a refugee in developed world, Europe and America. But let us pause a moment and imagine what could be the cause of such suicidal decisions, putting one life in danger by crossing those vast endless oceans with those kinds of boats we all have seen. There must be a true hell there and let me remember a bit of it, rampant corruption, high unemployment rate and insecurity, civil wars and humans' rights degradation, merciless hunger and famine, diseases and hopelessness among many man-made disasters.

They are escaping not because they don't love this most beautiful continent on earth, no, there is no beauty like Africa and Africans themselves but it is for the very simple reason that our leaders in the persons of presidents haven't taken charge of transforming the lives of their people for better and for that reasons the continent is still lagging behind in all socio-economic and political aspects. It is not about the help and aid but it is about leaders and leadership. Africa needs a true transformation in humans' capital parallel with another in infrastructures, education, healthcare, good paved roads...etc. Without new leaders of a different positive substance, Africa shall remain lagging behind the rest of the world and this can't be the option we have got. Let us all stand up for a better Africa.


**August 1, 2015**

**In a Nutshell**

I feel Gen. Kiir and his support base in their opposition to the provisions of IGAD plus peace proposal. They are seeing Dr. Riek Machar; the stone they tried shamelessly to trash and get rid of has become the cornerstone of any projected peace and political compromise. Juba and Kampala should now know that the whole world is not drawn under the sea of denial, impunity and injustice and that there is still a good part out there with a living conscience concerned with doing justice and achieving peace for all.

It is obvious that Kiir and his base are having a difficult time accepting Juba city to be demilitarized, to be put under international supervision and with Mr. Machar having 195 bodyguards with only 55 less personnel than Kiir neither it is a surprise either that Kiir support base in Upper Nile is almost going crazy, losing it to the opposition is something they can't afford to imagine but they should rest assured and subdue their feelings and let the peace materialized because their boss Kiir will also represent them within the 33% allocated to his base. Shouldn't we feel ashamed of calling South Sudan national resources, a Dinka's oil, a Nuer's oil, a Bari's Gold" isn't it the time we look at the mirror and see how low we have become?

On the other hand, it is a clear fact that South Sudan currently has no neutral national army. The two tribal armies and their allied militias will be kept apart until a gradual and careful integration process is complete. With its shaky tribal structure, South Sudan is in need of an educated and strong army oriented in strong values of nationalism and higher interests of this country and its nation in contrast to the current tribal army of Paul Malong Awan, Marial Changnon and Kuol Manyang Juuk. Not Mathiang Anyor or Dut ka Beny tribal armies that are being paid, trained and equipped through public funds but an army that will not be easily dragged into tribal politics and to commit heinous crimes against the very people it supposed to protect.

Peace belongs to South Sudanese people and those who are dancing upon the possibilities of SPLM/A-IO disintegration from within will dance even longer. While differences and disputes exist within the SPLM/A-IO on whether or not to strike a political compromise with Kiir as head of state albeit these differences will even strengthen the support to the leadership and won't lead to a major split. It is fundamentally known that there is no military victory achievable in the foreseeable future not only for SPLM/A-in-Opposition but also to the SPLM/A-in- Government and those who are fishing in the dirty waters using the latest decisions made by C-in-C of SPLM/A-IO will definitely fly up and land down to the same realization.

Delaying peace with devilish tactics is not going to work. Juba and allies are praying on the possibilities of the disintegration of SPLM/A-IO from within and they already have dispatches their agents and propaganda officers to spread their elements of confusion. Hence, it shouldn't be a surprise if Juba is being reluctant, confused and undecided about IGAD

Plus peace proposal since they are being told wait, it is just weeks and you will see Machar's movement crumble. Well, this won't happen and the illusionists should wake up. I know how ego and false pride have ended great people just because they have chosen for their heads to stays there buried deep down under the sand, they hated the truth and logic. Kiir and support base might reject the peace deal based on the same trend they waged this war upon. Isn't it the tribal ego and sick pride that is killing this country? It is.

In a nutshell, by now, as an independent country and nation, we should be enjoying the fruits of our hard-won freedom and the thrill of being our own and not burning under the flames of tribal egocentric mentality and those who have dragged us into this tribal war with one hand while robbing the country with the other in the name of tribe and clans. However, either peace or war, South Sudan has a learning assignment to do.

**August 2, 2015**

**In a Nutshell**

Why Kiir need to seize the golden chance of August 17th, 2015?

After the successful 2011 referendum in which nearly 99% of South Sudanese voted for the independence of their country, no citizen of South Sudan should live head down, dignity and pride smashed to the ground or begging for foods in refuge countries albeit the fake elite who are ruling South Sudan want to make sure they have created to themselves a fake class and false picture of heroism and masters of this country in which they have got away with power and resources of this country, using them as they wish and giving them away as they please. They are talking about rewarding us the leftovers from their foods and wealth and not about sharing the same fundamental God given natural rights of citizenship. Anyone who has a fresh memory could just rewind the memory back and recall how the liberation war was fought contrary to the ruling elite's claims.

Heavy weapons that were obtained to defend this country from any possible external aggressors are used to murder people in churches, something even the Khartoum that was waging war in the name of religion haven't done in sanctity of God's places. They have closed rivers from being used to carry foods to the starving needy and victims of their tribal war in Upper Nile's Wau Shilluk. They want to make sure the people of Yambio and greater Upper Nile, lives and comes on bending knees and as second class citizens. Something we have fought the mighty Khartoum for two decades and a half. This enemy disguised in our own skin is a no different and we will fight it until all South Sudan lives equally, dignified.

Gen. Kiir, his Chief of Staff, Gen. Awan and his Defense Minister Gen. Manyang has a golden chance to seize by August 17th. They need not be deceived by Gordon Buay or Lul Ruai Koang's assumption that the SPLM/A-IO is crumbling from within. This is not happening and I am so sure the regime won't decide upon the recommendations of these two. Kiir has proved to his regional and international allies and friends before his enemies that his leadership is the problem. He proved behind any reasonable doubt that he can't either deliver a thing or unite the people of Bhar-El-gazhal leave alone the people of South Sudan. Mr. Kiir that should be symbol of nationalism and unity of South Sudan is no more and has failed miserably.

I told some of my friends once, if the Dinka can't get along with their cousins, the Nuer than forget them getting along with the rest of the world. They might buy people with money and positions but that won't change any of behaviors and attitudes that have led to the current war. The same behaviors and attitudes will expel anyone around them. This is yet to be proven by time even though I do believe it is already proven. The scope of crisis is widening; it is not anymore fitting in the fabricated context of a Nuer' opposition. It is not anymore a Nuer vs. Dinka war. It is coming back to Mr. Kiir as it was originally. A South Sudanese case against Mr. Kiir failed leadership.

Mr. Kiir need to seize the August 17th peace proposal to save the little waters on his face by accepting the proposed reforms in governance, constitution, institutions and security sectors among others. Curtains and covers are falling apart, economic woes are here knocking hard on J1 doors and Malong's Army is causing troubles to his boss more than he can take anymore. Opening new pockets of rebellion are more likely in the coming days and as you have heard, the international community is finally fed-up and has lost patience.

When it comes to Uganda, Yuri Museveni is a no fool and I bet him and his people felt something unusual from the way Obama in his recent visit to the region, isolated a country like Uganda. This reflects at least that being guilty by association is not in the interest of Ugandan people if it is at least fine with M7. The Ugandan people has a strategic long term interest in keeping a good mutual relationship with the people of South Sudan not with a failed leadership that can fall anytime. The negative role of Uganda in this war will be remembered for generations to come and that's not worth it. Choosing to be politically blind might work sometimes but not in the long run and hence Gen. Kiir and Gen M7 needs to put their act together by August 17th or face the sure collapse.

## August 5, 2015

### In a Nutshell

Being a realistic politician is the right mindset where you start to adequately recognize the most powerful political figures and parties of influence at the level of personal and country political platform. This right mindset makes you do the math of power and politics right from the start. It serves as a compass for the skilled politicians to identify the areas of power and influence, directing them to where they can make political allies and coalitions in order to advance their political objectives as well as to enhance one's own political competitive advantage. It is the virtue that helps identify who would be a possible fierce political rival or would be a great political ally should there be elections but more importantly, it is vital for keeping the balance of power in order to keep the peace, unity and political stability of the country. No country ever survived or advanced without a political consensus of its political forces.

Albeit, Kiir and some of his political support base have failed miserably in this context and instead they decided to do the opposite, the math of weakness and the math of disintegrating our political unity into abyss of tribal and clannish molecules. By fighting and denying the presence of the influential powerful political figures and forces in this country and in contrary to Gerang's own political philosophy. Hence comes that disastrous decisions of bringing a coalition government down in one night and the attempt to ignore that the CPA and independence was achieved under the very fact of Garang-Machar reconciliations of 2002 and which served as the backbone of successful 2011 referendum, peace and stability until Kiir and Junta shamelessly and ignorantly decided to go against it on December 2013, putting us back to square one of 1983, 1991 cycles of violence and like never before.

All in an attempt to just get rid or block Mr. Machar from being a possible hire to the throne. However, if Kiir and base have ever done the math right just as Garang did to the math of successful referendum leading to the successful independence and recognizes the higher interests of this country and nation then this Macharphobia and all the war to shape a sad new reality is no better than seeing South Sudan at peace and progressing forward. Well, they need to get over it. Mr. Machar is not going anywhere.

Ironically enough, for some, seeing and admitting Riek Machar as a powerful and influential political figure who has shaped the course of political and historical facts of this country, for good or for worse (that's politics not holy heaven), they would better prepares keeping their heads buried deep down under their sand of denial and ignorance rather than coming out in the open and admitting Machar's rightful place and role in this country's political and transformational platforms. Denial, deception to themselves, to the nation and to the world is what brought us to this point of nowhere.

Kiir and base, come on folks, do the math right and admit Gat-Machar rightful place and let us sign this IGAD plus deal and get our people back to the joy of peace and our country back to the track of development and prosperity. Enough denial to self and enough deception to the nation. Politics is about doing the math of power right and in a country of 65 tribes, if it is not ignorance than it is an absolute craziness to run J1 with a crew of one clan leave alone of one tribe.

## August 7, 2015

### In a Nutshell

Based on the current rejection position of Kiir's regime to IGAD plus proposal, it is high likely that after August 17th deadline the war is going to escalate putting everything back to square one. IGAD or Troika are not in a position to impose a rejected proposal but it is likely that they will back-off a bit and leave the warring parties to sort out how they can/will bring peace to their people or win the war militarily on each other's.

Economic sanctions don't work on losers or those which wars are profitable business. The government must be backing its rejection position with a heavy military preparedness that will enable it to wage a full scale war on SPLM/A-IO strongholds, however this is also not winnable but at least it will usher into a new military or political realm that's different from the current IGAD plus' in which the government is finding itself cornered and swallowing the bitter political defeat ever.

The SPLM/A-IO should not be deceived by the current political and diplomatic victory upon Kiir and leave its military strategy unattended. It must have a plan B on post August 17th. Things are likely to head down the hell or hopefully some sanity will be regained somewhere beforehand. Those children, women and elderly who haven't reached a better safety yet should be best advised. Let us hope for the best while prepared for the worst.

## August 6, 2015

## In a Nutshell

Kiir thinks that IGAD plus is too much into his territories and if not rolled back then Walai, he will never sign it. Seeing Juba demilitarized, with Riek Machar only couple miles away with 195 strong guards versus 260 for himself and the vast oil in Upper Nile being put in the hands of SPLM-IO among other proposals, that's ultimately an endless nightmare. However, the real dilemma of IGAD plus from Kiir & Camp's perspective is that it treated both leaders with the same language and importance and hence giving them privileges and rights as well as the possible consequences according to this reality. This is making Juba crazy as hell but as a matter of fact, the two leaders are all rebels by now, something Kiir doesn't know. After July 9th, 2015, Mr. Kiir has rebelled against the democratic will of South Sudanese people and against South Sudan Interim Constitution by refusing to step down or by planning in advance this war just to postpone the election.

He is no more a legitimate president but only in his own eyes, support base and interest groups. The perception of the democratic world has changed after July 9th, 2015 and if he could read how the rest of democratic world leaders treat him or deal with him nowadays, he could comprehend the great change in attitudes and behaviors of those leaders. Well, our mad cows, here and there will rudely tell us, so...who care, we are a sovereign state and the hell with the world, well that is contradictory a stance to say the least. A sovereign state that its capital is under guard of foreign troops, its half of population are being fed by the UN, its borders of Abyei and Magwi being annexed slowly by the same foreign troops protecting the capital. Well, a sovereign state that is fighting its own citizens and can't fight the very foreign troops that are annexing its territories, what in the world is this sovereign state.

The second part is that Kiir's army wrongly named as South Sudan Army is not anymore by any standard a national army. Its tribal structure as well as its ethnic based war, and atrocities are all but documented crystal clear. Kiir as the C-in-C of SPLA, Malong as the Chief of Staff, Kuol Manyang as Defense minister, Marial Changnon as Chief of presidential guard, Marial Nour as the Chief of Military Security and the list is endless. Come on world, let us be a bit rational, this is a one tribe army with allied mercenaries from here and there and other interest-based militia that's no different from SPLA-IO with its tribal White Army militia and its tribal chain of command structure. However, the case of SPLA-IO is quite different, since they were singled out as the only target tribe being slaughtered and victimized as the scapegoat of the grand SPLM failure and fall.

Quantitatively and not qualitatively, Kiir and Riek are equal partners of this war and hence they are equal partners in achieving a durable lasting peace. The country is very much divided across their two political factions and armies and hence they must be all rewarded or punished at equal footings to put the fires of this war to rest and that necessarily doesn't mean we have no other stakeholders in this conflict to be considered.

IGAD plus is a serious and realistic bargain and tradeoffs, it doesn't really need to satisfy any party 100% otherwise it wouldn't be a compromise. It is leaving Kiir where he is and bringing Machar where he was and I don't see a reason why the two leaders would refuse to sign it. They will. Now let us come to the third part, what is in IGAD Plus for the South Sudanese people? Peace isn't it? Well, it is said that some of the duties of the first VP is to achieve those of reforms, accountability, restructuring and all that we been singing about since the inception of this madness. Let us hope for the best and wait how it will turn out to be.


**August 11, 2015**

**In a Nutshell**

Kiir and base shouldn't be deceived by their illusions and celebrate what they see as a possible collapse of the resistance movement. The differences within the resistance movement are not on the objective but on the methodology and accordingly Mr. Kiir by now has two enemies to worry about instead of one.

Therefore, and with the first enemy being the just declared new movement of the defected generals and politicians from the SPLM/A-IO or the far right extremists who have been accusing Mr. Machar of weak leadership, lack of ambitious working military strategy that should have reached Bhar-El-Gahzal region by now, exploitation of the movement to climb to his personal political goals among others. The extremists are not willing to strike any political compromise with Kiir as head of the state and believe in removing Kiir militarily or so they claim.

His second enemy of course being the less radical mainstream led by Dr. Machar that is willing to hit a political compromise with Salva Kiir as head of the state should the compromise incorporates reforms, restructuring, accountability and projected election date, separate two armies until an integrated national army is created among others. The impact of the split on the ongoing peace negotiations is not to be a major setback unless Juba decided as its hints, to exploit it and with August 17th, 2015 dateline looming and threats of sanctions around the corner, Juba no doubt also knows where its chances of survival are and it will seize them undoubtedly. Even though it is not known yet how many commanders or military units will join the new movement from the mainstream SPLM/A-IO, however, should there be interested cadres and support within the current ranks and files of SPLM/A-IO in which the defected generals were commanding top commanders then it is definitely about hopes that any disintegration of the SPLA-IO units will be less bloody.

Juba is hoping that the split will bring the SPLM/A-IO down to its knees, crumble and surrenders or at worst engage in internal fight with the new defected movement and hence for the SPLM/A-IO to lose its strength both in negotiations table and battle front. The end of SPLM/A-IO will mark the end of the most powerful rival that challenges the very thought of Kiir & Awan Kingdom-dit where all the 65 tribes of South Sudan will come on bending knees and Hail the Kings. Those are but mere illusions and will remains so.

If the defection was indeed for the love of Nuer blood that was cheaply watered down by Kiir regime than it won't make sense for the defected generals and politicians to water it down more, they could disagree with Machar and base but they should save their guns and capabilities to remove Mr. Kiir's regime, their very reason for defection as they said. However, they need to be cautious because they are likely to be approached by Juba regime in a way or another, manipulated by the politicians of Nuer Wew and those who want the whole resistance movement to fail. However, and in a serious note, irrespective of who is right or wrong, both Machar, Gatdet and Gathoth all their heads are on the top of the list of the most wanted by Kiir and camp, should any circumstances blinds any of them, the consequences are definitely dire. The SPLM/A-IO will pass this current test and many tests ahead and prevail upon Kiir even if it takes a decade long. Well, Mr. Kiir, the August 17th dateline is approaching at a speedy pace, you better think twice, good luck.

**August 14, 2015**

**In a Nutshell**

Dividing South Sudan on the tribal lines was a conspiracy in place right before independence. However, what is truly ironic about this is how the old divide-to-rule or conquer strategy still having its work effectively on African countries and nations which in just few years back waged a lengthy bitter struggle just to free themselves from the chains of servitude and slavery of the same divide-to-conquer philosophy. Unfortunately, South Sudan is a fresh example of such phenomenon which can be summed-up at best that Africans never learn from their mistakes or bitter past otherwise they could be in a better-off state of affairs.

Ironically enough, the new heirs of power from the old colonialists have instead placed themselves as the new colonialists disguised in our own African skin but with a mindset that is worse than that of the old colonialists' themselves. We have said it before and again that any ill-wishers with ill intentions on South Sudan knows and very well where to strike to bring the whole house of South Sudan to crumble. It is simple, just pit these two rival tribes, the Dinka and Nuer against each other and in few months there will be nation or country no more. In time where South Sudan is an independent state, there is a need to know that rivalry can't be to an extent of losing South Sudan and denying the young generations from what their forefathers fought and dearly paid for, enough should be enough and we all collectively have a country that need attention rather than tribal or individual interests.

There are two things South Sudanese need to revisit or at least to be mindful about, the sudden death of Dr. John Garang few months before he could successfully embark on the objective manifestation of his vision of united secular Sudan or self-determination of South Sudan. The second being this tribal war which in less than two years of our independence, we just found ourselves bathing in our own worse river of blood ever. I know it is not part of South Sudanese's nature to look at things in a dubious manner rather than to accept the will of God without any questions or maybe that of prophet Ngundang as his believers translates these events according to his prophecies.

However, South Sudan gateway to greatness or prosperity is not through tribalism in fact it is its sure demise that's guaranteed through the tribal ticket and those whose concerns is to make money or retain power through the same tribalism philosophy will have nowhere to invest the same bloody money but in the land of their associated foreign conspirators.

The negotiations in Addis Ababa has proved in a way our negative perception towards each other's and have proven that even foreigners are keen and concern on suffering of the people of South Sudan and on keeping this country and nation out of danger of disintegration more than their so-called its leaders. The benefits of reforms, restructuring of the governance, constitutional systems and our ailing institutions shouldn't be seen from the narrow tribal lens rather than the broadest scope of fixing what is wrong with our country and the need to reposition it onto the right direction which is imperative for it to be stable, at peace with itself and its neighbors and to prospers at a steady and consistent manner.

## August 15, 2015

## In a Nutshell

The defected SPLM/A-IO generals were against this IGAD plus peace proposal just like Malong and other Juba's hardliners who were against it, However Mr. Kiir didn't have the courage to oppose the powerful Malong and the rest of his hardliners and decided to save himself instead and not the suffering people of South Sudan. As for Mr. Machar, he proved that he is a leader and not a player, he dismissed his powerful generals and politicians that were standing in the way of peace, taking the ultimate risk for the sake of the suffering people of South Sudan and not for the sake of a VP position at this age as the Macharphobia crowds and Kiir's propagandists been singing ever since.

After removing them from their top positions, Mr. Machar was ready to reshuffle his defected generals in different capacities to make peace possible if the generals themselves have passed the test and waited as members of SPLM/A-IO without portfolios even for a short while, giving Machar the benefit of the doubt. However, in their quick reaction, they failed the test miserably and instead got confused by the crowds of Macharphobia and Juba propagandists and hurried to declare their defection and disowning Machar, a declaration that has no support from the ground as there is no single unit that has defected with them until this time of writing this "in a nutshell".

Now, Juba think it has won the game, hitting two birds with one stone, by dividing the ranks and file of the SPLM/A-IO and in the same time refusing the very peace it used to divide the SPLM/A-IO and subsequently we have seen Juba attitudes and behaviors in these days and in the wake of the defection news. the latest developments being the claim of changes of contents of IGAD plus said to be done by Museveni and that Kiir is not traveling to Addis Ababa to negotiate directly with Machar, and Wani Igga's front voicing itself through the Equatoria governors that peace should be suspended since it is going to be not inclusive because of the rebels split, laughable isn't it? I haven't heard yet of SPLM/A-IO units fighting each other have due to this so-called split.

Dear comrades, Dr. Machar has won the game and won it well and deep there, we and the world know by now what is the difference between Kiir and Machar. The latter is a true leader with his very people at heart and not a conscience-dead political player. You have seen them the players that are killing South Sudan in Juba and we are thankful that the IGAD plus proposal has unearthed who is who in the South Sudan political arena. The credibility of Juba's politicians and some who were secretly embedded within the SPLM/A-IO has come to test and failed miserably. The SPLM/A-IO is not in a weak position neither politically nor militarily and with that said it is not begging for peace but intentionally and responsibly seeking the peace, a just and an inclusive peace represented in series of serious reforms, restructuring of the state of South Sudan, accountability and in a political compromise with the same genocidal regime of Kiir Mayardit even though its hands are fully stained with the blood of thousands of innocents South Sudanese and this is just to halt the continuous suffering of our people. However, the conspirators seem not to have done yet with their genocidal project and they still deep in the game while our people are dying on a daily basis.

In a nutshell and with all due respect to the role played by our defected generals, they are free to form their movement, prove that they are better than the SPLM/A-IO by fighting Kiir and removing him and not by turning their guns to the same Nuer they claim to avenge and whatever will be the cost, there is no turning back. After August 17th, 2015 if Kiir and Juba failed to show any sign of competent leadership and continue to fish in dirty waters, unwilling to compromise to stop the bloodshed of South Sudanese people, the SPLM/A-IO under the leadership of the able Dr. Riek Machar Dhurgon will continue with the same line in both political and military fronts, undeterred by all the tests of defections and the illusions of Juba's players of its possible fall. The post IGAD plus will tell us a lot, stay tuned.

**August 17, 2014**

**In a Nutshell**

Sometimes we have to think about the future, about our young people who represents a new promising face in the world for South Sudan. The old folks surely are held strongly to their old worlds of tribal pride and egocentric ideas. Don't get me wrong, I don't mean that our young people don't need to know where they come from and where they should be heading but what I mean here is how to use the self and history conscious context toward a better South Sudan, a united and prosperous one.

You can't be a true leader without thinking about the future of your country and the future of your people. The youth are the future and we want to know where do the young people falls within the very thought of our leaders, Leaders who thinks about future generations do plans and acts responsibly, thinks progressively and work productively. They know their words and acts will either destroy or build the precious lives of young people who represent the future of the country.

As a true leader, you got to lays down a better world for them kids and young people, they got to lives in better world and living standards better than what the olds folks are now struggling with, better socio-economic and political standards.

These young people are the future, and what they live and experience now are also the very trends that make a bright or a gloomy future for this nation and country. What is leadership than without changing lives to better? The young and youth need to make sure they have a leader who will secure, build and achieve their futuristic goals. They can't be the ones victimizing themselves by just following and choosing blindly. The consequences are undoubtedly dire and certain.

The positive trends that we have seen from young people and the South Sudanese youth in Diaspora and back home indicates a promising future in all aspects of human activities. South Sudanese who are getting their PhDs in 20s, engineers and scientists professionals who have proven themselves in world class institutions, Icons of music, arts, modeling and more who are conquering the world and enriching its diversity.

When it comes to future making, give to Caesar what is to Caesar and what to God to God. Giving ourselves the benefit of the doubt, we certainly should start with there is no such a thing as the future will fall from the sky.

Our leaders' needs plans for the future, work together to build it make the collective wise decisions to shape the future for a great country and nation through the young people. That's possible and within reach.

If anyone of us claims to be fighting for this country to have a bright future, then these claims definitely void the very reasons we are fighting this disastrous war that is destroying the very future we talking about. One of us must be lying and doing the opposite. It is easy to spot the liars. Watch them whether they are delivering, providing the services the country needs, opening new developmental projects every time and then, laying down their short and long term visions and programs for the country and nation. We got to be real and lives real outcomes from these leaders through accountability and monitoring otherwise we the people, are the problem, we do not need to play with our lives and the future to satisfy none.

## August 23

### In a Nutshell

The ruling thugs in Juba are determined to lose it all and as losers as they might be, it is for sure a matter of concern whether they are looking for any national consensus, inclusive political national agenda or any compromise for peace or even yield for the possible international sanctions and the growing world's outcry for peace. All indicators point to the fact that they are opting for the police-security state approach, eliminating one by one their potential political and security threats to establish an absolute tribal dictatorship where Kiir is set to rule indefinitely and Malong and Manyang as the possible hires, therefore, there is no form of peace agreement acceptable to them but a total surrender to theirs terms and submission.

Even if they signed the IGAD peace plus in a one-week time to avert possible sanctions, international isolation and political setbacks in their camp, their plan B on how to make it ineffective and impossible to implement and finally make it fail is possibly in place and in which they will find a window to scapegoat Mr. Riek Machar again and the SPLM/A-IO as the reason. Juba thugs and allies, cunning and strategists as they are, it is possible that success might be of theirs until the full awakening of the rest of South Sudanese from the seductive power of positions and money. Well, by that time, it might be completely too late and too costly to defeat a dictator.

However, for those who still haven't got the big picture yet, South Sudan of Kiir and Malong is no more the one we fought for. It is now a private entity being ruled in shadows by allies of interest groups backed by Uganda military, Mathing Anyour tribal militias and the notorious security death squads. The recent sting of series of murders by "unknown gunmen", were not by any indicators but politically motivated assassinations that could tell us that the regime's bad boys are already on the loose or authorized to initiate the manifestation of the absolute dictatorship tribal state and the roadmap to Kiir-Awan indefinite rule.

The death list may include many active political, human rights and freedoms activists both within South Sudan and in Diaspora. The borders of the country may have already been sealed and particularly for those politicians and activists who are considered critical voices and opposing the regime policies and tribal approach within Juba and other states. It is fears, terror and death that rule the Kiir-Awan's country. God be of help to the innocent people of South Sudan.

Well, for those who still think that the regime still has a heart and ears to be awakened, they might be late and wrong in getting the true picture of the regime real objective. Neither, as we think that the possible socio-economic and political failure of this country is a matter of regime concern and it will force it to change otherwise a concerned government from the very rational point of view wouldn't initiate this kind of destructive war and insists on fueling it. Undoubtedly, the war from their perception is justified as a war to manifest the very tribal vision and project of those who are governing this country behind the scene.


**August 23, 2015**

**In a Nutshell**

Even Kiir Mayardit could be more rational than some of these so-called his die-hard and staunch blind supporters. Intellect does require us to adhere to the norms of rational and critical thinking since we assume, as debaters, that our collective objective from the political debate be it or other venues of debate is to arrive to some common ground or at least agree to disagree. However, being a blind supporter all the way (which you are entitled to) and particularly of a controversial politician such as Kiir in which judgment and performance are at stake, indicate at personal level some serious issues within one's judgment capacity.

Not to mention being a blind supporter of failed leadership strongly evidenced in its 10 years' performance and delivery (by statistics and empirical data). Rwanda in 10 years has transformed itself and became one of the best countries in Africa and the world so why not us, with the vast oil revenues and others resources which Rwanda doesn't even have. It is the leadership folks.

We have no personal grudges with the leaders of this country whatsoever but we must have held them accountable and constructively criticize them for their failures and shortcomings when it comes to policy, decision making and overall performance at socio-economic and political development of our country and nation. Our objective is to point attention to areas of weakness and failures, sustain the system and the leadership with ideas and thoughts in order to perform and deliver better. We are not vying for positions as we can't work for the same crumbling roof and please don't take it personal.

What would we gain from the failure and collapse of South Sudan? Nothing at all, and if you think in your comfort zone, that the problems with South Sudan aren't yours as a South Sudanese citizen then you might be one of the political mafia profiting from the same problems. We are not, our people are the ones dying in UNMISS compounds or refuge countries and hence it is crystal clear that we are different just likes the tale of two cities (of one city called Juba). What J1 says with its blind supporters isn't the same what Juba's UNMISS displaced people say leave alone their relatives wherever they are.

You can still be a supporter to Kiir or Riek but it would be great that if you add some rationality and reasoning to your assertions, opinions and defense of any of each. Our concern should be what benefits do the country and nation gains from any political, economic or social issue being debated and not a blind worshiping of a politician or a U-turn to personal and character assassination.

**August 27, 2015**

**In a Nutshell**

Less than 15 days as promised, Mr. Kiir has finally appended his signature on the IGAD Plus peace document, something we must give him a thumbs-up and some credits for being brave enough, pulling himself out from the range of evil influence of anti-peace conspirators and decisively breaking the chains he has put himself to or been put to, by the enemies of South Sudan (giving him the benefit of the doubt). This time and around he has chosen the side of ordinary people of South Sudan who are in dire need for peace and decent life.

Whether this is a temporary tactic or a short-term strategy to let the mounted pressure of the UN and the international community ease a bit where a U-turn to the bloody business as usual is possible whenever and wherever a window to that is possible, or whether it is a self-realization that his own survival and power relay on this IGAD plus more than the lies of Gordon Buay, the madness of Makuei Lueth or the military might of Paul Malong's Mathaing Anyor, whether this or that, Mr. Kiir has now survived or at least for now and the Kiir must go has been put to hold until further notice. However, Kiir Mayardit is now in hot spot as never before.

A hot spot between four forces that he might need to either play it responsibly and skillfully or the possibility of getting off-track is even more likely. The first force being his new internal enemies within his camp, the dissidents of IGAD Plus who will continue to work tirelessly to undermine the agreement whenever and wherever there is a window to that, setting obstacles and hurdles in front of its full implementation or creating chaos, conspiracies just to below it off at any time and space of their chosen, well unless Kiir himself is willing and able to protect his part, there is no reason why these anti-peace ring of gangs should try their chances.

The second force being the SPLM/A-In Opposition(IO), SPLM-G10, SPLM-DC, the rivals and the partners in the peace agreement who are expecting the agreement to be implemented and honored as it is. Any attempt to dishonor it will for sure take the whole course back to the bloody square one, given the fact that the two armies of SPLM/A-IO and SPLM/A-in Government(IG) are left as they are until the full integration in 18 months. The third force being the international community that is waiting with all the technical know-how, financial resources, and the will to help or enforce the implementation of the signed peace agreement regardless of the SPLM-IG or SPLM-IO reservations, that's, should there be an attempt to dishonor the agreement, the sanctions and other harsher measures are in place and ready. This time, the international community is serious as they have asserted, we wish.

The fourth force is the South Sudanese people, where the real deal and difference can be made. Kiir and Machar, Igga and Akol, Pagan and the rest of leadership has a unique chance to apologize to the people of South Sudan through repositioning their focus on what the collective leadership has failed to deliver in the last 10 years. The blame game need to be subdued and put aside, they have consumed most of their lifetime on themselves and their political differences. South Sudanese, this time and around, needs to see, lives and enjoys what smart leadership can build, deliver and transforms. We are done with tribal politics and wars, personal rivalry for the last 40 years and the only redemption for all the misery and crime done upon the people of South Sudan will be through successfully putting this nation and country in the path of success again where unity, peace, security and prosperity should be the priority focus of the day not upon the grudges and political feuds of the past.

An ambitious socio-economic and political transformation program must be adopted in short and long term time frame. However, and before anything else, this nation needs a massive healing program where all the necessary stakeholders should play their role effectively and where all the underpinning causes of tribal hatred, culture of failure and all the ills in context of socio-economic, cultural and political aspects have to be thoroughly addressed and confronted. As a matter of fact, we are not heading nowhere without healthy minds and souls but back to the cycle of destruction and violence. We must have institutions for healing the mentally and psychologically sick before we can mistake them for heroes or whatever they see themselves they are. A massive education revolution that should transform and engineer a new society with less bias and social ills should be adopted through a well-defined, results-based education system, we can't expect people behaviors and attitudes just to change automatically, let us try some other magic and education is one that I recommend.

Well and in a nutshell, Mr. Kiir as the head of state needs to take a leading role in all this. However, for Mr. Machar and Igga there is even a more vital role than Kiir's, this time and around it should be through a clear mechanism where what is going wrong or what is expected to go wrong must be corrected and confronted head on through the created mechanism and system. I wish we all have learned that one mistake from a leader is as fatal and deadly as the war we have all seen.

## August, 30, 2015

### In a Nutshell

Welcome to the peace era and don't be surprised if some guns haven't stopped yet and are still being heard here and there, they will. Neither Mr. Kiir nor Mr. Machar can reverse the gear of peace train and so are their subordinates unless a new rebellion from the dissidents of IGAD Plus within either camp shall declare itself as substitute armed rebellion, well, while that's also likely, it will be of less significant in term of military and political might compared to both the then warring SPLM/A factions. However, both leaders are quite content with the IGAD plus peace agreement not because of anything else but because all of them have finally got what they want and the rest will just fall in place in the process.

Don't get me wrong before I explain myself. In my previous in a nutshell opinion titled Justice should start with the reinstatement of Dr. Machar into his rightful positions in both party and the government. I explained why that is and how it could bring back the peaceful co-existence Mr. Kiir's wrong decisions have destroyed. However, some were quick to decry my statement that this war is not about Dr. Machar in which I also do agree with them. However, the only misunderstanding between us in my opinion is how Dr. Machar does fit in, in this particular context. Here is how; the 2002 reconciliation between Dr. Machar and late Dr. Garang was not a mere gentlemen agreement between the two leaders but it was a reconciliation and reunification of the most powerful political and military South Sudanese factions in that time namely SPLM/A and SSIM/A under the leadership of the said leaders. A reconciliation that has made the CPA peace agreement with North Sudan possible and hence leading to the successful conduct of referendum vote in 2011 with a vote of nearly 99% and the then the triumphant independence.

In the 2002 reconciliation, Dr. Machar wasn't there representing himself but the vast political and military base and movement that any an informed and expert on how South Sudanese politics works cannot ignore or underestimate. The removal of Dr. Machar in 2013, both at party and government level was a serious breach and dishonor to the 2002 reconciliation agreement and so how come it wouldn't split the nation, the army, the security organs or say at least the whole country? It did and with costs and consequences for reachable than that of the 1983 and 1991 respectively. IGAD plus has revisited and identified the straw that broke the Camel back 's and finally it has succeeded, so far.

Our politicians must be aware of this fundamental fact which is, in a country of 64 tribes, it is the art of how one does the national politics to bring about the national consensus and paint everyone equally with the colors of South Sudan's flag and not the other way around by seeking the dominant of a single or two tribes claiming to be the majority and concentrating power and the resources of the whole country on the few privileged by a tribal concept while marginalizing others. South Sudan itself was born out of marginalization of North Sudan so how come would the South this time and around do it to itself and by the very same people who have taken arms to liberate the very people they are now marginalizing. Ironic isn't it.

How about the post-Dec. 2013 conflict ushered hopefully by the IGAD peace plus? Did we have learned anything of value? Did we know and learned how we are going to keep the balance of power and resources sharing and distribution among the all 64 South Sudanese tribes or is it the same business as usual that gives one or the two majority tribes the lion shares in everything? How about if we reverse the order, giving minorities tribes the lion shares this time and around? They are South Sudanese like anyone.

Those who have called for reforms and to be different than the old system has credibility at stake because they have to prove that they are practically different by putting what they have been singing into actions. The SPLM/A-IO have to champion a true transformational approach in a way that never before and this is how it will win the minds of South Sudanese and not only that, it will also pull the SPLM/A-IG to do the same, encourage it to compete with great values, effective performance and deliver results in order to keep its competitive advantage in the political game.

The backbone of any country is the civil and administrative services, not politics. If we create a skilled, educated, non-politicized civil and public administration then we have created a sound foundation for the country that can survive any political differences and politics of divisions and tribes. Firing or appointing people in the civil service based on political affiliation is a grave harm to the country. The criteria and mechanism of selecting the civil servants must be away from politics, tribalism, nepotism and all types of corruption. On the other hand, education, qualifications, integrity and technical know-how should be the underpinning ingredients of a public and civil administration that would run the country in the right direction and add value in context of socio-economic and cultural development. The SPLM/A-IO can make a difference if it avoids sinking in the same corrupted and troubled waters. Good luck.


**September 3, 2015**

**In a Nutshell**

If you think it is easy and better for Gen. Kiir to get away from the chains of IGAD plus than getting away from the chains of Paul Malong Awan's Mathinag Anyor then you might need to think again. The IGAD Plus implementation roadmap will be executed as planned and monitored phase by phase and clause by clause, within the designated timeframe, allocated resources, and the expected results. The implementation mechanism might be already in place in which the AU, UNSC, the Troika and the IGAD will provide all the technical know-how in project management to make sure the agreement is a success. There is nothing much Mr. Kiir or Mr. Riek can alter after they have signed it.

However, Kiir's interest in both IGAD Plus and Paul Malong is his own strategic survival and not for the beauty of both. The IGAD plus has given him an opportunity for survival which is the same interest and objective he sees in keeping Paul Malong Awan's Mathaing Annyor and Museveni close. However, the question is whether Paul Malong apart from his Mathaing Annyor militias will be still important to Kiir given the fact that Malong's secret plans and power ambitions do worries Kiir more than Riek Machar. Unless Kiir himself is the one grooming Malong to be a possible hire to him otherwise things should be working differently now. However, most of Kiir current political and military allies such as Malong, Kuol and Makuei Lueth, Igga, Lomoro and countless other whom positions and interests are at stake are against the IGAD plus.

Kiir has to tell us the truth, whether he is facing a rebellion within his own camp or whether he can't control his army. The sporadic fighting here and there just days after he signed the peace agreement are a clear message from Malong, his generals and the die-hard supporters that Kiir signature on IGAD plus have nothing of significant meaning on the ground and that the final ceasefire signed days after the agreement will not hold whatsoever. The newly appointed governor of Upper Nile, Gen. Thon and his support base might constitute a challenge to Kiir and to IGAD plus. The Apadang or Akoka Dinka people in Upper Nile have a question of interest of what is for them in the IGAD Plus agreement in term of power sharing and resources distribution in the greater Upper Nile Region. However, as a matter of fact, they can't be ignored because they are a fundamental part of Upper Nile leave alone that some of the oil fields are located within their area.

Strategically, Mr. Machar has a vital interest than Mr. Kiir in winning the Dinka of greater Upper Nile to his side and gives them guarantees that they will be represented fully in all the SPLM/A-IO administrative and political structures. This is very strategic for the peace to succeed in Upper Nile region before anywhere else leave alone that the exclusion of Dinka people of Upper Nile opens a wide window of exploitation by either Kiir or Malong to destabilize the region and the country as a whole.

Mr. Kiir doesn't see his rule ending soon and only God knows how he will manage to win or avoid failure in the coming projected elections. However, in the process towards the elections and the enforced implementation of IGAD plus, Kiir may either need to change the perception of Paul Malong about the IGAD Plus which I see is not possible since Malong sees IGAD plus as the document that has denied him the opportunity of taking over from Kiir in a way or another. Gen. Malong sees the war as the only ladder where he can jump all these so-called SPLM line of seniority and succession or the SPLM Political Bureau, hence, such a document from his perspective, is a sell-out and not acceptable.

In addition to that, the IGAD plus is also giving Malong and support base the best conditions and claims for a military coup against Salva, however Mr. Kiir is not sleeping and is keeping his friend Museveni informed or maybe it is the Museveni that is reading the threats of Paul Malong with his Mathiang Annyor and the political support base.

Until he gets rid of Malong, Kiir will continue to play on the reservations card which in fact, has no effects. However, getting rid of Malong is not that easy and we will wait to see how Kiir will manage to get rid of Malong's grip control over Mathiang Annyor and transform the Mathiang Annyor to his army that can support him in the peace era or if there is a possible return to the bloody square one, to summed-up, Kiir need the Mathiang Annyor without Paul Malong. As for Kuol Manyang, he seems to be of no significant threat to the King's throne and also might yield to work with Kiir in era of the IGAD plus as his main objectives of avenging the 1991 Bor massacres seem to have paid off more than double with Riek Machar's hometown destroyed and the people of Bentiu has been subjected to the worse atrocities ever by his right man over there, Gen. Jok Riak.

In short, the ball is at Juba's court and the cards of the game are with Gen. Kiir. The way he will play it in the next few days will shape the path to the 90 days before the start of implementation of IGAD plus and SPLM/A-IO has to be in full readiness, militarily and politically. If Gen. Kiir chooses to yield to his own survival option, then expects decrees and reshuffles of his military and political allies within the government, demoting or removing who he deemed to be threats and promoting or appointing those he sees would be allies in the new era. Otherwise if he chooses the defiance path and to keep the old alliance, then expect the notion of ceasefire violations, the possibility of full-scale war and then the IGAD plus being dishonored at end of it. Well, this or that, Gen. Kiir Mayar will have a little nightmare until he decided fully which way to go at the very watch of the powerful Paul Malong Awan.

**September 19, 2015**

**In a Nutshell**

First let me offer my sincere heartfelt condolences to the victims of the shocking Maridi deadly incident.

The deadly incident in Maridi does tell us why an effective government and leadership are needed in South Sudan and that the current public policies are inefficient and ineffective. Simply because such unnecessary huge loss of innocent lives could have been prevented and avoided if we have an efficient and effective government and leadership in place and where its first duty is the making of the lives of South Sudanese public better, safer and secure. However, this is not the case now and our current government is the last to know, the last to act and react when it comes to public policy, lives, and future. Unfortunately, this is not the first or the last of tragedies because in J1 there is nothing as such as effective policies and leadership. Take my words for it as a simple concerned citizen.

This is the very reasons why critical media and pens are needed to point to areas of weakness and shortcomings in government and leadership albeit Kiir's security agents have assumed that such role is undermining the country's rulers tight grip on power and therefore they have been shutting down media houses, kidnapping and beheading journalists doing the very job of cautioning and alerting the leadership and society to where attention is needed most and where government scrutiny is demanded.

A society without a free media is conscience-dead and lacks the very tools that awaken its mind and conscience in time of lost and stray and J1 is completely out of touch with what is happening to lives of South Sudanese in both inside and outside of the country. The situation does tell us that we are people without a caring government now and in fact, it seems that J1 is our public enemy number one now. Tragedies happen and they might get anyone off-guard, however, for such entities as a local, state or federal government, the degree of immediate respond to such a deadly incident could help reduce the frustration and instill some confidence in the nation's hearts and opinions that their government is there in the time of the utmost need despite any shortcomings. But to the very dismay of the world, nothing of such has happened in the shortest time possible and the SSTV is the last to report and the last to inform. Where were Wenna Lueth, Makuie and his own SSTV?

The job of the first responders such as the police, fire squad team and medical ambulance dispatchers are to make sure the first aid and life-saving items and procedures for the immediate victims are provided and that incidents that could escalate to a wider scale causing a wider damage and additional victims that are caused by fire, explosion, extreme and massive violence …etc. are contained to possible minimum effects. This is what we consider a good respond from an effective and efficient government that fears failure and that is subject to public accountability and its shortcomings are questionable and subject of the investigation under the laws of the land.

The first thing that would jump in the mind of an effective government be it local, state or federal is whether the public is safe or not and particularly in a situation where a tanker carrying tons of flammable fuels and that is involved in road accident in which the fuel is pouring everywhere and where the innocent crowds gathered to siphon out the fuel unaware of the imminent coming danger. Government officials and particularly the police or other security forces could have prevented the public from even coming close to such a dangerous place of incident, evacuate them leave alone watching them or letting them gather around it and like nothing is going to happen. Well, our government is last to act and the last to respond leaving the dear public lives to chance and mere luck.

If the lives of ordinary South Sudanese are really valued than we would have a caring government that plans for emergencies, safety, security, food sufficiency and other services ahead of time and not the last entity to know whether the public are starving and 80% going to bed without dinner, dying in hundreds with cholera outbreak or acute malnutrition that is awaiting to take 50,000 lives of South Sudanese children on a yearly basis or that 400,000 children are now being wasted without schools, scholarship students in foreign countries are on streets, hungry and haven't been paid for several months, crime and insecurity are on the rise ...etc. South Sudan is now the highest in military expenditure in the whole East African region, spending billions of dollars in war that is destroying its very own people. Don't we need a different thinking and a different culture of success? Why do we have to insist in our own collective demise?

There is a need of direction and policy change in J1 in order for this country to reposition itself onto the right direction and before it is too late or is it already? I hope not.

May the victims of this avoidable incidents rest in peace and to their family comfort and support.

**September 22, 2015**

**In a Nutshell**

Apart from its enormous benefits, Psychology is also one of the most destructive sciences which humans' race has ever used to destroy each other's. Psychological warfare has created as results; man-made criminals, the mentally ills, the drugs and alcohol addicts and whatever the self-proclaimed so-called the dominant race is it or tribe ...etc. has initiated and perceived necessary as tools to dominate upon another human. Inciting fears and terror as a way of making other submissive to their will and selfish plans and hence some culture, political ideologies and even some religions were spread through fear and terror.

Well, we South Sudanese should know about this better than any other black people, particularly those who were living in Khartoum during the war or other refuge countries of different people. However, a society that is just out of such an ordeal can't claim by any health measures that it is mentally and psychologically sound. What does our seat of power and leadership, J1, know about this? At least I heard Dr. Machar once saying in a visit to Omaha, that most if not all of us South Sudanese are traumatized by the lengthy liberation war and its various psychological and physical effects and we need healing in the post-war South Sudan before the trauma, the alcohol, the guns, the HIVS/AIDS, the allure of money and all that you know could end us up. This should be a first thing first right after independence for a caring and knowledgeable government to embark on. Well, that wasn't and still not the case and one would wonders what J1 is all about? Definitely it shouldn't be about kidnapping Journalists or terrorizing the people of South Sudan again but J1 role and job should be about identifying problems facing South Sudanese or what would be possible causes for future problems and in that context, work on solutions or preventive strategies. Well, in my simple opinion, J1 now is the biggest problem and not a solutions provider to this country and nation.

If we haven't learned anything from the current bloody war, then there is no reason why unfortunately we could come back to the same bloody chapter. There is a serious need for both the leadership of opposition and the government to be more serious and realistic not to repeat the same policies and behaviors that led to the current bloody conflict. The leadership must insist in creating a real, sound and solid foundation for South Sudan as a nation and a state without tolerance to what could stand in the way of such an important need. I realize that we all need to get rich quick and be somebody without due process and in that context we create corrupted behaviors and policies that could appear to be right or personally

155

deemed success while in fact we are destroying the very foundation that could create a true rich country and wealthy nation. The fundamental fact that is overshadowed by greed is that actually as a nation does not need harmful shortcuts. South Sudan is a rich country by nature and hence every south Sudanese is blessed accordingly. How?

It is a matter of committed and good leadership and this country and nation will fulfill its dreams both at national or personal level. The petrodollars and technology if managed well, this country will witness in a very short relative time unparalleled development and growth in both socio-economic and political platforms and this will for sure make South Sudan, the Saudi Arabia of Africa, a position that has its enemies and friends within the surrounding region and the world. Paul Kgame of Rwanda has done it and done right and well. But Rwanda doesn't have the vast oil and other resources like South Sudan. However, through committed good leadership and governance, Rwanda has developed and changed positively in every way and it is now ranked the most effective government in Africa and 7th globally. If we could put all this unnecessary noise aside and embark truly on what should uplift this country and nation, the results will certainly be great and in a very short timeframe. However, healing the nation from war-time effects, be it psychological or physical and replacing the culture of violence with a peaceful one, finding effective ways to disarm the civil population and reviving their trust in a well-educated and trained national army, police and security agencies could usher into an era of great country and nation we all dream about. Your take!!!

## October 27, 2015

### In a Nutshell

If we carefully and diligently worked out the details and the terms of IGAD Plus peace agreement, a return to war may not be likely and we could finally enjoy a permanent peace that would usher our country and people to an era of long term stability and peace where socio-economic, political and cultural development would be possible and where our children can enjoy uninterrupted education life and not end up in the usual cycle of poverty, ignorance and violence. There are many indicators that new war zones might emerge anytime soon particularly if the decree of creating the 28 states went on without addressing the grievances of those who think their land have been grabbed and annexed to other tribe's territories.

However, the IGAD peace plus agreement as we have emphasized on previous "in a nutshell" opinions are here to stay. Not because it is a perfect peace agreement but it is the best that we have at the moment and with time and efforts, it definitely will usher our country to a new era that could build trust and mutual understanding that a war cannot. Hence, how the IGAD plus will be translated, its details applied and implemented, that's definitely what makes the difference and most importantly are the details that could prevent, avoid and minimize any direct confrontation between the armed forces and security operatives of the two armed warring parties.

If by any chance, such a possibility is likely, then the question is how it could be defused, deescalated and prevented not to mess up the whole environment in a split second and take us back to the bloody zone. Therefore, a clear and an effective mechanism are needed and must be in place anytime and at the most of the volatile meeting points of the rivals' armed forces. Because any such incident, happening in our current very much hatred and tribalized charged environment, could make a return to the bloody square one high likely. A rush to Juba without the right formula and the right substance that makes all the formal and informal dealings and the communication channels of power sharing crystal clear is not at all, recommended. To minimize such incidents, formal engagement and communications should be done without confusion and with less or no grey areas at all.

As we have seen the blame game and fingers pointing of who started this or violated that during the course of the current bloody conflict and as many signed ceasefires being violated before the signature ink could even go dry. It is also high likely that our local and external enemies of peace will not miss to exploit and manipulate any little window to perform their usual business of propaganda of confusion, conspiracies theories and sabotage in a wish to bring the whole process to a crumble. In this case, most if not all the communications and dealings must be official and in a formal means. Sensitive positions of engagement must be occupied by people who are committed to this agreement to be a success. Those who have the abilities to reason, act responsibly and have the capacity and skills to deescalate any possible confrontation and disagreement. Remember, the fire of the current civil war that has come finally to burn the whole South Sudan was started by people who has neither the skills to prevent it or the capacity to manage or to read its immediate or long term disastrous implications. Both warring parties need to be always mindful about who is there and with the right training and information of what need to be done if such situation arises.

IGAD plus Peace agreement is a work in progress and in the process, it will meet some setbacks and obstacles here and there but the need for permanent peace in this country will have to make all of us, hopefully, think twice and make use of our peaceful tools to co-exist together in peace, prosperity and harmony. Destruction, war and under-development are never the right choice of any nation on earth and definitely it is not what we are here for. It is a time for South Sudanese to define what they truly need after decades of bitterness and for sure, war is not one of those at all.

## November 7, 2015

### In a Nutshell

In 70s, 80s and even at the peak of Sudan civil war in 90s and with Anya Anya-2 and SPLA clashing on ethnic lines, South Sudanese were still at large in a rare harmony and living side by side and particularly in big cities like Malakal, Wau and Juba. In families like the one I grew up at, we have the Chollo, the Nuer and the Dinka living and sleeping deep side by side and snoring as hell without the slightest fear of one another. However, one would wonder whether it is a possibility now in the deep ocean of planted tribal hatred, revenge and bad blood. There is no doubt that the war has attempted to destroy one of the most homogenous African society ever, society that was well-woven and beautifully intertwined in a rare social fabric across the centuries but now, brothers have turned against brothers in the worst tribal war atrocities and cruelty ever.

Recalling back the good collective heart of South Sudanese wherever you go, branded by a unique hospitality that exceed even the expectations of the visitor, it is unimaginable that we could have lost the road and all those great virtues and the cohesion of our people in a split second. However, I wish we all have come to the undisputed conclusion that war is a true menace that's like no other, it is built on hatred, on inhumanity and it turn the supposed to be God-like human into a complete beast of no slightest mercy.

But don't worry that much, the devil has failed and will always fail in South Sudan. Its tests and temptations won't last that long because we are people that can choose to be good or worst at will and close our minds or open it as well when our ego are or no more in the line. We are Nilotic with ego that can be above the logic, wisdom and the precious life sometimes. We have proved in this war that we can destroy precious lives and things just because our ego and prejudices are insulted, messed up with or put to shame or tested. Don't wonders if a stranger asked this question; why are you South Sudanese fighting and killing each other for things that don't make sense and you have a blessed country with so many blessings and if the stranger added, you guys can make wonders and go to the moon in so short a time if you want to. The answer is that we have much ego that blinds us from all these and I wish that destructive ego can give us a chance to think twice, have second thoughts of the best alternatives rather than violence and destructive explosion. This ego must die for South Sudan to live or at least it has to be nurtured to a more meaningful and useful force.

Education and culture of peace can do as a great favor and that's a work of knowledgeable leadership whether in government, institutions and civil organizations that can collectively transform the society and shape it to a more tolerant, wise-thinking driven society. Politics that feeds on hatred should be a crime. Nations are also protected from exploiters in the name of politics by laws and constitutions that work for all not particular group(s). The thing is, without internal cohesion as one nation, we are never to reach anywhere.

in a nutshell, whether it is a new approach for our political power houses to build their stay in power and leadership on segregation and pitting of tribes against each other, it is never a good political strategy for the nation-state building process, in fact, it is the very destructive substance that surely and swiftly bringing all of us to dead end. It is the cohesive not conflicting tribes that make the great nations. Our politicians must get back to political parties and movements with better socio-economic and political substance, promises and programs, inclusive enough and has a nationwide approach not the ones that are shallow, shortsighted visions dwelling on tribe of who or clan of whom.

**Nov 18, 2015**

**In a Nutshell**

Being aware that the expected transitional government is coming to effect soon which will make the exercise of executive powers of decision making to be shared or at least consulted within the presidency between the SPLM-IO and SPLM-IG, Juba has been in a restless state since the day IGAD compromised peace agreement was signed. Juba has been doing crazy things inconsistent with the spirit of peace and is saving no time, rushing, defining everything before the SPLM-IO guys could even land their feet on the capital soil. This is not a good sign neither it reflects a spirit of readiness for reconciliation nor it indicate that a new era for our country and nation is about to kick off.

Our expectations were that the political notion and the tone in Juba could have changed ever since the IGAD Plus compromised peace agreement was signed and hence the suffering people of South Sudan has expected both parties to embark on creating a conducive environment and the positive public opinion for a successful implementation of the Compromised Peace Agreement. That's by changing the political offensive and all the related activities, negative rhetoric in media and in the executive decision making. But this has been not the case, in fact if it wasn't the good resolve and the keen interest of SPLM-IO for the people of South Sudan to regain their peaceful life and rebuild their shattered lives, the IGAD Plus compromised peace agreement could have been a gone case by now.

With the expected coming of SPLM-IO, President Kiir and his base in Juba are still acting out of fears of losing power and control. Hence, everything they have been doing since the IGAD Plus peace agreement was signed point to that context. To mention just few that came to light since then, such as the creation of 28 states and the dissolution of SPLM-Juba leadership structures leave alone what we don't know in the hidden Juba's conspiracies clubs. Every presidential decrees issued since the peace was signed indicate a clear defiance and an attempt to derail the whole process. We have expected that the SPLM leadership structures were dissolved to accommodate the expected new changes created by the signed peace accord and hence, one should expect a new direction to the country and the nation accordingly.

But to our dismay, the recent appointments of SPLM-Juba secretaries has now made it clear that Mr. Kiir's fears of losing both the party and country leadership seat are still in place, the same fears of December 2013 that has caused all the turmoil for the last three years. Therefore, out of the same fears, Kiir has opted to bury Arusha re-unification bid and instead he insisted on the creation of his own version of SPLM with his supporters and in which he is the dominator and the king without the slightest threat of a rival.

Well, this shouldn't prevent the go ahead with IGAD Plus compromised peace agreement. In fact, in my opinion, this is a healthy breakup for both the SPLM factions if done peacefully and without the resort to violence and out of the fact that the post-liberation SPLM is never the same SPLM that was formed to liberate the land and the people of South Sudan in 80s. The SPLM is now a political party with many conflicted interests and visions and its breakup shouldn't be a surprise.

The thing is why these wrangling SPLM leaders are not courageous enough to change the name of SPLM with other names that are appropriate with the demands and the facts of post-war South Sudan? I remember that in one of my status' posts I suggested for Mr. Machar to change the name of

SPLM-IO to a name that represent his vision and his strategy to transform South Sudan. This will brand him out and so his followers from the rest of SPLM and as long as his vision is right and working for South Sudan, success and victory should be his in the course of the time.

The historical SPLM/A of Dr. Garang have done its job quite well. Unfortunately, it has died with the untimely death of our late leader, leaving the nation and the country in continuous orphanage until we luckily find another leader in the capacity of Dr. Garang. People shouldn't be worried about changing the SPLM name neither, because the South Sudanese people today look at the SPLM/A differently from the one in the past liberation days and in addition, we should be a progressive nation that is dealing with the demands of the present and the future not a nation that is stuck in the past and its deadly grudges. A right name in wrong hands is worse than a wrong name in right hands and after all it is never about the name but the vision, the mission, the programs and the political strategy of the political party represented by its leaders.

In a time when Kiir's party meets a true good challenger in the political arena, this will be the time Mr. Kiir will think twice and act accordingly to win every tribe, every vote and every opinion otherwise his rival will seize his weakness and wrong policies. True democracy could be the next realm we could be exercising if both Kiir, Machar, Pagan, Lam stood out with their separate parties and the rest of political parties will surely join. You can't mix all the bad and the good stuff in one pot and still complain and cry why your stomach should be hurting. It is the time for each SPLM's leaders to brand his/her vision out of the crowd, a time of multi-party democracy in South Sudan.

## November 21, 2015

## In a Nutshell

Before dividing the country to whatever number of states deemed necessary to answer the questions of federalism, equal distribution of power and resources or so they says, Mr. Kiir could have tasked professionals, historians, engineers to do the necessary feasibility study that could address all the socio-economic and political aspects related to this matter and should have sought help from former colonial entities to provide him with maps, references documents and books that define the historical territories of tribal lands throughout the history of South Sudan when it was still part of Sudan. Nothing was created today, the tribes with their land territories and borders were documented before Gen. Kiir was even born to the world. That's, dividing South Sudan land is not a simple political decision that can be taken overnight at some Juba club but it is a very complex one that need a lengthy and careful process of research and tracing of history of tribal land territories and all the geographical and historical aspects related to it.

However, while the decree of creation of the 28 states may have caused serious concerns and could derail the current IGAD peace agreement or led to eruption of potential new tribal wars let us also note that it has answered some problems and wishes in some parts of the country such as Jonglei and other parts of Equatoria and Bhar-El Gazal. The real problems and wrangling are in Unity State and Upper Nile state and some parts of Bhar-El Gazal states where some communities complains about their historical lands been annexed to other tribe's territories. The 28 states decree is a problem in both ways, in its creation as well as its requested annulment. If Mr. Kiir decided to annul it or withdraw it today, you will see the supporters of the decision take an expected stand against Kiir and I think, Kiir know that very well and accordingly he just decided to go ahead with it irrespective of its serious implications on the national security of South Sudan.

But here come the questions: should the SPLM/A-IO suspend the implementation of IGAD Plus and go back to war as a result of Juba defiance and decision to go ahead with the constitution amendments to accommodate the 28 states decree? Is there any possible political compromise that can be reached in that context to avoid going back to the bloody square one? Is there any role to IGAD mediators and the international community to play in bringing about a compromise or consensus in that context? We can't deny that 28 states decree is a serious problem now that needs to be handled and considered seriously by the opposition, the IGAD peace mediators and the international community. It needs a proper addressing before it spoils the expected IGAD Plus peace implementation or even create new bloodiest ones.

Those who are saying the decree should be completely withdrawn need also to slow down and consider those who are supporting it and those who are saying the decree should go ahead with its current form need also to slow down and consider the grievances of those that are opposing it. I think there is a middle ground here where all the opponents and the supporters can meet and compromise. That's, we need a political process that may lead to a peaceful agreement and not war and blood that can roll back the little progress made in peace and reconciliation efforts.

The fact is neither the 28 nor the 21 or even 50 states will come without opponents. They are all a work in progress that can be improved, amended, fixed and corrected in order to answer or accommodate new realities. We just need to sit as a family in a democratic mood and see why this or that won't work here or there or why this is not fair to who and who. There are many political ways for us to reach a consensus and agreement rather than war and destruction even when Mr. Kiir closes all doors we need to believe there is a way to make him come to his mind.

## Nov 25th, 2015

## In a Nutshell

In less than two months two major defections occurred resulting in the formation of two new rebel groups mainly from Chollo and Equatoria regions. Land issues created by order 36/2015 in one and repressive and grave human rights abuses in another are stated to be some of the reasons for the recent defections. This is happening when the SPLM-IO were preparing to send its advance team to Juba for the start of peace implementation. However, the government still insisting on the 28 states creation and have closed its ears to logic and reasoning.

Hopes for a peaceful settlement are now diminishing, the scope of conflict and war seem to be increasing amid decrease of prospects for peace. The country economic situation is alarming, insecurity, hunger and malnutrition are also striking hard around the country and particularly in the most hit hard conflict areas. Nevertheless, Juba is heading the other way, insisting on the implementation of its own political program that is strengthening Mr. Kiir and his own interest's groups in a clear defiance to the spirit of the newly signed peace agreement and showing not even the slightest care for the collapsing country and nation.

If you can send your imagination to figure out the big picture out there for South Sudan, I have no doubt that you would agree with me that it is not promising at all, in fact, it is very troubling. The man who we hope that he might wake up and return the country to normalcy, Gen. Kiir, appear to be completely out of touch with all these alarming indicators and hence the country is slipping down the road and he might not be aware of it. Something is seriously missing here and Juba words and actions regarding peace and reconciliation don't add up either

Now some are arguing hard that only return to war and to the agenda of removing Kiir by force is the only way out and opportunity for South Sudan to have an able competent national leadership. I have no doubts this is happening particularly if Juba insists in its own dictating actions. Juba needs to recognize that the only way out is a nationally driven debate and consensus on relevant issues of contest. Juba unilateral program is not going anywhere and the dictatorship nature of government, its bloody security approach and grave human's rights abuses must stop for rebellions to stop.

## November 26, 2015

### In a Nutshell

We have said it from the very inception of this crisis that the problem in South Sudan is a national one and that Kiir attempt to label it and execute it as a war against the Nuer was a divisive strategy of divide to conquer. All sound minded South Sudanese with unbiased judgment and analysis can trace how the crisis started within the SPLM party and until it ended unfortunately by the genocide against the Nuer. The 1991 split and its consequences were used as a pretext to unearth tribal hatred and to justify the Dec 15, 2013 Nuer massacre. This has succeeded temporarily and the Nuer took it upon themselves, and fought both Juba government with all the national resources and capabilities it wrongly used to try to wipe a single tribe leave alone the support of its regional allies symbolized in Yuri Museveni of Uganda.

Internationally and should there be any connection with the history and the past than the conspirators must have thought that we have forgotten those who have bombed and leveled down the great Ngundeng pyramid in the beginning of this century to try to erase the great cultural symbol of the Nile people out of fears and jealousy of an emergence of a black prophet and religion in the parallel. We haven't.

Nevertheless, the Nuer stood firmly and strongly until they brought their misled brothers and sisters to the fact that this is never a Nuer problem but a wide malicious conspiracy against this promising great nation and country of South Sudan. The conspiracy was that after they finished the Nuer, they definitely will come to the Dinka, the Bari, the Chollo and everyone. The sole objective of all this, is to divide South Sudan from within, prevent it from consolidating itself and realize its great potential to be the Kuwait or Dubai of Africa. But Kiir thought and still thinking that it is all about his power, the presidency and that attractive chair in J1 and hence he used the

Dinka against the rest to protect his throne but he is the most person who has done an enormous damage to the Dinka people. If you want to build a great Dinka, you will instead show a great national leadership that will build both nation and country of South Sudan to greatness and if this was the case, he definitely will find the support from the rest of tribes first before his own, the Dinka.

Unfortunately, this wasn't the case. All indicators point to a serious failure of leadership and management of country affairs. In his 10 years' period as president, Juba alone, the capital of the young nation still has no running clean waters or electricity and with nearly 100 of billions spent. The unity of nation is at its zero level and each one is heading far from nationhood backward to tribalism and clannish sections. The nation and the country today are at a very miserable shape at both socio-economic and political ends leave alone the future that look even more gloomy.

Being the president, the man in the driving seat and the captain of the ship, he is the man to blame and take the consequences of the failures not his subordinates or the "president's aides" and accordingly, his die-hard, interest blinded supporters must accept that truth and stop running into all justifications and the support lies because by this, they are not doing any good to the president and the country but more misleading and failure. It is very childish thinking for those who think this is an attempt to fail Kiir and bring Machar to presidency, it is not.

Amidst all these, there is a little hope that president Kiir is aware that the country is socially, economically and politically no more and if we give him the benefit of doubt that he is aware than he simply doesn't care whether this country or the nation are sliding into a sure hell. His false immediate aides and interest groups are not telling him the truth rather than feeding him the lies of false greatness and successes and this is the problems of all the dictators. They are kept there by money and blood aides and they never depart their comfort zone until the country and the nation are no more. Sadly.

## November 28, 2015

## In a Nutshell

SPLM former detainees are back to Juba without their leader Cde. Pagan Amum and the question of course is whether it is a final return or is it just being part of JMEC inauguration. None in Juba political horizon is showing any indicators or positive trends that Mr. Kiir is putting the country into a conducive mood for the implementation of IGAD compromised peace agreement. Recent appointments of SPLM-Juba's leadership structures and the controversial constitutional amendments for more presidential powers and accommodation of the 28 states creation are just few hard examples that Mr. Kiir is in a different path of his own.

Accordingly, the former detainees, unless being a party and political movement of their own, I don't see Kiir is dissolving his new loyalists SPLM party in which he is the sole King without a threat to accommodate those he deemed once trying to oust him from power and the true igniters of the current crisis.

Kiir is better off to go ahead with his new direction than being convinced again into a valley of his fears and hence the reunification bid seem to have reached a dead end. The question of course is where the SPLM-FD fits in the new political process and how they will independently operate in the very watchful eyes of Kiir brutal security operatives. Additionally, I haven't heard of them forming a new party or political movement or any possible merger with the SPLM-IO or SPLM-IG. These serious questions and speculations could be the very reasons of Mr. Amum absence and of course his own security amidst the last threats when he returned to Juba few months ago.

Can Mrs. Mabior in her capacity as the mother of the nation convince Kiir in a different approach to back down from his own survival agenda? Well, this is politics and everything is possible. However, Kiir political math and calculations are all based solely on his survival and how serious is the threat of whoever is trying to come close to his seat of power in J1 regardless of who they are. In fact, his new allies with whom he survived the 2 years political and civil war ordeal are awake and won't save a minute to interfere. Hence, what direction the SPLM-FD political future would be apart from being part of the IGAD compromised peace agreement or the expected transitional national government is but still a puzzle.

With the new constitutional amendments and the controversial 28 states, the SPLM-IO has been pushing through the IGAD mediators and the international community to make Kiir reverse his unilateral amendments and decisions that are clearly standing in the way of peace agreement implementation. However, with Kiir saying "Walai" no such a move will ever happen, some are arguing a return to war is likely. Well, we just came from the war and in fact, the killing is still ongoing in a way or another and accordingly, the SPLM-IO is trying to be strategic by resisting not to be dragged into the valley of rushed decisions and reactions.

However, burying heads in the sand and let go of the winds is also a never good working strategy to deal with dictators. Confronting their bias and defiance would be a better way instead particularly to the SPLM-IO. It will be a valuable asset to the SPLM-IO to have a known culture of no compromise when it comes to its core values and the agenda of reforms because the overall objective is to achieve a realizable change on the ground. Well, with all the Kiir's new obstacles and road blocks, it might be a time to rescue the collapsing country with a new approach, conquer Juba once more time and fix it from within and of course with all the security risks attached.

## December 2, 2015

## In a Nutshell

Juba leadership has proven to be irresponsible and incompetent and has a lack of national vision or long term national strategy on the state-nation building track and that's why we are here at a point of nowhere. The opposition leadership has two options to successfully deal with Juba leadership, the first is to adopt a policy of containment through knowledge and good leadership rather than policy of confrontation.

The second, is to have a better leadership and performance through better peaceful alternatives that gradually but surely bring the country and the nation back to normalcy, peace and stability. But it is not easy, there are many internal and external elements out there that are awaiting to blow-off every good chance for success. However, what will make the difference is whether the opposition leadership has known the mindset of Juba's leadership and how to deal with it successfully without assertion to violence. It is like dealing with an immature adult who will spoil the very peace he so badly need.

In South Sudan, destructive ego is a serious character factor both at personal and leadership level. Dangerous and unpredictable as it maybe, two of a kind will set South Sudan on ablaze. Our two different leaderships need not be at the same level of ignorance. At least one must contain the other through knowledge and wider understanding and the ability to predict immediate consequences and negative end results should there be any misunderstanding along the road of the peace implementation.

This is the art of politics and professional politicians and this is as well the very reason why South Sudanese people must make sure who and who is occupying sensitive leadership positions. Professional politicians and administrators with clear positive records on sound decision-making not immature adults with quick temper that can put the country onto a risky dangerous road and situations like the one we are in now.

While the general frustration is at its level high due to the shattered dreams and the hopelessness triggered by tough living conditions and a gloomy future amidst war, incompetent leadership and tribally divided society and nation, there is no alternative road but to conquer our fears and differences and hold tight on our unity and possibility of change for a brighter future. Giving up is no option.

In a nutshell and as we embark on a new road of restoring our lives and country back to normalcy, let us be reminded that it is not all honey and easy out there, in fact, the anti-peace crusaders, the war propagandists, the conspirators and the elements of all evils are but awaiting. But if we are truly willing and have what it takes and the knowledge of where we should be heading than the arrival to the safe shore is sure and certain. Good Luck.

**December 3, 2015**

**In a Nutshell**

We have liberated South Sudan and we are free to do whatever we want to do with it, rule it, sell its resources to whoever we may please, dry its banks at day and night and keep the money in foreign countries, buy the best mansions aboard. We are sending our kids to the best schools, best colleges and universities aboard and we are going to attend the best treatment in the best hospitals in the world, said the new gallant liberators.

We have our mighty SPLA that we won't change its name even though we are no longer part of Sudan anymore out of fears that our ego may got lost and vanish the day we abandon the name and accept the name South Sudanese People's Defense Forces. Our mighty SPLA is going to kill any South Sudanese who dare to ask logical questions such why we have fought the war and end up like this? Didn't we fight the war collectively altogether, small and big tribes? Didn't we all liberated South Sudan? Nope, if you dare to ask these irritated questions, we won't just kill you, but will burn to ashes your villages, towns, castrate your young boys, rape your young girls and teach the whole of your type a lesson they won't forget, said the gallant liberators.

Have you heard of Nelson Mandela of South Africa, Sam Nijman of

Namibia, Fidel Castro of Cuba, Abraham Lincoln of America and many more real liberators who escorted their people out of chains of servitude, slavery, poverty, ignorance and colonialism? Have you heard them doing what you are doing now to your own country and nation you claim to have liberated? I don't care, get out of my face and I don't want to hear more of your nonsense you Nyagati, said the gallant liberators.

Oh come on, nearly 200,000 are refugees in their own country, living in dire conditions and dying on daily basis, children and mothers are severely malnourished, 7 million are under threat of hunger and sure famine, about 3 million are refugees in neighboring countries, banks are dried, insecurity at its worst, Upper Nile and Equatoria regions are almost gone. Nonsense, nonsense you Nyagati. Everything is well and good as long as J1 is secure and as long as there is clean water and electricity in J1 than all is well and good, said the gallant liberators. Our gallant liberators are surely from a different world. God saves South Sudan.


**December 8, 2015**

**In a Nutshell**

In those doom days of December of 2013, Madam Angelina Teny has also run for her dear life and if she was found that night, the matter could be a different sad story by now but God never let it happened. Early from the very inception of this crisis she wore the military fatigue alongside her husband. Dr. Riek Machar and the then second most powerful couple next to the first couple of South Sudan became the first couple of the rebellion of what we know now as the SPLM-IO and accordingly they also became the most wanted couple by Juba regime, none of them if found, could be spared.

Mrs. Machar has been there days and nights witnessing and being an active part of the formulation of the SPLM/A-IO while in the same time giving the emotional support to her husband and to the cause of people of South Sudan. She has been doing it not only in the time of rebellion but through his career and leadership. She is one of South Sudanese well educated women, a career politician and leader who did held many ministerial posts and been in forefront of South Sudan Women leadership and rights advocacy. The daughter of late veteran South Sudan Politician Thomas Kuma Khan and anyone who had been in Malakal and close to South Sudanese politics knows very well how Gat-Khan has positively shaped many today young politicians and leaders lives and future.

It was yesterday when she was appointed as the head of SPLM-IO head of defense and security commission. First, we congratulate her for this much well deserved appointment crowning her role and contribution in the movement for change and reforms as well as her active role in South Sudanese Women empowerment and rights advocacy. However, the appointment has triggered mixed feelings and reactions from within the SPLM/A-IO leave alone the usual adversaries and opponents of SPLM-IO. Some pointed out to the fact that she is the wife of the SPLM-IO leader Dr. Riek Machar and her appointment is a bad precedent on how the SPLM-IO claims to be advocating for reforms while doing the very nepotism, one of the core corruption factor that has brought the house of South Sudan crumbling down to its knee. The other part of argument is on context of what are the qualifications of Mrs. Machar and what has she done so far to make her deserve such a complex and high demanding post of defense and security where a career military and defense personal should fit best. They further argue that she should be appointed in Women Affairs, education or social and gender positions where women are seen best fit from the very poor perspective of a man dominated society such as South Sudanese.

Come on folks, let us be fair and give our women the dignity and the recognition they deserve. Education is what should make the difference, not gender. Performance and service delivery is what should make the difference not gender. You don't deny a qualify person a well-deserved post because she or he is your partner in a marital relationship. The question should be whether Mrs. Machar is qualified or not and not whether she is a wife of Mr. Machar or a woman. The appointment of Mrs. Teny has answered both qualification requirements; hence this is far from practicing nepotism of employing unqualified relatives and I encourage those who are criticizing the decision to find out about Mrs. Machar's CV and Resume.

In a nutshell, Women today are not only assistant ministers but great presidents, defense ministers, universities lecturers and commanders in combat zones...etc. The old concepts and perception about women don't hold waters anymore and our male dominated society must accept this fundamental truth. Example of women who has been active in politics and still and whose husbands or fathers were career politicians and great leaders are all around us from Mrs. Clinton of USA, Rebecca Garang, Rebecca Joshua Akuchi of South Sudan, Late Indira Ghandi of India, Late Banazier Bhutto of Pakistan, Aung San Suu of Myanmar and the list is endless. A society where women take center stage in leadership is likely to be one of the most peaceful and prosperous societies. Congratulations Mrs. Machar and to South Sudanese people.

## December 12, 2015

### In a Nutshell

Mr. Kiir has the keys of normalizing all the nation's political differences if he has the capacity of behaving as a national leader and if he has the will of restructuring the political environment to accommodate a peaceful transition, no one is above him in South Sudan echelon of power. What if he just accepted the return of the 600 advance team of the SPLM-IO two weeks ago, what if he opened an honest reconciliation and healing bid within the SPLM party and across the nationwide, what if he committed himself to corruption free new direction that will attract the donors and investors alike, what if he worked hard to stop the insecurity and what if….., endless. Kiir is not acting as president, not acting like he has powers to use positively for this country and nation to be at best.

But instead, his enemies turned loyalists are playing with his fears, he is a hostage at best guess and best benefit of the doubt hypothesis. Otherwise what is holding president Kiir back from what he has power to do? To change this nation for better, to develop this nation to the best, to make it united, peaceful and prosperous? Why is Kiir choosing instead the wrong and destructive path? Whose interests is he advancing by destroying South Sudan? Couldn't he have maintained the same power by working in positive direction? Isn't that a puzzle?

Mr. Kiir is in dilemma between choosing to compromise the political power with others or go all the way in an absolute bloody dictatorship, between breaking down the SPLM and reviving the Arusha reunification bid and in which at both ends he wished the results must have assured that he stays in power. He is reluctant between inviting the same threats of December 2013 in which he wished will go away with plunging the country into tribal bloody war and political chaos but to his dismay, everything and everyone is still here, the competing other SPLM members are still here as well as the Nuer he attempted to wipe out are all but here.

The confusion and reluctant of Juba is so obvious and reflects a house in disarray to an extent we start to doubt whether Juba as a government is capable of anything more than advocating for its stay in power while the country is no more. Juba is in constant fears of losing its control on power, it is therefore reluctant in implementation of peace agreement as well as whether to accommodate the former SPLM members of political Bureau. No one wants to loss his/her post, not the party or in the government.

Accordingly, fearing to lose his new loyalists with whom he survived the last 3 years' political turmoil, he therefore may try to keep his current SPLM structure and holds on power as long as he wants with an iron fist. But such a choice is likely to breed the same confrontation and infightings of 2013 leading to the current war. Well if he chooses to go along with his new loyalists and pushed the former detainees and the SPLM-IO to be separate SPLM wings, the fact is any political activism is a recipe for real troubles. Juba political atmosphere is uncertain; it might explode again if not handled well and this time with wider consequences, hopefully not.

## December 14, 2015

## In a Nutshell

There are no answers for questioning the madness that took your precious lives in a split second, the ignorance that cut your dreams short, and the cruelty that left your children orphaned, the heartlessness that let your spouses' widowed and your country destroyed. You won't believe it if we tell you in the afterlife that it was done by the same people you were eating, playing and joking with.

You won't believe it that it came from the very same people who know you at best. Your peers in the army, your colleagues at job sites, your classmates at schools and your playmates at childhood grounds and your neighbors at the neighborhood. You won't believe it, that it was done by the in-laws, the cousins, the uncles and the nephews in the name of their tribe. You won't believe it. That is why it is an absolute "Madness".

This is a nation that has gone strayed. A nation that has taken from ego a way of a life and replaced knowledge with ignorance, truth with false, love with hate, light with darkness and humanity with cruelty. So don't wonders no more why you have gone too soon. It is an absolute "Madness".

You may ask what happened to those beautiful people of the Nile, the tall and the dark skinned people that I know. Their hearts are so pure full of kindness and love, strong yet merciful, intelligent yet humble, independent yet caring and brave yet meek at the core. Again, what happened to the people of the Nile? What happened to the children of the Nile? Oh. Did you say "Madness". Oh, I see a total "Madness"

May your souls rest in peace our December 2013 victims of the total "Madness?"

# December 15, 2015

## In a Nutshell

This is the day when our nation was divided, with part of this nation as mourners and other part as the celebrators. This is the day when the unity of this nation was killed by few greedy folks, when the union of this one nation is no more, when all our historical bonds and ties were brought to halt by few greedy souls. This is the day when the dreams of this new nation were brought to ashes just for the interests of the few lost souls to flourish.

This is the day when South Sudan was made to bleed forever by its own leaders. Money and power has done its devilish magic, altered their hearts, seduced their minds and poisoned their souls and now they live in a realm where the death of their fellow countrymen is but a source of celebration and joy. But remember, those you made cry today were never least brave and were never least patriot if not that you have chosen a war of the coward and to be the coward at best, you came and stab them from the back, kill them with the same weapons that were meant to protect them and the same army they thought it was their defense shield. You caught them by surprise, showing them your ugly reality.

Those you have brutally murdered in this day have gone but they will never be forgotten. History will hold you accountable in front of their orphaned children and grandchildren, widowed spouses and battered relatives even in thousand years. This land forever will remain theirs as it been for centuries and it is never the illusions and the fairy tales of the few greedy souls that will ever make it not. So celebrate and kill with our stolen power and wealth at least for now but not forever.

But just a little reminder while celebrating and having the joy of your devilish victory, we remind you that our dream is still alive, stronger as never, in fact you just made it even stronger and this nation will continue to sacrifice the precious to make that dream a reality. You have misunderstood us, underestimated us, misjudged us and we know for sure that you have closed

# December 17, 2015

## In a Nutshell

As we remember the victims of December 15th, 2013, the pressing question to all of us is: What plans and actions taken to prevent genocide from happening in South Sudan? When the underpinning factors that led to December 15, 2013 are all but still here and thriving as hell. The failed leadership that has plunged the nation and country into the bloodbath is still but here, holding on power with iron fist and is even more determined and thirsty to a more bloodbath massacres.

Guns and tribal hatred are all but still here as well. The tribal hatred is destroying from within the body of the once one nation, paralyzing it and diverting its attention from what it need most to what is destroying it. Tribal hatred seems to be the ghost in the political machine and thought that is moving each one of us foundation of thought and what our politicians are building their political foundations and strategies upon. Meanwhile, guns and sophisticated weapons are still pouring in into South Sudan in a way like never before and everyone seems to be well armed to teeth. That includes young children as young as 10 years and the ignorant who want to repeat ignorantly what they see in the movies and wipe out their portrayed enemies like flies in a real world.

In the light of such clear indicators and trends, the likelihood of future genocides and mass killings in South Sudan is but certain. Hence, while we are commemorating the victims of December 2013, it is important to reflects and think, suggest and workout some effective ways and alternatives to try to prevent or at least minimize the likelihood of occurrence of such a large scale humans lost in future.

Since the leadership and the government are both suspects and complicit in being the major cause of such mass murdering, South Sudanese cannot throw their whole trust and have the gut in the same time to ask the same leadership and the government for protection or prevent and strategize ways out for stopping the likelihood of future genocides.

However, looking to the reality on the ground where the country is currently divided and well-armed on ethnic lines, minimizing the occurrence of mass murdering will solely be on the type of leadership of those ethnic-based armed government, opposition movements and militias. The way they behave and the manner they control their respective tribal forces and popular base will have a sure impact on whether or not future genocides are going to occurs. On the other hand, Juba government must come to define itself accurately that it is solely tribal to the core and it doesn't have a bit of ground as a national government both at policy making level and direction nor on its very tribal establishment and hence it is a major part of the problem and that fact won't change until a real national government, army and security forces are in place.

Therefore, the only authentic hope for South Sudanese people is a neutral third party that its mandate is truly to protect the civilians and the vulnerable masses. The United Nations has already a mandate and sizable forces claiming to be just doing that. Nevertheless, the ways and policies and even the distribution of its forces around the country seem to be unrealistic and won't deter such threats of future genocides. Hence a more working research and approach is needed as well as an effective mechanism of distribution of its forces around the vulnerable masses of South Sudanese. The African Union has yet to act realistically and enacts plans and strategies on how it will address and uproot the threat and trend of ethnic genocides in this tribally structured continent.

In a nutshell, South Sudan will remain a timed bomb until the present factors and the clear dangers are no more and hence the African Union along with the UN and the international community must stay awake and with an active long-term working presence in South Sudan to prevent or at least to minimize future mass slaughters.

## Dec 18. 2015

### In a Nutshell

We are not against capitalism but this is not the way capitalism is created, at least not in Africa. The South Sudan's new social rich clique, the Kiir & Co., has finally decided to mitigate the accumulated stolen wealth for the last ten years and use them to steal even more from the same people they were stolen from at first place and hence bringing together its two faces, the one who is being managed by bad boys or the black market and other one being managed by their smooth criminals or the Central Bank. They decided finally to take away the little resources left in the hands of the struggling South Sudanese masses by floating the South Sudanese Pound against the US Dollar and as a result of this greedy act; unimaginable hike and increase in the prices of commodities, the transportation and the fuel as we have seen it at the quick rise in NilePet fuels prices and nearly in every commodity. I need not to remind you who own and controls those businesses nor the companies and hence I don't have to remind you who control the shaky economy.

Our new rich social clique must be celebrating by now since by floating the Pound against the Dollar, the $100 became $300 in a split second and still counting, they have tripled their revenues while the loses of the ordinary South Sudanese tripled upward as well and if the situation persist, all the poor's money in few months should land in the hands of our new rich and the foreign traders. You will be left with nothing and these rich will come in another role to employ you and force you to work for them in a way or another and squarely just for your living". No, we are not against capitalism, but we are against the malicious ways these people have acquired their capitals and wealth and the way they are trying to invest it on the same people they have stolen it from.

As a citizen of this country, you should wonder how this new social rich class did form itself from nothing within ten years and now we have billionaires and millionaires who didn't have even a goat in the last ten years. Wonders not, it is not the hard work nor it is the smart guts or brains but it is the magnitude of theft, corruption, fraudulent practices, fake contracts, fake companies, public money laundry to our most corrupt neighbors where South Sudan money has made whole villages a hub of leisure and first class life. We have nothing in South Sudan; everything has been robbed and saved in foreign countries. We are fed and supplied with imported food items and the entire most needed daily life items through contracts that has been bought and sold in fraudulent ways and no one care whether those commodities or products are good for consummation, safe for health or outdated. It is not those who make money of these fake contracts that dies and bear the health effects leave alone the financial burden but it is the ordinary South Sudanese who by the grave circumstances of the situation, forced to consume and use these outdated products without other options.

Floating the local currency against the dollar is an act always taken by a producing country, with sustainable economy, that's at peace and prospering. Are we currently producing anything? Is the oil sector working effectively and producing its 98% share of our revenue? Aren't we at war that has consumed nearly everything and our 2/3 of the population being fed by the UN? How do you float your local currency when you don't have a solid economic foundation on the ground and no effective competing market forces that can compete to lower the dollar rate against the local currency in the long run if this what they mean? In an ailing and unsustainable economy, the so-called $20 million injection from the central bank to commercial banks are not enough and are not sustainable hence the 20 million and what will be taken from the poor South Sudanese are all ending in the hands of the rich and their greedy regional friends.

The poor South Sudanese, while consuming the little they have to survive, will find that they became poorer in few months than before and while all these money ends up in the hands of the falsely rich and in the foreign countries, South Sudan will find itself ultimately broke and in a total collapsed economy sooner than later. Well, unless the same hawks of corruption and war reversed their decision or has decided fearfully to let the peace agreement to materialize as scheduled, where oil production will resume and where the international donors and the investors may offer an emergency conditional funding for peace implementation and rescue to the ailing economy if not the collapsing country, and there we might have a chance of good survival even though with that, the falsely rich clique will have gotten away with what they have already stolen.

## December 29, 2015

### In a Nutshell

I think we aren't into the CPA2 implementation phase yet. Are we? If not, then when will the official implementation phase start? The delay tactics are deliberate and as I said before, Kiir is using the little time he has before the CPA2 official implementation kick off to change South Sudan platforms and structures of power, resources and population demographics that existed before CPA2 signature and implementation. Things he won't be able to change when the power sharing between him and the SPLM/A-IO goes into effect.

The CPA2 didn't clearly barred Kiir from taking advantage of the period before the official implementation to change everything to his favor through presidential decrees rather than the general assumption that the same ground that existed before the CPA2 should be the same it has to be implemented upon. However, Kiir was quick to use it and drastically, dividing the country into 28 states and adding more excessive powers to himself. With Kiir current attitude and if the trend persists in future, I doubt whether the SPLM/A-IO has anything to do at this moment or after it became part of the system to make any realizable changes except going back to war fields to pressure Kiir to back off from his latest decisions or in future nor I see Kiir is giving any consideration to IGAD or international Community. That's, deadly conflicts and bloody disagreements between the two warring factions might be wait in store for this nation and country. Hopefully not.

Unless, a serious change occurred within its leadership ranks, I doubt that the SPLM/A-IO is ready to return to war fields and even Kiir himself does know that with the current state of affairs within the SPLM/A-IO and this is one of the reason making Kiir acting as he has crashed the SPLM/A-IO already. However, if the SPLM/A-IO decided to go ahead with the implementation of the peace accord and with all the uncertainties surrounding the present and the future, the questions are, can the SPLM/A-IO reverse whatever Kiir is changing or decreeing now or in future or yield to implement the peace agreement on Kiir's own carpet? If so, then Kiir already prepared the ground for himself to have the upper hand in executive, legislature and judiciary and with that said, how will the SPLM/A-IO enact its reforms? Reasons with Kiir? Be equal partner in decision making? It is not likely that it will succeed on that track too and hence I think it became apparent that Juba main objective is to gradually and surely dump the CPA2 into recycle bin anytime soon just like the David YauYau agreement.

Well, unless the whole thing is about bringing the self-wrangling SPLM together again and where each member from here or there will take back his/her position and rank and the rest is history. In that case, whatever is happening in the SPLM-IO or SPLM-IG is meant for one thing, don't be fooled.

# CHAPTER 4

## 2016 ARTICLES

**January 5, 2016**

**In a Nutshell (5 points)**

-Hopes hanging on JMEC to order/convince Gen. Kiir to relinquish his 28 states decree and back to the 10 states structure. Would he? What if he won't? What JMEC can do?

-SPLM-IO doing everything based on the 10 states structure, sending everyone to Juba, appointing and submitting their MPs and ministerial nominees. Alright but what if Mr. Kiir never agrees to rollback his 28 states decree? Don't tell me people are coming back to Pagak. (Juba is always a one way for those opposing Kiir)

-Kiir already annulled the 10 states structure, put the 28 states into effect, appointed governors and some resumed work already and some won't leave but upon their dead bodies.

-My people are dancing and overjoyed with their new positions and already wetted in the heavy rains of congratulatory messages. That's awesome but where to? 10 or 28 states?

-Well, at least there is a bit of scam here, someone is cheating and some people are being cheated or are it a one man's illusion. I hope so too but only time will tell.

Congratulations, it is peace in anyway and the advance team of Facebook warriors is on their way to Juba.

**January 6, 2016**

### In a Nutshell

Kiir and base has a complete surprise to the SPLM-IO, the IGAD, the international community (Troika) and for all of us whose expectations in the next coming weeks is the complete CPA2 implementation in the letter and the spirit and as signed on August 17th, 2015 in Addis Ababa, August 26th, 2015 in Juba respectively.

Unless the SPLM-IO has decided to give in to the endless obstacles, hurdles and defiance awaiting her from the side of Juba, the likelihood of peace collapse is higher than we might think. Unless Gen. Salva has destined himself from the hardliners and anti-peace gangs within Juba, who in a way or the other, will continually attempts to fail the peace process, giving the benefit of the doubt that he is not one of them, our hopes for final peace could be in vain.

Kiir and base, want to make sure the SPLM-IO don't get away with any key post or state that they will use as a tool to threat Kiir's power and rule. Hence, comes the 28 states, changing the population demographics and the political representation that gives the dominance in all the three branches of the government and the political power, the executive, the legislature and the judiciary to Mr. Kiir.

Kiir and base has a serious misconception about how this war has ended. They misunderstood the need for peace and the importance of ending the bloodshed that has driven the SPLM-IO ever since to overlook on some prerequisites of a genuine peace. Juba has taken this as a weakness and hence Juba is acting as it has defeated the SPLM/A-IO militarily and that the opposition is rushing in to avoid possible serious divisions and wrangling within its ranks and file.

Accordingly, Juba thinks they have every right to act unilaterally and not necessarily on CPA2 accordance. Keeping its 28 states, choosing for the SPLM-IO what to have and what not to have from ministerial key positions to all the powerful positions and ministries. Therefore, whether for this peace agreement to hold and last is not a question that depends on how long and how serious is Juba in its provocative anti peace actions and agenda rather than it is a question that depends on how long can the SPLM-IO take the heat and to what extent can they compromise given that some of their recent actions are definitely irreversible. Let us wait and see.

## January 8, 2016

## In a Nutshell

Whether he was truly a suspect or not, Riek Machar's apology for the 1991 Bor massacre was never accepted except by few and particularly the family of Dr. Garang Mabior and a handful few from Bor and the Dinka community at large and this was clearly evidenced on Salva Kiir, Kuol Manyang, Makuei Lueth and many architects of 2013 Nuer massacre who has based their reasoning and the strategy on revenge to 1991 Bor tragedy.

The war went on; killing thousands, burning homes, destroying the three states of Greater Upper Nile, displacing millions within and without the country and has almost brought this nascent country to a total collapse. The wide world was appalled on the nature and extent of atrocities and cruelty of South Sudanese upon themselves in one of the ugliest crimes against humanity ever, putting the image of this promising young nation worldwide into doubt.

Yesterday Mr. Kiir courageously swallowed his ego and apologized for the Dec 15, 2013 Nuer massacre and its aftermath destructive war. I wish it is sincere and real and not one of his usual emotional breakdown and rhetoric that we have seen before but never have any real meaning. This country need a new beginning, a complete fresh start based on such apologizes, healing and reconciliation but they have to be genuine and put into effect not a mere face-saving games. Our hearts and minds should never be the same if there have to be a new brighter dawn for this nation and country.

Our leaders must acknowledge the current sad affairs of this nation on which they have planted a deep tribal hatred, bad blood, tribes against tribes, clans against clans, brothers and sisters against each other. It is a nation against itself in a war that they are the fuel, the victims and the losers at the end of the game. A new beginning is needed with a new vision and a new drive based on an inclusive, national reconciliation and healing process.

The questions are; would both leaderships of the warring parties initiate such a most needed and vital process or is it the business as usual? What would make Mr. Kiir's apology works and authentic if Dr. Machar's apology was never taken seriously and real? Wouldn't be another war based on revenge to Dec 15th, 2013 Nuer Massacre?

## January 9, 2016

## In a Nutshell (7points)

- When the wrong and right become one thing, none of them should complain anymore about the words and deeds of the other and so is the

SPLM-IO, the SPLM-IG and the SPLM-FD reunification bid.

- Challenging Kiir within umbrella of one party was proven before as non-working, risky and dangerous business. It was the root cause of December 15, 2013 massacre of members of Machar's tribe and the aftermath bloody destructive war. Tell us, how it is going to happen smoothly, effectively and peacefully this time and around.

- Within the reunited SPLM, Machar will still face the same strong opposition and challenges in his bid to become both chairman of the party, front runner and the flag bearer of the party in the presidential elections scheduled for 2018. In fact, Machar could be dumped aside in a doubtful democratic process and which he will have no say. Still he needs to figure out how he will defeat or convince Kiir/Igga to step aside or retire, and by the way, should any of you resort to military solution again, the people of this country are tired of SPLM's wars and massacres.

- SPLM reunification closes the only great door for democratization of the country. Mr. Machar, a strong rival force and base to Kiir's and base. This country could be better off if the two has separate democratic parties that compete for better performance and better socio-economic and political development program and agenda. Their merger would kill all that.

- I have said it before, that a man who usually add his way of life, vision and mission into another man's authority, loses the logic, independence and has no reason to still complain why his views and opinions are being dominated and ignored.

- Vivo Dr. Lam Akol, for being brave enough for changing your party's name, staying yourself and accepting the reality that the first step for being true is to work under a right and a true umbrella. South Sudan doesn't afford cheating ourselves into short, temporary and non-working marriages.

- Well, for my SPLM-IO, leaders, colleagues and supporters please call me in when the final funeral rites to our great SPLM-IO are about to be sealed under the so-called reunification. That day I should look for a different political party and someone else that truly fight for truth, reforms and real change in South Sudan.

**January 11, 2016**

**In a Nutshell**
**a response to Gabriel Pager Ajang**

First of all, the Nuer never went to bush because of 30% ministerial allocation and there is no justification whatsoever for the Dinka to have 60% of ministerial posts or the rest of 63 tribes to have 10%. Let us refresh our minds and go back to Khartoum when we were all slaves and subjects of Khartoum's successive oppressive regimes. Could we justify our current injustice to our own brothers if we couldn't justify Khartoum injustice to us all? If yes and on what bases? This is not what we fought for; this is neither the country nor the system that about 3 million precious souls perished for. We need to roll things back, bring back our sobriety and conscience which have been lost in the ocean of greed, tribal hatred, nepotism and all social and political ills and corruption.

The SPLM-IO cannot be a carbon copy to the SPLM-IG tribal approach. It should be the alternative no matter what are the challenges. It must exactly bring forth the right formula and structure on what true South Sudan democratic and diverse state should be built upon. This is the bases why we are against the re-unification, something is meant to correct the wrong should not again have brought under the very umbrella in which it is against. The SPLM-IO has a very promising future if it would build itself into a national inclusive movement meant to change South Sudan and accommodate all the South Sudanese in one identity regardless of their tribes. A true one nation.

When it comes to community decision on leadership and leaders, first of all leadership is a competitive endeavor in which individuals who see in themselves the qualities of leadership and who think they have visions and transformational agenda do compete for their constituents' votes and choice be them on local or national level. I don't know about a collective agreement in any community to replace leaders of generations (A) with leaders of generations (B). Through other process than free and fair democratic elections and naturally. Any dictated decision or unilateral process will be against individual's free will and is a recipe for divisions and wrangling in the concerned community.

Those individuals you mentioned can't be barred from leadership through a community decision in other form but through free election and in a fair competitive democratic process. How about if they are still productive and have in themselves the will and the drive to lead. Let us compete in a democratic environment, bring on your vision and socio-economic, cultural and political programs, your transformational agenda, no matter how old are you (look at the American candidates of election 2016, from Bernie Sanders age (75) to Marco Rubio age (45). This clearly indicates that it is not about how old are you as long as you still physically and mentally fit and have what it takes to lead.

Our leadership dilemma is not about age or this generation or that. I believe leadership principles are personal and those who seem to be hitting right and left has no leadership substance from the very core of themselves. The case here is how do we select our leaders? What are the criteria of selection? What qualities and values we are looking for in a leader/ Do we select our leaders because they have transformational agenda or because they are members of our tribes, clan, family and no matter whether they are corrupt and visionless? We have seen in America and Kenya how competing candidates' debate in front of the public about issues and programs in a process that give the voter a clue about a possible leader and based on that, the voter shall make his political choice.

Our dilemma is deep and to have it diagnosed accurately, it need political scientists, social engineers, psychologists and nearly every professional and from there we can re-engineer our society and position it onto the path of political and social health and wellness. It is a complex task that many of our leaders who inherited leadership because they have fought the liberation war minus any other leadership qualities are not aware of or lack the accurate understanding for its underpinning causes. Our current forefront leader could have been the person in the driver seat, driving the car to the destination, safe and sound but unfortunately this wasn't the case and what made the matter worse is that he has the support of those who think they are the democratic majority; however, a 99.9% of wrongs don't make the wrong right.

## January 14, 2016

### In a nutshell

The typical African democracy has been inaugurated today with Mr. Kiir 's new SPLM party even though the scenario of ruling South Sudan for hundred years was initiated several years ago. I don't need to remind you of the typical African democracy where presidents stay in power for life, 30-40 years and where the incumbent president win election with 90% votes neither I need to remind you of how state's constitution are amended and obstructed to allow our eternal presidents to make it to their 6th or 8th terms in the office with each term set to be not less than 5 years. That doesn't need a reminder; it is the constant world of majority of Africans.

Well, this is what Kiir and his next successors who also will rule for another 100 years has initiated today, democracy of one party within a security/police state and that will always win in forged, rigged and fake elections and the examples are many in East Africa alone and most of our battered continent. But look at the puzzle itself, this is happening and when there is only one day left for the January 15, 2016 deadline given to the political parties to register so they can be eligible to participate in 2018 projected elections. Does that make any sense and while the SPLM-IO and other opposition parties are still out of the country and in a time where all efforts are being geared to stop the ongoing war and suffering of South Sudanese all around the country?

However, it is not that complicated what Mr. Kiir and his new SPLM party are up to and he already unveiled to us the true course and objective by telling his supporters to elect him in 2018, seriously? Well, I remember in the course of the debate surrounding this Dec 13, 2013 conflict, I once told Cde Muorter Majok and Cde Garang Gong that Mr. Wani Igga must not deceive himself that he will succeed Mr. Kiir at any given circumstances and I asserted that when the time come, excuses and reasons will be made up as why Mr. Igga can't be president just like they did to Dr. Machar. Well at all these, there is something good and clear about Mr. Kiir, that's he has been telling people his true intentions to rule as long as he want and he is doing just that. The other intention is that he is a tribalist to the core that is committed to uplift his tribesmen on the expenses of other South Sudanese and he has spent vast blood and money on that, Period. Hence, it is up to those who still don't want to get it right or fight it but not Kiir.

Well, learning of Kiir intention to run on 2018, I don't know how our Vice president Wani Igga reacted today but I am so sure he heard it and loud as well but the man has been a true resilience through the period of liberation movement otherwise he could have faced the same challenges and opposition as Dr. Machar. However, Igga's chances to stay as a Vice president for life are about to start. As for Dr. Machar and as I outlined in my previous "in a nutshell (7 points)" that he must not accept to be lured into a fake reunification where he will be dumped aside later in a doubtful democratic process that he would have no say at all. Well, today Kiir must have vindicated us since a group of opportunists within the SPLM-IO always manipulates our analysis and readings and quickly labeling us as traitors while we maybe the honest guards to the substance and direction of SPLM-IO. Anyway that's politics, no regrets.

As for our suffering South Sudanese, I know you are a peace loving people who have been living in peace and harmony for centuries but our current president's policies and actions can never pass without creating tribal wars and land disputes and I hope God won't let us down. The future of next generation seem to be gloomy as well and with 51% of our children not attending schools, about 3 million externally uprooted and hundreds thousand internally displaced to UN compounds and depending on UN food assistance, mortality rate at its highest among young children due to acute malnutrition and hunger, I believe our president has proved that he is a person that may not need to be challenged rather than he may truly need a serious help and a different approach to save this country from real disintegration.

## January 16, 2016
## In a Nutshell

The SPLM-IO need to come to the term that they are an opposition movement and whatever military power they have got doesn't give them a constitutional power to enforce their decisions and agenda no matter how good they are; they need to be a government first to act as a government. Yes, we have an illegitimate government, a corrupt and misguided one in Juba but let us admit that it is the government of the day regardless of what we or the world think about it. It is the one that executes the daily businesses of the state of South Sudan and it is the one representing it internationally and regionally despite its bad image, poor performance and the worse of them all, being the killer of its own people.

Yes, it is a failed and a bad government but it is the de facto government of Republic of South Sudan. With that in mind, let us not forget what is in the capacity of Juba as a government to decide and do in the name of government of South Sudan, for example; It is still within Juba to expel diplomats, UN representatives, borrow money and all that but the worse we could expect is what if Juba went crazy as it does always and decided not to deal with the Chairman of JMEC and regarded him as persona non grata? Rounded up the members of advance teams and the rest will be a tale of the tongues. Well, I know many of us think that it is not possible or is the worse and the craziest decision Juba can ever take, however, as a matter of real prediction, it is likely in any time through the troubled road of CPA2 Implementation.

Sending 100s of SPLM-IO members as advance team including high ranking leaders such Gen.Taban Deng Gai and rest and then deciding that the leader of opposition Dr. Riek Machar will not go to Juba if Kiir won't roll back his decree of 28 states creation is a very risky decision and it could have dire immediate implications. We expect by now that the SPLM-IO must have known what type of government and regime they are dealing with and hence, they should have a better approach and strategy since half of their trunk is already in Juba and the other half is in Pagak, Taban and other high ranking SPLM-IO leaders are in Juba, I see no difference, which means Dr. Riek is already in Juba.

But didn't Mr. Kiir created the 28 states before the advance team could even travel to Juba? If the creation of 28 states was an as red line and a clear violation of CPA2 as many of SPLM-IO has argued, then it should have been resolved before any advance team could have traveled to Juba. Now, the decision of leadership of SPLM-IO not to let their chairman go to Juba as a pressure to Kiir to revoke his 28 states decree is clearly putting the safety of all advance team into a clear risk and danger and you can't rely on the UN and International community for protection either, recent history and events around us do emphasizes that.

On the other hand, deciding to pull out the advance team is also a clear declaration that the next thing to it is a resumption of war. Then why would you think that the regime would let heavy weight and high minds of the movement get out its own eyes to wage a war on her? In fact, this is an additional card they will use to the maximum to achieve some of their anti CPA2 goals. Hence, the SPLM-IO's leadership either is just kidding or still not getting the game right. Realistically, the SPLM-IO possible option is to negotiate with Kiir and find a common ground on the 28 states and act in a way that doesn't put the lives of its advance team in jeopardy. The parties the agreement need to admit that there is a need for more states but it highest purpose shouldn't be tribal allocation rather than to achieve social and economic development and integration of South Sudan. A solution disputes to current 28 states can be negotiated out with direct involvement of those whose land and tribal territories have been annexed and where the international community can provide help in judgment, presented with documentation, maps and references to resolve these issues and grievances.

**January 18, 2016**

**In a Nutshell**

Dear Mr. President: The War Will Burn Down the 28 States too

Now that the 28 states issue became a dual redline; they are Kiir's red line if Dr. Machar and base tried to ask or work on their revocation and they are redline of Dr. Machar and base if Mr. Kiir insist on imposing them on Machar's camp and the rest of South Sudanese. Well, unless the redline in South Sudan politics has become politicized and became with less meaning than what we know but If the redline still means a point of no compromise, war and death, then Machar and Kiir has already declared war. I believe leaders and politicians whose lives of their innocent people hangs on the very words they echoed or actions they initiated should be very careful and cautious enough since every word they utter either can make war or peace or at most it can't be used against their own credibility and trustworthiness. However, since us as country without accountability, where leaders can't be impeached or required to answer for what they say or do, it is the norm and not the exception.

But why drawing redlines when there are still enormous possibilities of political solutions and compromises? Doesn't this negative notion in our politics reflect an acute political poverty in our politicians and leaders' political capacity and philosophy in dealing with national issues of sensitive importance or are we a nation of sudden strangers who never lived in harmony and co-existed in peace and unity before? Since when did the blood and death become our politics and way of life and then only what we hear are redlines? Look at the geographical distribution of our people and tell me if there is any single ethnic group that is living in an isolated island without sharing a border or the same land with one or more ethnic groups. Go to our map and territories and see for yourself what beautiful diversity God has created and what lost humans are trying to destroy. South Sudan is one country and its nation was one and has been one and will again be one. The red lines, the 100 states are all nothing and this nation and land shall be as it was.

Now let us suppose that Dr. Machar called his advance team back to Pagak and decided to resume the war which means that we are back to bloody square one. That's high likely but what is next? How are you Mr. President going to achieve development and your vision in the 28 states when there is an ongoing war that is burning the land and killing the people? War means the death and destruction of the disputed people and the land respectively isn't it? Within the war, there will be no 28 or 21 or even the 10 states that will be existing nor functional or populated since the remaining South Sudanese will be forced again to catch up with the already uprooted externally or displaced internally. The destroyed Greater Upper Nile and its uprooted and displaced people should be an example. Did the president ever visited Malakal or Bentiu or Bor since the war erupted? I haven't heard of that.

Kiir may not need a full rollback of his decision of 28 states, it is not that all bad neither Machar may not fully disagree with the 28 states decree. I believe there are certain areas of disagreement and these are areas that need to be identified, tackled and resolved as well as an increase or decrease in the number of states can also be proposed. It is very imperative that our politicians believe that one nation must not adapt the policy of war and blood rather than policy of compromise and consensus.

Let us be honest about the land of Chollo people that have been annexed. The Chollo people have been accommodating all South Sudanese in their Land, Malakal mainly and its surroundings and Mr. Salva should be very thankful to Chollo people instead of stabbing them in the back. Malakal has given Salva just like many of us, a home, a career, and a future he couldn't afford if he grew up in Warrup. Annexing the land of Chollo to either Nuer or Dinka is a grave injustice and no matter they are a minority, they haven't given any choice but to depend and bring back their grabbed land until the last man standing. My advice to Dinka of Akoka and other whose land and territories are overlapping with Chollo is that they need to sit down, talk as a family and avoid themselves pools of blood. It is their children and future generations that will be still living there not Juba's politicians.

The SPLM-IO has shown a keen and consistent willingness for peace while Juba has cheated the world and the South Sudanese as well. Because before the signature ink went dry, Juba initiated several presidential decrees, restructuring the country geographical and demographical distribution existed in 10 states structure plus adding powers to the already powerful president. Well, Juba may see itself smart and powerful in her own eyes and whatever it has done after it signed the peace agreement on August 26th, 2015 was a well calculated plan to derail the peace process in which it accepted unwillingly. The SPLM/A-IO has all the options on table and this time and around trusting Juba must not be one of them.

**January 21, 2016**

**In a Nutshell**

The Jieng Council of Elders and the Making of Jieng Country

Part of finding a permanent solution to South Sudan conflict is that we must unearth what is in the minds of Jieng Council of Elders (JCE), the group that is said to be the architects and political chefs of Gen. Kiir political tribal program. Since 2013, the systematic nature of many controversial drastic events that has made the promising, newly independent state and nation of South Sudan a field of tribal wars, tribal political chaos and the high likelihood of its disintegration has raised serious questions, whether such events were results of inexperienced political leadership represented by mere military generals who have nothing in their leadership storage but the legacy of having fought the liberation war or whether such drastic events where the fruits of a well-planned long-term political program of disguised, underground movement that has approached the then hero of liberation war, Gen. Salva Kiir Mayardit, and succeeded in convincing him and used him as a tool to implement a vision contrary to the one the majority of South Sudanese fought and voted for.

Most of us believe a sudden change to Gen. Kiir political beliefs has occurred at the wake of 2013 and this wasn't necessarily because of Dr. Machar quest for power rather than the hypothesis that Machar himself and unconsciously was a card in the game in which its real players were behind the scene. The mathematical scenario supposition was that, had Machar stuck with Kiir and never declared his intention to challenge Kiir in both party and the projected election nominations respectively and instead worked to maintain his close ties with Kiir and rejected the rest of SPLM members (G10 later) unproved coalition with him, Machar could be still a trusted Kiir's political ally not a projected fierce rival and things could have been different by now. However, the hypothesis continues to define the real cause of Mr. Kiir sudden change as a part of the game as well, that's, Kiir was also a card in the game just like Mr. Machar himself. Well, the questions then are; who were/are the key players of the game and what was their objective?

Had Gen Kiir stayed the course as we have known him or at least as we have believed him to be, a man for South Sudan and all South Sudanese people in the liberation days, then we could have been in the true path of translating and manifestation of the South Sudan that we truly dreamed about and fought for and we could have traveled that great path with a more realistic achievements and landmarks on our socio-economic and political transformation for the last 15 years. If nonsense and bias were put aside, by now we could have much of our grand projects and dreams in place, the billions of $$$ that we have rendered here and there and the international credit that we earned hard during the liberation struggle could have made a country of our dreams comes true. Electricity, clean water, phone lines and other communications system could be mostly everywhere. Our country could have much of itself well connected by paved roads, good bridges and highways and the trade and businesses could be booming between our people in their safe and secure neighboring territories.

Unfortunately, this wasn't the case. The sudden change of the Gen. Kiir of the liberation days, where he was well known as a hero who has given best of his lifetime to the cause of his country and people to the current Kiir guided by JCE, has definitely ruined the dreams of all South Sudanese if not most of the Africans in that region who were waiting eagerly for the independence of this blessed promising country and nation. I bet most of us are looking for the causes and what made that drastic change to the man we mostly knew as consistent and faithful to the liberation cause and to the leadership of the late founder father of this nation Dr. John Garang.

Some has argued that it is the influence of Jieng Council of Elders (JCE), which consist of group of influential Dinka elders with aim of establishing a Jieng dominated country and governance ruling system. The JCE has been on the surface and forefront of political events and helms since the Juba massacre of Nuer ethnic group with much of the country accusing them of being behind the tribal program that has positioned this country onto the path of tribal hatred, wars and its possible disintegration. This kind of suspicions and unsupported accusations to JCE were even re-enforced further with the presidential order 36/2015 establishing 28 states in which 12 out of the 28 states are given to Jieng and with claims that some large parts of other communities' land territories have been annexed to Jieng's newly created states. Well, to understand what are behind JCE's motives and intentions, we need to know how the JCE was formed, its structure, who is who analysis of its members which could give us a clue of why did JCE penetrated the SPLM from within, rocked it from within and finally set it apart from within. Are they truly serving Jieng's interest? What is the nature of their relationship with Kiir and who is using who? I recommend the reader to do his/her own analysis and to get the answers.

However, whether those claims are supported or not, JCE has admitted that only 24 out of the current 28 states were from their original proposal to the president and they are not aware of the other 4 which they said were made up in J1 by the president and maybe with his own immediate political friends. Most South Sudanese believes that the true objective behind the creation of the 28 states has no connection to the claim of taking government to people or any socio-economic development and that this is a part of JCE transformation program of one dominated tribal country. Now, on the other side of the coin, similar questions are being asked and debated about the extent and the role of Machar's 21 states, their demographic distribution and geographical structure and what political gains did Machar made through that? Did the 21 states helped in any way to pump up the idea of 28 states into JCE or Kiir's Mind? I leave the answers to the readers

Coming back to the JCE's master plan and to make the whole scenario short and, if such a claim is true that the JCE is the one running the show with sophisticated plan in place, then such a plan must be a long-term one, that must as well have a powerful enforcement mechanism and tools, a well trained and equipped military, a brutal police/security support, a viable political elites and financial resources support base that is able to lobby for its cause in international capitols. If such a description does really fit what JCE is and about, then Dr. Machar and his SPLM/A-IO must change the way they are dealing with the realities of situation in South Sudan and a better, well thought out approach and strategy may be needed.

☐

# CHAPTER 6

Pre- CPA 2005 Articles

## What Makes Kiir's Administration so Unique

By Chuar Juet Jock*

September 1, 2007 — our president Salva Kiir Mayardit is a man with a constant standing in our modern history and the struggle for freedom and better future. A man who stayed the course firmly in spite of all internal and external conflicts that have affected the liberation movement since its inception. His role in realizing the Comprehensive Peace Agreement (CPA) is great and will be recognized in our modern history and throughout the future generations

In fact, he is the first administrator of our autonomous southern Sudan following the tragic death of our first president Dr. John Garang. The death of our hero Dr. John was a heavy lost and unbearable for our suffering people and all the world freedom seekers. The expectations of our enemies were great that with his tragic death, the CPA and the liberation movement all will crumble and that our bitter collective struggle will end in vain, winding back to the domination and suffering circle of these injustice and domination powers.

But, Kiir Mayardit and the rest of our gallant leadership in our liberation movement have proved the opposite and contrary to all evil wishers dreams. They have stood the tragedy firmly and have calm the situation holding the vision of the late leader and assuring our people that the vision will stay alive. In fact, we don't know if our leader Dr. Garang great life was stopped by an act of foul play or it is accidental but all we know is that his vision will be carried on no matter what, not by this generation only but by all the rest to come.

Being the first administration after two decades and a half of bitter civil war, Kiir's administration as I like to call it, is unique in every direction and tasks that it will shape or carry out accordingly. The huge responsibilities and heavy tasks plus the great challenges of the implementations of the CPA, the long awaited and high expectations from our people that have paid the price of freedom so dearly and have endured all the inhuman treatments and conditions during those years, all these factors make Kiir's administration so unique and also vulnerable of misjudgments and unfounded criticism in the post war southern Sudan history and future.

With Kiir's Administration leis the future of southern Sudan in all aspects, simply because it is the administration that should laid the foundations and the platforms of modern southern Sudan state. How this administration visualizes the future of southern Sudan will have a great impact to the future of this part of the Africa that has suffered a lot from domination and isolation.

Starting from nothing but a land that has nothing but the remains of the few infrastructures destroyed by the war, a land that its people were subjected to systematic killing and uprooting for decades, there is absolutely nothing to start from, this land have to be made alive again and its people must be returned and healed at all cost and its infrastructures have to stand and flourish once more no matter what.

All these demands and responsibilities need a unified and determined leadership, understanding and united public, viable technical and human resources, effective and efficient means and ways, philosophy and policy that convince the world and its conflicted system of politics. But mostly a policy and a philosophy that would effectively works with and tames the reluctant and defiant National Congress Party (NCP), the de facto partner that has the share of lion in the Government of National Unity (GoNU),

Besides being a partner in the implementation of the CPA and the democratic transformation of poor Sudan. It is really important that, those people who do judge and criticize Kiir's administration performance for the last two years put in mind and thoroughly consider and always the type of partner this administration is dealing with.

Here are some stops of what make Kiir's administration particularly unique in the history and future of post war southern Sudan.

locally, Kiir's administration has succeeded with some degree in its policy to unite and reform the house of southern Sudanese from within particularly in terms of power and wealth sharing, reconciliations and normalizations of relations with others southern Sudanese political and military powers, tribal leaders and former foes, these all comes in the quest for southern Sudanese consensus and unity, leaving no place for our enemies to sabotage and prevent the implementation of the CPA. Without the unity and consensus of southern Sudanese, the CPA would be judged as exclusive by the enemies of our freedom it is really important that the administration continues to balance and distribute the power and wealth among different political and ethnics groups of southern Sudan.

Agree with me or not, the administration also has given a considerable positive role in quest for a peaceful and political settlement of Darfur conflict even though its role is being affected by the defiance of NCP and the disunity of liberation movements in Darfur. On the other hand, his administration didn't neglect Nuba Mountains at all, guided by the vision of New Sudan that must be carried on parallel with the autonomy of southern Sudan and recognizing that the realization of new Sudan depends greatly on the realization of achieving just and last peace in the whole Sudan

Regionally, the Kiir's administration enjoys a great recognition by the neighboring Intergovernmental Authorities on Drought and Development (IGADD) countries that helped greatly in realization of the CPA. It is really important that these countries have to share benefits of realizing peace in the region and that by investing in newly rich economic and development opportunities. It is also worth noting that the role of Juba in the realizing peace in neighboring Uganda led by our vice president Dr. Raik Machar has to be empowered, supported and realized. Strategically, without peace in Uganda, the peace in southern Sudan is still incomplete.

Internationally, it is important that Kiir's administration weigh every step into international arena, we are really in dare need to strengthen ties with our allies and friends in the developed world especially north America and western Europe, Australia and Scandinavian countries. Those who have stand by our people in the bitter times of our struggle and still, should have the priority in our international approaches and interests.

However, the bigger task ever this administration has faced and still facing is the return and complete repatriation of southern Sudanese Internal Displaced Persons (IDPs) in Sudan and refugees in neighboring counties, Western Europe and North America. With too many responsibilities that all comes as priorities, the shortage in financial resources, and lack of effective technical means still hinders the success of this task. It is really worth noting that Kiir's administration recognizes the important of accomplishing this task as soon as possible, before the proposed elections, census and referendum.

Good and effective governance needs viable and efficient institutions and systems, the poor performance represented by the delay in provision and deliverance of services, rampage corruptions and wide insecurity, failure to pay government employees in a timely manner, inadequate regulations and laws that governs and regulates private sectors in term of provision of services and products, inequity in the employment system, all these errors and failures are due to the lack of efficient systems and trained and responsible human resources.

Kiir's administration first and unique job is to establish a strong foundation for southern Sudan, a foundation that will make this rich part of Africa and its people play the role they should in reflecting a new face of Africa. A face that is not just known as corrupted, AIDS affected, tribally divided, and the famous beggar of foods and Aids in the international streets, a face that is not only known by hunger, malnutrition, diseases, genocide and human right abuse. A new face of Africa must emerge and a free and dignified African must be born and there is no right place to this but southern Sudan.

To construct and create this new face, Kiir's Administration will need to create effective institutions with efficient systems designed just to achieve this task, institutions and systems that know how to accomplish the tasks and that are sophisticated administratively and technically. This includes all aspects of life in southern Sudan, in political, socio-economics context, defense and national security as well as foreign policy. Some will say the creation of institutions and acquiring systems with that quality and efficiency is too expensive. But the fact is that the absence of effective institutions and the lack of adequate systems is twice expensive than creations of these institutions.

Constructive criticism is necessary to drive and correct the process of implementation of the CPA, sustention of good governance and awakening of government attention of failures and errors here and there. In the process of this constructive criticism let us always acknowledge that Kiir's administration burden is huge and unique in terms of time, responsibilities and demands.

Well, clearly what make Kiir Mayardit's administration so unique is that, it has started from nothing and in a time that need solid leaders and achievers to put together a shattered nation and ruined land in the path of peace, unity, development and stability and at least the next administrations will start from something that is definitely built, founded and designed by his administration

## The Road to democratic change in Sudan

## By Chuar Juet Jock

November 19, 2008 — Yes, Barak Obama victory in the United States presidential elections does inspires, invokes the feelings and the dreams for positive change not only in the situation of so dominated black people of the world but also in a peaceful reconciliation in the so deteriorated racial relations and ethnics tensions among the diverse human races and ethnic groups of the world. This century will always be marked as the century where race, tribe, and ethnic backgrounds were and still the leading factors for civil wars as well as regional conflicts and that has resulted in a grave and mass human lost as ethnics cleansing, genocide and crimes against humanity became the tools of quest for power and control.

Unfortunately, our country, Sudan, deeply fall within the troubled countries and states where policymakers, lawmakers and their enforcers has used ever since the race or religion factors to create and engineer constitutional and political systems as well as socio-economic systems based on racial, tribal, religion or even gender profiling factors, systems that, glorify and enrich some humans while marginalizing and humiliating other in the same time, resulting at the process end in a society that is divided to itself and that's engulfed in social ills, violent and hate crimes as the man made economically disadvantages tries in vain to catch up with the man made economically empowered.

As Sudanese, we definitely do agree that a fundamental change in the way things were and still are in our country is not just a mere wish but a must have requirement, the vast majority of Sudanese do agree that this country is not in their hands, neither its rich resources are used for the benefit of the Sudanese people and that this country has been and still being ruled by powerful minority that has been installed during the transition period given this wrong name as independence day.

It is also well known that the racist minority rulers in Khartoum has always seized the opportunity of being the heirs of power from the Anglo-Egyptian colonists in 1956 and from that point of time, Sudan was run by minority that claims themselves as Sudanese, while their deeds, from actions to policies in all the history of their successive regimes denounces this such claim. Yes, we are in dare need for change in Sudan, changing the brutal bloody regime in Khartoum with all its racist constitution, political and socio-economic systems, that means defeating the racist National Congress Party (NCP) originally known as National Islamic Front(NIF) in the upcoming projected elections in 2009.

As Sudanese from various walks of life, different political colors and religious and ethnic backgrounds who have fought, opposed, and resisted this regime policies and brutal deeds in its twenty something bloody years. We do consciously acknowledge that bringing about regime change in Khartoum through popular uprising or other democratic means has proved to be too risky and unsuccessful as the dictator system has installed itself firmly through harsh means and have transformed the whole country capabilities and institutions such as the then national Sudan Arms Forces (SAF) and various security forces to just forces for its protection and survival.

Change will not happen if this minority powerful ruling class in Khartoum is not removed from power, we have been hoping for a relative change in their conceptual world , in how do they view themselves and Sudan as country as well as its indigenous people, simply because these concepts and visions are what divide us, held us prisoners within ourselves, it is also the same concepts that driving this minority to carry out all these brutal ethnics cleansing, genocides and crime against humanity, against their brothers and sisters.

Therefore, the only golden moment for real change in Sudan , all Sudanese are intelligently asked to seize is the 2009 projected elections, it is the moment where all the Sudanese should unite and make this democratic change possible and prevent their country from breakup, a moment for real defeat for the long time exploiters of our country and its resources and a moment for a glorious victory for the longtime agents of the real desired change who love this country and don't want to split on the bases of race and religion, these are tools that the ruling minority has used even since to rule the vast majority of Sudanese and keep them divided.

It is never easy to defeat this powerful racist minority that has been ruling the country through military coups or exploiting Islam to form a religious state, simply because throughout times of their successive dictatorship rules, they have accumulated financial and political power that is behind any description leave alone their strong backers here and there around the racist countries and systems of the world. Our problem in Sudan is not a religion neither it is race, but our problem is this racist regime itself.

For twenty something years Omer Al-Bashir and company did has an absolute control on country resources and wealth, they have controlled every single power base, owning and directing the full Sudanese economy, all the major companies, financial banks businesses as well as oil companies, they have formed a strong military and Para military that is ready to intervene to prevent any possible change that will overhaul their racist system, in addition to a bloody secret police and security organs equipped with the best tools and technology that has made it possible for them to conduct this systematic genocide and massing uprooting throughout the country.

We do deeply acknowledge that none of us did democratically elected Omer Al Bashir as president of Sudan, neither his racist party the National Congress party (NCP) formerly known as the National Islamic Front (NIF) to be the ruling party of our country, in fact we all do remember clearly when the NIF was defeated at last democratic elections in 1985 and how they went to work underground to toppled the last democratic government of Sadiq Al Mahdi on Friday, June 30th, 1989 by a military coup d'état.

Though this is how this racist group did seized the power, most apparently the NIF was secretly sabotaged and penetrated and though its Islamic agenda was used by a group of racist Arabs nationalists that has ties to other Arabs Nationalists Movements in the neighboring countries or others like Iraq or Syria , which might be the cause of the serious rift and divide within the NIF movement between the Islamists and Arabs Nationalists resulting in the formation of NCP of Omer Al-Bashir and the Popular National Congress (PNC) of Hassan Al Turabi and therefore the imprisonment of the most senior leaders from African ethnic groups and hence the mass uprooting and ethnic cleansing of African people of Sudan, in South, Nuba Mountains, Ingasna and Darfur.

This group has used Islam extensively as a pretext to pursue its racial agenda, downplayed with the fears of the innocent Sudanese Muslims that Islam is being targeted by western world through South or Darfur, a devilish tactics and cheap lies that sooner were proven to be mere cover up. When the Islamic Sharia laws was introduced in Sudan in 1983, most victims that were put to death or their rights hands and legs got imputed were African Sudanese, Muslims and Christians, from the marginalized areas, from Darfur, Nuba Mountains and Ingasna and South of country, it is the racist system in Khartoum that marginalized them and it is the same racist system laws that is punishing them at the other end, what a controversy, additionally, the racial, ethnics cleansing, genocide of African Sudanese Muslims of Darfur that is keeping the heart of humanity in aches and pains on daily bases is a clear prove to that.

We in Sudan do know and very well that there is no most devoted, true Muslims then the Darfur people in all Muslim world, it is Darfur that did make it possible for Islam and Arabization to reach South and other parts of Sudan leave alone Africa and the world. Unfortunately, the worst systematic mass killings, rape, ethnics cleansing, genocide and all the ugliest crime against humanity that happen in Darfur didn't happen but by the racist regime in Khartoum that has claimed ever since Islam as their constitution and political Ideology.

All these fall in the attempt to change the demographics and dynamics realities of Sudan, to reduce, weaken the mechanical and majority of African Sudanese (Muslims and Christians) and hence preventing it from any formation that will led into its unity and accordingly its empowerment.

We do firmly acknowledge that in a real and true democratic state and system like the one we want to have, a political majority can be attained through various political means and agendas, it is though acknowledged that even though the African are 69% or the Muslims are 60% that doesn't mean always that a racial or religious majority will always be the winner of any democratic elections, in fact, the well-being of Sudan and its all people should be what constitute our political visions and agendas.

In the democratic country and system that we wish to have and where majority rules and minority rights are protected and guaranteed, the fears of minority will have no place whether it is a racial, religion, tribal or any kind of minority base simply because any form of power abuse will be firmly prevented as well as the balance in constitutional, legislature or executive powers will be guaranteed by the supreme national constitution of the land and the people of Sudan.

The present state of our country which does tell us that more work is needed in order for Sudan to change, Sudan must be restored by its people from the this racist minority grief control, the 2009 project elections will be the best and the golden chance in just doing that, to make it happen , we as Sudanese people will need to critically think about the past, present and the future of our country, each of us will need to think seriously about the 2009 elections ,what this elections means, what it could change, how it can be made more secure, effective and successful with a trusted results.

The 2009 elections will impact the future of our country in a great deal, it could mean an end to a brutal bloody regime that has been our nightmare for twenty something years, and that has made our country but the worse place ever by all terms of insecurity. In 2009 elections we the Sudanese people, (southerners and northerners) will meet head on with the longtime exploiters in Khartoum and their stooges everywhere in Sudan, it is each of us vote that will make the change possible, it is each of us vote that will make the long awaited freedom and liberation to prevails.

Hence , we ought to know which political party does represent the change we need and define clearly what actually need to be changed in Sudan, and who have the keys, the capabilities and abilities, leave alone the will to make that change possible in other words who are the major forces that drives and moves this change process forward, what are the forces of resistances that are preventing this change from taking place and how they can be overcome, defeated or changed, is this change the desired one for our country, how this change can be realized, , and how it can be protected if realized.

Dr. John Garang de Mabior, was the first Sudanese from south of country who ever thought big about changing the whole Sudan through South and by South, something that was seen as unrealistic by Southerners themselves resulting in fierce internal rifts within the liberation Movement at its early ages and hence dividing the forces of liberation into unionists who fight for major change in the racist system that run the country, and the separatists who does think the problem is a southern Sudan problem and its Christian majority therefore see the total solution in separating the South from the whole country.

Dr. John Garang de Mabior and his colleagues founded the Sudan People Liberation Movement, Sudan people liberation Army (SPLM/SPLA), a political movement as well as a people Armed Force, with one clear and distinct objective in mind, liberation of Sudan and the Sudanese people. A critical look at the objective of SPLM/SPLA will definitely lead us always to the question that will define clearly our collective and common enemy, Liberating Sudan and its people from whom? Since Sudan was already considered as independent and liberated as well in 1956.

Though the vision of the SPLA/SPLM does sees Sudan and its people as a colonized, robbed, stolen country in one hand and colonized, enslaved, dominated, bandaged people in other. The other parts of this question will then follow in one mind consecutively, who is colonizing, enslaving the land of Sudan and its people as well as how the Sudan and the Sudanese people will be liberated, answering this questions also will define the path the great leader and his gallant colleagues has chosen to liberate Sudan and its people.

The SPLM/SPLA has waged a lengthy bitter armed struggle as well as an effective political campaign against the racist minority rulers based in Khartoum for twenty two consecutive years, In 2005, it did signed the Comprehensive Peace Agreement (CPA) with the de facto government of Omer Al-Bashir of National Congress Party (NCP) which was formed as a result of serious divide and rift in the National Islamic Front(NIF) between African Muslims and a group of Racist Arabs Nationalists resulting in jail and exclusion of the main effective figures in the NIF Party from African Ethnic groups , a turning point that has unearthed the real face of the racist movement that has been ruling Sudan for a long time by proxy and under the slogan and pretext of Islam.

However the CPA has created a one country two systems as a temporary accommodation for this troubled country until the fate of the union is decided in 2011 when southerners will decide to secede from the rest of the country or remain in the union, with the projected 2009 elections that is seen as the golden chance that can save the country from real breakup in 2011, The SPLM share in national power doesn't give it any mechanical majority, neither constitutional power to make the desired change happen, the SPLM will need to gain new political grounds and more constitutional powers to furthers its agenda of democratic change and transformation.

If the SPLM is the agent of change and the change advocate here in this stolen and exploited country, then the SPLM has to be effective and efficient enough to be able to make that change happen, by being a true democratic movement that cherish democracy in its institutions as well as in its already controlled southern part of the country, its performance, successes or failures in this testing time will impact its future and competitive edge in coming elections.

The voices of change in Northern Sudan need to embrace the SPLM, in fact the core debate about change in Sudan is meant to wake up the conscience of our brothers in north of the country, liberate their mind set from the dangerous concepts the minority rulers have been planting, no single Sudanese is really benefiting from this manmade disaster in Sudan except its makers and that is definitely the deformed ruling class in Khartoum.

For the SPLM, as a people movement for the desired change, rendering the masses of Sudanese people into powerful one nation, fully aware, politically conscious in socio-economic causes of the problems of this country will be an effective part of its strategy to win the upcoming elections, you can't defeat a powerful mass that are well informed about what is going on in the country neither you can make choices against their own future, interest and well-being. In fact, they are one that is paying a huge price for all what Khartoum has been cooking from wars caused by racial, tribal and religious hate policies.

SPLM cannot rely on luck and chance in this final battle, they are not an option, the SPLM need to strategize and very well in order to win, by opening up the whole bitter struggle history of Sudanese people since 1955 and beyond, it must teach the Sudanese masses about the lengthy unjust and inequitable political, socio-economic systems and situation of our country, these masses are not well informed enough, they were misled for more than fifty years, they are confused and their religious fears are what the NCP always downplays particularly in northern part of the country, In southern part and other marginalized areas of the country, tribalism is sickening their minds and is preventing them from thinking big, standing in their ways to come together to give a final death certificate to the racial system in Khartoum. For the SPLM, indeed it is time to liberate people minds, change concepts and old ways that the old minority system has been preaching throughout its long ugly present.

The Sudanese masses can come together, work together to achieve the desired change but that is not an easy thing to achieve without a viable leader and organizer and this is the first main task that the SPLM should be really doing, bringing the masses together, put them to work together, empower them with the necessary information about what has been and still going on in Khartoum and the important of their vote to make that change possible in Khartoum, equip them with the necessary communications and media tools that increase their awareness and strengthen their faith in the upcoming change, The SPLM will have to be the all good party, a true honest agent for the desired change that Sudanese masses have to trust. It is most likely that internal power thirst and competition, tribalism, corruption and other ills will always try to stray the SPLM from its glorious objective and course, which is the total liberation of Sudan and its entire people.

A conceptual change campaign will be a necessary strategic tool for SPLM to change Sudan peacefully and from within, it could save Sudan millions of wasted souls and financial resources as well, because any relative change in conceptual world of this racist minority will greatly mean a lot, the way they see themselves as a unique race that is here to rule but not to integrate with the locals, that sees Sudan as a land, rich of resources that have to be exploited and used to empower their international political cause.

It is these concepts that is keeping our people in Darfur in misery and hell as it does before to the African people in South as well as in Nuba Mountains, Ingasna and the East, it is these concepts that sees Sudan as land that have to be emptied from its vast majority of its indigenous people through uprooting, marginalization, domination, and even committing mass killing, genocides and grave crimes against humanity, they want this land empty , and that is the big project that Omer Al-Bashir and his gangs were all about for twenty something years.

Any change in these inhuman concepts of this minority and its powerful backers around the world is a saving for Sudan, is a peace for its so exploited people, is a stability and prosperity for this rich country, is a beauty for so diverse and colorful land, any change in these inhuman concepts is a peace for the whole world.

But how a change can be achieved and accepted in so deformed society, where preachers of this inhuman concepts holds the daily breads of the rest, where the inventors of this lies and inhuman concepts have surrounded themselves with all kinds of powers and where just saying no to these wrong concepts generate a condemnation to death.

In fact, it is not just only a society that is so deformed but it is a society where change is the only thing made impossible. Something that Southerners had clearly in mind that even if they decided for unity in 2011 what are the guarantees that another Omer Al-Bashir will not emerge after all the golden chances are missed and put us back to square one.

It is fundamentally true that it is not just a regime change that will change Sudan it is also the change in concepts of how Northerners view themselves in part and how do they view the rest of country in other, especially its indigenous people, this country won't come together if we didn't erase the dangerous racial, tribal or the religious intolerance concepts that the racist system in Khartoum has built its house on, no human being, in any time and space, no matter what his/her color, race, tribe or religion will ever accept being looked down or rated as second. A homogenous society that is in peace with itself cannot be realized without a peaceful conceptual realm being created by the government and other social, religious and educational institutions, in fact our government in Khartoum is just putting more oil on the fire by teaching all kind of hostile concepts and teachings, which does just benefit its racist agenda and survival.

Even though we have strong belief that the majority of Sudanese will vote for change in 2009 upcoming elections, we can't guaranteed that, a clean smooth elections will take place and accordingly will produce a trusted outcomes and results, as elections fraud to prevent a real legitimate change from happening through a popular vote are always known in countries being controlled by brutal dictatorships like the one we have, therefore an international supervision and monitoring system will be a must have requirement in order to make this elections achieve a trusted results and outcomes.

There are major problems that need to be solved first in order for 2009 projected elections to be inclusive, legitimate and successful, first will be the problem of Darfur. Without a final solution for the Darfur problem and other insecurity problems around the country, the 2009 projected elections will be incomplete and hence its results will be illegitimate and waste of resources and efforts. In other hand, the NCP will try to keep the fire in Darfur aflame in order to prevent, or at least delay the 2009 projected election something that it will apparently put the blame to fragmented Darfur movements. A critical thinking and a wise move is expected from these shattered movements, to unite, negotiate, and rally its bases to join the SPLM and other democratic forces to make it possible.

Eventually, Election system will need to be inclusive, effective and secure, that won't happen without the help of international community. We still have hundreds thousands of Sudanese in diasporas, other millions are displaced internally, an election system that will include every citizen no matter where they are will be the system that will achieve the desired change.

For you as a Sudanese, northerner or southerner, wherever you and if you are really keen enough for a peaceful democratic change in our country then 2009 elections is the chance to overhaul the whole racist and deteriorated system in Khartoum and bring about a responsible national government that is keen enough to make the change happen, it is not just change of a constitution, political, socio-economic systems but it is a campaign of change in the wrong concepts and opinions that are keeping this great Sudanese nation apart, please mark your calendar, 2009 elections day is the day for change.

## Why South Sudanese need to change?

## October 1, 2007

By Chuar Juet Jock*

The laws of nature tell us that you can't ask for the conditions and the environment that are surrounding you to change since you are not changing yourself nor the ways and habits you are used to, neither the beliefs and concepts that guides your current life. Change is the norm of life not the exception and the change that I am writing about here in this topic is the positive change, a change toward a better and a fulfilled life, a change that will take oneself to the realms of accomplishment, happiness and satisfaction with oneself and with life itself. Smart people always adopt a lot of changes in their lives whenever they discover that the current ways of life and the direction of things are not in their best interests, time is crucial for the right decision to make the necessary change. things also don't change overnight neither old habits die easy, there is resistance and a price to pay but surely with determination and strong will, victory is assured.

I was thinking about how we as southern Sudanese can reach our collective and common higher aspirations and goals, after signing of the Comprehensive Peace Agreement (CPA) which brought this relative peace that we are enjoying today. The CPA has renewed, ignited and motivated our long suppressed dreams and hopes, dreams and aspirations that we held since the very birth of our visions to the world. Most of our generations fought and died and never have a chance to see these dreams materialized. It is our responsibility to make them be a reality, a sacred duty that we owed to honor our martyrs and heroes.

To realize these dreams, a clear identification and definition of our higher and common goals must be in place and accordingly, a road map must be clearly drawn and pursued, a set of necessary changes in our negative ways of life, beliefs and concepts must be adopted. Every habit or belief that is standing in our ways to reach these higher goals must be sidelined; the overall goal is a good life for every southern Sudanese, a life that is fill with fulfillment, success and joy. This won't happen unless we all south Sudanese have to change and work together for change, government and people, tribes and clans, individuals and institutions.

In term of mentality, a free South Sudan, won't really be free if our minds are not set free, we have undergone a systematic brainwash and mis-education for decades by all the successive central Khartoum regimes, a mis-education that its intentions and goals is to keep us in the state of servitude and weakness, a brainwashing that its main intentions are to keep us divided and in poor state so we can be easily ruled, dominated and poor in our own rich land. Our whole problems and shortcomings are all rooted to this brainwashing and mis-education systems. We cannot have a sound and healthy life since our minds are not sound.

The ways we see and judge ourselves is but a reflection of what our minds were shaped and brainwashed, though how come I see my fellow southerner as different as it is used to today in some of our communities. Why on earth that we look to ourselves as strangers and enemies while the reality says we are not. No doubt it has something to do with what we have got in our minds and hearts and that is the brainwashing and mis-education that I am talking about. Unfortunately, as a result, we have lost too many innocent south Sudanese souls as victims of this shameful ignorance and self-unconsciousness as a nation.

The fact is that as southerners we have a high degree of unity and homogeneity than any nation in this earth except China and other Asian nations otherwise the consequences of this brainwashing could never be less than other African dilemmas, which have fallen as victims of this colonists' conspiracy. However, a useful advice to every southern Sudanese, accept it or not, we are one nation, diverse but one. give your mind a chance and ponder on our similarities, history and common roots and backgrounds, I have no doubt that you will find nothing but a nation that is meant by God, the creator, to be one

We are coming out from bitter war, a war that has transformed us and everything in our life; we have seen and endured a lot, the worst side of life and human behavior for more than two decades and a half, death, hunger, diseases, terror, slavery etc. we have been uprooted to all different parts of the world. There is no doubt that our hearts did bleed a lot and were affected by all cruelty of these conditions and hardship yet we have seen and touched the real world. Therefore, armed with this bitter experience and reality we have overcome all the miseries and more than that we have positioned ourselves to succeed and build a new future. However, we will need to clean our hearts once more time in order for us to reach our novel destination, without healthy and clean hearts we can't built a peaceful civilization that its pillars are peace, justice, unity and prosperity, let us forgive the cruelty of the world but never forget it. God has done its part to us by giving us the beauty and strength and this beautiful and rich land and thankfully what is left is our part.

Our ways of life and habits need to be checked if we need the positive change to happen, south Sudanese are too engaged in politics more than into establishment of their own businesses, vocational or technical centers or companies. That is a major weakness that has helped to make us powerless in resistance to economically empowered northern Sudanese. We are all waiting to be ministers, presidents and so on but none of us dream to be the most successful business person neither a famous technician nor a scientist. The advancement of any society is measured by availability and quality of various services and goods, these are provided through a service or product businesses. We, south Sudanese are expecting the government to provide and do everything, well that is not true, private sector is the real core driver for prosperity and development, we need to own and managed our factories and companies. Government should only regulate and engage in provision of public services that cannot be provided efficiently by private sector.

There are vast opportunities for all of us, our country is richer than our total population number, yet some of us out of ignorance and greed are fighting for position of a minister or commissioner which salary might not be the same with owning a business or a factory, so to speak and just a simple question, which job is really more secure? I bet if you can stay for 10 years as commissioner but I am sure you can stay as Chief Executive Director of your company as long as you want. This focus on government positions need to be changed.

The role of government and nongovernmental organization in conducting and achieving the desired change are parallel, all of them can pursue this change through their institutions and their policies. Institutions such as educational institutions, media and religious, social planning and youth and culture all should work in conjunction and coordination to achieve the big picture of the desired change, every department and division of government should do its part in this process, school curriculum and substance should be aimed to build new directions of culture, morals and values. Religious institutions should do their part in arming a generation of peaceful and healthy souls and minds, social planning institutions should plan for a society that is homogenous in culture and structure, a society with less social bias and ills. Health department should plan for a healthy nation and for future generations that are not crumbled by AIDS and other endemics diseases, department for youth and culture should create and design a unified culture that gives us a clue for the direction of this change and so on

The greater change that will really help our situation a lot and will save a lot of efforts and monies is self-decided or individual change, south Sudanese who are really keen enough to see their country and people having a great future and life have already done so or are on the way to do so. They have positioned themselves to a South Sudan that is based on values of justice, equality, freedom and good life for every southern Sudanese. They believe that these are the final aspirations of all human kinds and no matter what, what is right is right. Yet we still have few that are still wondering in realms of negative tribalism, greed and hatred

South Sudanese has fought bitterly against marginalization, injustice and inequality, yet in their very autonomous government created and gained as result of this bitter struggle, crowned by the CPA, different intended and non-intended forms of marginalization and discrimination are on the surface. On tribal, gender and individual level, some ethnics and tribes are hardly represented in different level of local, state and regional or central governments, while some tribe took it all. On individual level some highly educated and qualified southern Sudanese are left out from being considered for employment or representation just because they lack strong tribal or political backing, on gender level our women, the beautiful face of our country are still not represented fairly nor given their right full place in leadership, this is absurd and need to be change. Otherwise there are clear contradictions between what we said we have been fighting for and what we are now

Change is gradual, as one of my friend told me and also has a price that need to be paid, well, however we just need to begin the process and set ourselves right from the start, there is no doubt that with an excellent management, a good and strong will we will accomplish the desired change, reach the South Sudan of freedom, prosperity, equality and justice and where everyone of us shall have a good and a great life.

## How South Sudanese can shape their very own future?

By Chuar Juet Jock

November 12, 2007 — If Sudan was ever in good hands through its modern history it could spare its innocent people all the bitter suffering that they have undergone and still. It could spare the world from being sick from the daily inhuman scenes and news of the current systematic killing and uprooting of its African citizens, it could be one of the richest, peaceful and prosperous countries in the world due to its huge natural resources, unique location in Africa and the world plus its big fertile land that is blessed with the longest river in the world, the river Nile. Unfortunately, you can't expect anything then the current poor, miserable situation in a country where young children are taught nothing but hatred, racism and tribalism.

Good citizenry is not just a work of chance as our de facto caretakers in Khartoum may think, it is an outcome of well-designed programming and installation of the good into the would be the future and the face of the country- the children. It is a process of shaping the very minds and conscience of the young children so they would be good and loyal citizens to their country and their worldwide family of humanity, but our de facto caretakers decided to do the opposite, by programming the future of Sudan on violence, racism, tribalism and religious intolerance and unfortunately as a result, Sudan has failed itself as well as the humanity.

As Southern Sudanese, we must avoid by all the cost to fall and wind in the same end, and that is by accurately and adequately investing in our children future if we really want them to be good citizens that will work for the betterment of the future of our country as well as the future of Africa and the world. Southerners who are really keen to build a new prosperous and a brighter future for their country must very well engage in a long process of programming their children to be good elements for the desired positive change and prevent our enemies who really want to control and shape our future into their own direction through our children.

There is no doubt that Southern Sudanese real keys for a brighter and peaceful future for their country are their children. Children are always they would best, they would be whatever the adults want them to be, positive or negative elements to their very society and humanity in general, they would be whatever they are being told or taught or shaped upon. The world that is being shaped into their very visions is the world that would be theirs; therefore, we shouldn't be surprise why children and women are the most vulnerable victims and targets of the Khartoum racial wars, simply because they are easy to be change and transformed into different worlds. In fact, the systematic killing of men and the abduction of children and the rape of woman are not but just some of the tools of racial extermination that the regime in Khartoum is conducting to shape and change the future of Sudan demographics, as the raped women will breeds children of aggressors' race and the abducted children will be brainwashed and programmed into different people that won't know their history roots let alone their language and culture of origin while the killed men will vanish forever, though, a clear race elimination process.

However, how to shape or make the future of our country out of our children that is what we are here about and let us together reflects on the vital institutions, the right substance and the necessities that should be involved in this important process. I believe providing the right environment for our children to grow up in good mental, emotional and physical health should be given a priority because neither education nor technology or science could be of benefit if they are being digested by people let alone children who live in a hostile environment. Therefore, we need to work together to provide the right environment at home and the other institutions of learning and development so our children can grow, learn and develop to become good future citizens.

Educational institutions as well as spiritual and social ones are all institutions for integrated development and correction of children as well as adults. For children, what is being provided in those institutions is what shape their minds, behaviors, attitudes and at the end characters and personalities. Therefore, we must emphases on the food that our children eat on daily basis from those institutions, I mean by the food here the curriculum and the materials that are being digested by our children's minds and souls, and the substance that is being taught in those schools, churches and other social centers, simply because this is what make the difference and that is what shape the future of our country young citizens.

Our children can't live and interact with the world when they are set or left behind in term of technology use in every aspect of modem human life, therefore southern Sudanese, government and people alike, must heavily invest in field of technology and that is by bringing fresh and up-to-date technologies and train their children on the Know-how techniques of these technologies and systems, if Juba university or any southern Sudanese universities are not equipped with modern computers technologies than how the students and instructors alike will interact with foreign universities where having a good knowledge of computing is a required just to do any assignment or research, hand written assignments or research are no longer acceptable. Neither our children can't have a sound knowledge in unhealthy bodies, therefore southern Sudanese, government and people, must invest adequately in private and public healthcare sectors and make healthcare services available and affordable to all citizens and on both counties and states levels. Health education must be included in school curriculum in early years of elementary education, making early awareness possible for endemic diseases such AIDS/HIV, the new tool of the early African death phenomenon and that is bringing Africa down to its knees.

On the other hand, Physical education is very important for creating healthy and creative future generations of southern Sudan; this must be encouraged through building viable physical education facilities within educational institutions as well as standalone and separate physical education and wellness facilities that will transform the whole nation to a healthy and creative nation and that will have a great impact in the quality of performance of future human resources, also teaching values of tolerance and peaceful co-existence are crucial for southern Sudan of peace, respect and dignity of everyone, our own hard learned lessons from slavery and discrimination of Khartoum did show us how destructive is to put someone down because of his/her color, gender, tribe, religion and else.

Discrimination is not Godley and is a sin that is no less than sin of murder itself. The worst murder at all is the emotional killing that is caused by discrimination, injustice and inequality; our children must change the world and that by having the strong education of the very pillars of democracy, freedom, justice and equality. Any citizen of southern Sudan must take his/her right place based on free will not because he/she is forced to, our constitution must guarantee the rights and freedoms of all its citizens and those rights and freedom can't be changed by the outcome of any elections or government.

There must be strong and solid laws and rules that guarantees and works for the unity of southern Sudanese society and that prohibit any kind of national trends to encourage negative tribalism and clanship and that threats the national interests and security of southern Sudan. Negative tribalism must be regarded as a national security threat; this should be in defense of our country from outside enemies that uses our tribal differences as tools to destroy our national security and unity through our shortsighted brothers. We must teach the value of positive nationalism to our children not those of destructive tribalism.

Time has already make the unity of southern Sudanese stronger, tribes that did abolish the tribal marks, tattoos, piercing and so on of features that distinguishes this tribe from another, has become closer, and now-a-days, it is very hard to differentiate between Sudanese from Darfur, southern Sudan or Nuba Mountain let alone within the southern Sudan tribal structure. Intermarriages also have made our unity more solid, African woman in Sudan and elsewhere in Africa has a divine role in bringing these shattered tribes of Africa into one related and united nation. in shaping the future through the next generations, it is really important that government and people of southern Sudan work together in changing some of our tribal traditions and customs that make our unity weak as well as those that encourage us to be discriminated within our society let alone other societies

Southern Sudanese have a high degree of homogeneity that can make them the most cohesive and united nation in Africa if it did find the right nation's constructive builders of politicians and intellectuals. Our country is blessed with more precious blessings but those blessings could have turned to be a curse if it didn't fall in the hands of the constructive southern Sudanese and instead in the hands of destructive ones. In Africa bad politics and governance always plays on the strings of tribalism and clanship unconsciously and consciously sometimes. Both negative tribalism and clanship are viruses that eats slowly our strong nation body and if not dealt with in proper manner, it is likely that we wind in the same venue of the unforgotten African tragedy of 1994 in Rwanda, where the entire world has witnessed again how really could human destructive ideas and behaviors could harm and destroy the humanity very co-existence and peace

It is of important that the people of southern Sudan know that they are ultimate decision makers of their future not governments, those governments that don't work in the interest of people must not be allowed to stay, they must be change. People of southern Sudan must make it happen for their life to be peaceful and prosperous and their rights and freedoms guaranteed and protected by protecting democracy and its very pillars of freedom, justice and equality for all through their precious votes, wise nations never gives their votes to incompetent leaders that sooner or later will deny their very own electorates rights and freedoms.

We belong to our motherland, Africa, and as matter of fact we are connected to this beautiful continent by heart and mind. It is of imperative that, government and people of southern Sudan strengthens this connection in hearts and minds of next coming generations by making it possible for information and communications between us and the rest of Africa be of priority. As part of East Africa, we are requiring to interact economically, socially and politically and the most useful methods to make that possible is to teach Kiswahili as a language subject to our young children in all their schooling years, these will make them more connected to their brothers in east African countries as well as in the rest of Africa.

As Southern Sudanese, our future is in our hands, only when we work tirelessly to make it possible for our children to live in a world that is different from ours, a world with no war, discrimination, inequality and injustice and where all humanity can work together and put their focus on other issues of common interest, such a world is only possible upon our realization that all men are created equal.

# What Justifies Sudan's successive military regimes?

By Chuar Juet Jock

October 14, 2007 — Sudan did never have a chance for a real and fair democracy since it was proclaimed independent from the British and Egyptian colonists in January1956, since then successive military regimes have follow like stream of water, from General Ibrahim Abbuod to Jaffar Nyimery, Suaar El Dahab, and to the current most brutal and Hitler of Sudan General Omer El Bashir. It was only and for some brief intervals that weak and proxy democratic regimes did have a little chance and which unfortunately the minority dominated military have toppled them all in clear coup d'état.

The fact that this minority in Khartoum cannot attain real majority votes through any given clean and fair election process in the whole country is the reason and the clear justification for all the military regimes that came to power via bloody or peaceful coup de tat, forming authoritarian and dictatorship rules that their core goal is to transform Sudan into Arab and arabized country by an Iron fist. Using Islam as a pretext and philosophy that sustain their racists' goals and until today Sudan is considered an Arab country and its flag is but a representation of Pan-Arabs colors and all its foreign relations, political interests and economic investments are directed toward the Arab world, represented by the Arab league in Egypt, the former colonist of Sudan that have together with Britain planted this oppressors in the so-called independence in 1956 to systematically rules, kills and uproots our people, besides being the strong backer of Sudanese Arabization scheme, the shameful false reality that contradict the true reality that Sudan is an African country with 67% African Black Sudanese out of its whole population

The mechanism that these minority rulers depend on to dominates this vast poor African majority is the same theory of divide to rule of their former master, the English. Many factors are used for creating divisions among the communities of the African majority. Religion has played a major part in widening the gap between African Christians in South and African Muslims in North of Sudan, tribalism was until these days an effective weapon in South's multi tribal communities and throughout its bitter history the war against Khartoum injustice and domination was portrayed as religious war between the Muslim North against Christian South. the minority Arab rulers in Khartoum used this to mobilize an army of African Muslims to crush the African liberation movements in the south by the name of protecting and depending Islam from the conquest of the infidels represented by the international Zionism , the West (America and western Europe) and its agents in Sudan(southern Sudanese Christian mainly).

The minority rulers orchestrated a wide Ignorance and deep cultural and political unconsciousness among Africans in Sudan and which have contributed greatly in the success of Khartoum divide to rule system to rule the divided and economically poor and socially unorganized Africans in the whole Sudan. The little power and wealth that Khartoum minority rulers provides for each part of these divided African majority whether in Southern Sudan, Nuba Mountains and Blue Nile, Darfur and eastern Sudan were mainly used to deeply widen the tribal divisions and feuds, putting some tribes up or down politically, empowering this and weakening that, and accordingly creating tribal rivalry and competition that have blinds the local poor Africans from even what their real oppressors in Khartoum have in store for them. It is this policy and pressure that some tribal chiefs and sultans have allied themselves to the Arabization scheme and went further to annex their people areas to northern Sudan, out of political ignorance and unconsciousness, creating the today disputed areas in border between south and north Sudan.

There is a good chance for Sudan to come back to its people, particularly with current increased awareness and political consciousness of the majority of African Sudanese, that the real issue of the Sudan is not religion but it is this racist minority oppressor in Khartoum that always comes in military coup dictatorship. Though the real problem of Sudan has nothing to do with religion as the Muslims of Darfur and Nuba Mountains African ethnics cleansings have already indicated. It is a racial problem at the first place. In its fifty years of age as an independent or so they say, Sudan was never ruled by an African Muslim president leave alone a Christian one. And accordingly the claim that a Christian can't rule a country with a Muslim majority is a baseless. Nigeria and Tanzania are all African countries that falsified this minority claims

However, any country future and stability is build and guaranteed through its national constitution, which is the supreme source of all citizens' rights, responsibilities and duties. The national constitution of any given country should be the first source of healthy co-existence of its entire citizens, and that provides fairness, equality, justice, freedom, democracy to them all without any room for discrimination or exclusion of any individual or group based on any form, race be it or religion, gender, culture, origin, any form at all.

For Sudan to change, it constitution must be changed or if changed according to the Comprehensive Peace Agreement (CPA) then it have to be translated into reality and action, the recent SPLM pullout from government of national unity (GoNU) is a clear indicator that the changed constitution is not being honestly and completely implemented neither the CPA other terms. The former constitutions were the source of all Sudan problems, they weren't inclusive neither doing they provide the very equal pillars for co-existence of its citizens. Clearly, any efforts or calls for democratic transformation of Sudan without a healthy and fair national constitution are but just a waste of time.

Chances for democratic Sudan are many, when there is a fair and healthy constitution in place, and hence the people of Sudan will exercise their rightful rights, duties and responsibilities to form their political ruling majority on any bases they want and accordingly there will never be any marginalization or domination or exclusion of any minority, since the rights of any individual or group are protected and guaranteed by the constitution and doesn't depends or change on or by the outcome of any elections at any time and space.

To win a fair, clean and inclusive elections in democratic and secular Sudan, there are three chances or forms of political majority any political party could advocates for, a political majority that is based on Islam and Arabization, and this is mainly the old type democracy that didn't prove itself to be worthy of governing Sudan, where the old two major parties the Umma party, led by former prime minister Saddig El-Mahdi and Union Democratic Party UDP lead by Mulana Ahmed El Mirgani did have the upper hand. However, the current minority National Congress Party (NCP) also is pursuing the same direction but in a dictatorship manner. The failure of this form of political majority was due largely for the call of establishment of an Islamic state guided by Islamic constitution and that is a lack of clear and inclusive vision and political project for Sudan and its multi diverse backgrounds plus their failure to deliver what they promise to their constituents particularly in marginalized African areas.

The other form of a political majority is the one based on the Pan African's majority of Sudan, and which is represented by those who have been dominated, marginalized and suppressed by Khartoum successive based minority military regimes or the proxy democratic systems. This majority has been the force of change in Sudan for decades and is likely to form a solid and real democratic Sudan which they have fought and still fighting and paying for it so dearly, these are the 67% African majority, from southern Sudan, Darfur, Nuba Mountain and Blue Nile eastern Sudan, and which the Sudan People's Liberation Movement (SPLM) and Sudan Liberation Movement (SLM) or Justice and Equality Movement (JEM) does have the leads. Any possible unification of SPLM, SLM and JEM is a big tremendous success for the marginalized people of Sudan and no doubt that they can win big and easily in any fair, clean and inclusive elections.

However, for this African majority to rule Sudan, their bases and masses have a dare need for political and cultural awareness and consciousness, a dare need for united vision of a new Sudan that is based on democracy and secularism and where a healthy and inclusive national constitution is the supreme source of all equal and just rights, duties and responsibilities of all the citizens

The African Sudanese conflicts are not separated, although they are reflected to the world in that way by the media of minority Arabs rulers, in fact they are all black people of Sudan based conflicts, mainly Southern Sudan, Nuba Mountains, Darfur and Blue Nile, which form the 67% percent of Sudan total population. The unity of this black Sudanese majority is not in the interest of the Khartoum minority, neither does Khartoum welcome their political or economic empowerment nor their political awareness and consciousness. It is the interest of Khartoum that this Sudanese Africans majority stay divided in their tiny and poor states, divided tribes or as divided Muslims and Christians so it can continue the killing and uprooting project, gradually and systematically and by their own hands (Africans Vs Africans) according to the theory -kill the slave by a slave.

This minority ruler's philosophy is well reflected in the way it is handling all the conflicts of vast marginalized African people of Sudan, negotiation them separately and signing proxy and false peace agreements with them separately, CPA for Southern Sudanese, NPA for Nuba Mountain and DPA for Darfur and EPA for eastern Sudan and the list goes on. One would simply wonder why there is no APA (Arab Peace Agreement) or NPA (Northern Peace agreement). In fact, the case for the black people of Sudan if not in the world is one and has the same common goals and objectives which the quest for freedom, equality, justice and democracy are its most obvious pillars.

Black people of Sudan will never get their country back unless they unearth all the mockery and the covers that these minority rulers in Khartoum do hides and works through them, they won't be free if they don't eliminate the already set mental, cultural and tribal and religious barriers and that the minority oppressors has put and planted between them for decades. It is highly requested from the leaders of African people of Sudan's liberation movements to adopt a unified vision and strategy to lead their masses into the light of freedom and dignity and to take their country back once and forever. South Sudanese leaders and people need to do more about Darfur then what they are now, it is the utmost duty of these leaders to advocates for the new Sudan parallel with the interests of southern Sudan, they have the support of their poor majority people as well as the whole black people of the world and definitely, they are the real leaders of upcoming democratic Sudan.

The final possible form of political majority under a just and fair secular constitution, and only when the people of Sudan gain the political maturity and put their all differences and divisions aside they can form a political majority based not on a religion or race but on other common aspirations such as freedom, unity, justice, equality and prosperity and others that make Sudan more democratic, united and prosperous.

Otherwise when the iron fist control on power by the minority rulers in Khartoum seem to be undefeated and their defiance and unwillingness to the transformation of Sudan on democratic bases continues, then the best solution option for Sudan dilemma will be the current one, one country two systems or three systems when Darfur Peace Agreement (DPA) creates another system to the already available south- north two systems and which might lead at the end to two or more Sudan

We are not calling for a reverse racism or oppression but our call is that Sudan must be back to its people and that it should be formed on new sound democratic bases that will make it a country of all Sudanese irrespective of all their differences and origins or backgrounds, and only on this conditions Sudan will be real prosperous and united country on map of the world.

## Why Omer Al-Bashir should go back to Hush Banaga?

## By Chuar Juet Jock

November 22, 2007 — There is no doubt that the innocent Sudanese people could and once more be at door steps of an all-out war if the first vice president of Sudan and president of Government of Southern Sudan Lt. general Salva Kiir Mayardiit toke Omer Al Bashir by his mockery and insult words last Saturday November 17, 2007 at Wad-Madni town and during the 18th celebrations of birth of the National Congress Party's(NCP) infamous Popular Defense Forces(PDF), a terrorist jihadists army that they co-founded with the help of Bin Ladin in 1989.

Any keen Sudanese mind or an honest observer who did have a chance to hear, read or watch the should be national leader and so-called president of Sudan talking to this bloody terrorists paramilitary have only one thing to say and say it out load and that is that Omer Al Bashir should voluntarily quit the presidency of Sudan and go back to Hush Banaga, his home town in Shendi north of Khartoum where he should go back to take care of his mules and donkeys the only skill he has proven so far to be qualified for. He did prove behind measures that he does not fit to lead a nation so good and civilize as the Sudanese people neither he has the qualifications necessary to lead Sudan as a united diverse and peaceful state.

Omer Al-Bashir, has forget one thing, a very fundamental thing, and that is, he, Omer Al Bashir, is neither a legitimate ruler of Sudan nor an elected president by the people of Sudan, he is just a power robber since he came to power by a clear coupe d'état when he toppled the last democratic government of Sadiq AL Mahdi, on Friday, June 30 1989.

From the day one of his bloody and shameful rule his face was painted by the blood of the innocents Sudanese people when he started by mass murdering and execution of more than 58 officers from the Sudanese Armed Forces (SAF) in a clear day light and the signal that have early informed the Sudanese people about the upcoming curse to the land of Sudan called Omer Al Bashir and his racist party, Ingaaz. Omer Al Bashir is not the bravest man in Sudan let alone in the world as his illusionist mind may tell him so, in fact he is the second sickest person in control of power and destiny of a country and people a world has ever witness after the former brutal dictator Hitler of Germany, and like the later he is going to let the Sudanese people free with a bloody record and a list of more than 15 million innocent lives, murdered, imprisoned, tortured and uprooted from their country by his bloody regime.

In the time of Omer Al Bashir Sudan was overhauled by his regime to be one of the worst place in the world in term of human rights and insecurity, his regime has been the first every Sudanese government to engage directly in a well-planned systematic genocide of the African Sudanese in the whole Sudan or what is called of national comprehensive strategy of Ingaaz and which the Southern Sudan, Nuba Mountains, Blue Nile and Darfur are it main targets.

His irresponsible words during last week celebrations in Wad-Madini of the bloody terrorists PDF has indicated to us that the differences between Kiir leadership and Omer's are now so obvious, while the first vice president Kiir was looking for a peaceful means to resolve the pending issues in the implementation of the CPA in his two weeks visit to United States and Kenya where he met with the officials and statements of the two countries that are concern about the worse political situation in Sudan, Omer Al-Bashir the supposed to be the national president of the whole Sudanese people was shamefully launching and engaging in a very racist and war mobilization of his PDF jihadists and celebrating the 18th anniversary of the emergence of this terrorist wing of NCP.

In fact, what the world doesn't know is that if there is any likeness to PDF in the history of crime against humanity it would be clearly the SSS of Hitler. The PDF are really a state within a state and an army within an army, they are the actual policy and strategy enforcer of the NCP, they are the one who are in control in Sudan and since 1989 they have conducted a brutal cleans up in government and non-government institutions and now-a-days, their control of economic, military and political institutions is at its momentum. More importantly if the world is really serious about punishing the genocide and crime of humanity propagators than it should look with focus on the PDF, they were the horse riders that have burned complete villages and women and children alive in Southern Sudan and they are the present Jinjaweed of the Darfur Genocide.

The dilemma of Sudan is a matter of leadership, since its independence, the de facto successive presidents in Khartoum were the makers of policies of division, racism and oppression, instead of being the leaders for goodness, unity, and prosperity of Sudan, they were the civil wars fire igniters not the peace makers. they weren't even leader at all but just power robbers and thieves of nation's wealth, This is because they were not elected or chosen by the people but they are the de facto leaders who always came by bloody coups, though lacking neither the legitimacy nor the mandate by the very people they are acclaiming to rule, and as a result they have to create internal and external troubles and wars to give them reasons for staying in power and control and this is the fundamental reason why we have been in this chaos and war situation in Sudan for fifty bitter years.

Lack of wisdom and collective responsibility of our successive de facto presidents has caused too much destruction and agony to Sudan and its innocent people and in the light of president Omer Al Bashir last Saturday, September 17, 2007 words of insult to the Southerners, we out to ask ourselves these questions: Did our leaders learned from the hard lessons of fifty years of wars and destruction? Does it really worth it to pursue war methodology as the means for solution of problem of Sudan? Are our leaders incapable of resolving the nation differences by peaceful and political means or did they lost the touch with the people and the facts on the ground? What is the purpose of leadership and what are the higher aspirations of any human nation on this earth, is it just only war?

Our leaders, now and in future ought to know that Sudan problems will only be solved by more stability not more instability, a stability that will create more sustainable and equal development and prosperity, and that will eradicate poverty, marginalization and illiteracy and that will heal the bitter wounds of the past wars and that will change the hatred into love and fears into confidence, and this won't ever happen but in peace and only in peace. We need a long peace that is guarded by leaders such as vice president Salva Kiir, a long peace that will make it possible for all the blessings mentioned above to be a reality and president Omer El-Bashir should join the guards of this peace not the destroyers and the bullies.

The NCP party doesn't have to create wars so to find legitimacy to stay on power and shift the attention of Sudanese people and the international community away of its crimes against humanity in Darfur neither it should stop the implementation of Comprehensive Peace Agreement(CPA) so to avoid the proposed general election it will never win nor should it believe that after 18 year of systematic killing and uprooting and all sorts of injustices and inequalities did it successfully change the solid good conscience of Sudanese or its demographics.

The message of chairman of the SPLM Salva Kiir Mayardiit and his first deputy Dr. Riek Machar in respond to the words of insult uttered by Omer Al Bashir was a great balance of responsible leaders who have led the war of liberation for 21 years and have known by experience what war really brings. They are well aware that war is the last thing Sudanese in general and southern Sudanese in particular could ever think about. The NCP should not act upon these peaceful reactions as a ticket to more insult and defiance. The SPLM is not weaken neither it will be, but the SPLM doesn't see the war as an objective itself but a mean to regain the stolen freedom, justice and equality of Sudanese people by the Khartoum successive military regimes, Al Basher included

However, the SPLM must not be carried to believe the lie that the NCP will relinquish the power peacefully and through clear and clean national election or that the NCP will fully implement the CPA through peaceful means, this could be a clear and dangerous illusion, the NCP will never do any of those as long as there is oil money and as long there is China in United Nation Security council. The SPLM should not just sing the song of peace, this won't ever guard the CPA, it should build the peace, protect it by building a good governance and training the SPLA. Peace means being strong and being ready, being the hope and the answer and being recognized as a strong partner, peace is a balance of power, it is not just an emotional gesture. The SPLM must be realistic if it wants to be respected as strong peace partner otherwise the SPLM will never have an effective role on the table of governance of Sudan neither in the mind of its defiant political partner the NCP.

Our country is really calling upon all of it sons and daughters to avoid war and make Sudan a no return to war country. All Sudanese should join hands to make this dream a reality, let us differ in whatever aspects we want, let us compete for power and interests but let unite in making Sudan a no return to war country, it is only possible in everlasting peaceful Sudan that every dream and aspiration of each one of us will be attained and no doubt we will realize the Sudan of freedom, prosperity, unity and Justice.

## Darfur in the realm of consciousness

### By Chuar Juet Jock

November 5, 2007 — a new dawn in African Sudan has emerged and Darfur has come into the realm of consciousness and is in intense search of its lost identity and roots as its sisters of Nuba Mountains, Blue Nile and Southern Sudan did before. African Sudanese in Sudan and after all this long wander and lost in the realms of unconsciousness are finally realizing that neither speaking Arabic nor being a Muslim make you an Arabic man nor speaking English or being a Christian make you a white man, in other words, religion and non-mother tongue languages can't change one's origin or ethnicity as it was played upon by the successive Khartoum minority rulers as a philosophy of the Arabization and misleading scheme of these African tribes. With this realization, the African people of Sudan has marked a new dawn of self-consciousness as well a beginning of continuous and costly war to liberate themselves from the control of dominant powers in Khartoum let alone the bias of a decades long scheme of Arabization and misleading, and as a result of this mental revolution, Sudan will never be the same as the late visionary leader Dr. John Garang has declared and upon his true words, the gloomy days of African Sudanese in particular and all Sudanese in general are all about to be gone and a new Sudan of dignity, freedom and democracy is the new born child of the new found consciousness.

For Southern Sudanese who think that Darfur is a separate problem and that it was the main region where the aggressors or the so-called Sudanese Armed Forces (SAF) manpower's comes from and that as a matter of fact the current problem of Darfur is not their main concern. Well this is completely not true and it just reflects a shameful lack of clear understanding of the problem of African people of Sudan as a one project that was being executed and still by the minority rulers in Khartoum in different timeframes and with different techniques and tactics. On other hand, this opinion is but a complete reflection of a mere lack of clear definition to the objectives and goals of the minority rulers in Khartoum Arabization scheme as well as the degree of efficiency of theories of divide to rule and kill the slave by slave respectively within our primitive African communities. The barriers and the separate walls that where built between us and the rest of Africans in Sudan are many, they were well crafted in our minds and reflected in our very own thoughts and opinions and simply without liberating our minds from such bias the struggle for New Sudan will be in vain and the cost and the time of total liberation of the people and land of Sudan will be too high and lengthy respectively.

The African people of Sudan have to know that these divide to rule tools including religion, tribalism and others, were employed by the Khartoum rulers to install themselves upon their vast majority and Darfur is just but a clear victim of this policy of Khartoum successive systems of governments that did put Darfur completely into a different course against itself and apart from its sisters in Nuba Mountains, Blue Nile and Southern Sudan. The strategy of the minority rulers in Khartoum was and still is to kill us separately and apart, their policy and strategy was and still is to help us incommunicado within our separate borders, and use all possible differences among us to widen the disunity and until recently neither Southern Sudan could interact with Darfur in the west nor with Nuba Mountains in the center.

The Darfurians were recruited into the SAF by misleading strategies and exploitation of their much imposed poverty and ignorance, they were mobilized against South Sudan out of their wide ignorance of the hidden agenda of the racist Khartoum rulers and who did use the religion factor as a pretext of its racist war. Southern Sudanese must not watch Darfurians dying as a result of false reasoning that neither Darfurians nor Southern Sudanese are responsible for it, we are all victims of the devil in Khartoum nor it will be unforgivable mistake that we let Darfur down for whatever reason we may acclaim. Surely and strongly, Darfur is a fundamental part of New Sudan and the Sudanese dream.

Any real change or realization of the New Sudan will come through solving the conflict in Darfur, Darfur is a fundamental part in achieving the right democratic transformation of Sudan, it has already decided and paid and still paying so dearly that Sudan need to change, it did already join the dignified march toward new democratic Sudan. The poor people of Sudan have great expectations in both leaders of the liberation movements in Sudan led by Sudan People Liberation Movement (SPLM) and Sudan Liberation Movement (SLM) and Justice and Equality Movement (JEM). This should make these leaders be up to the aspirations of their people, they must carry out the dream of not only African Sudanese but all the marginalized people of Sudan in coordinated responsibility and must unified the vision of New Sudan and be above the shortcomings and the barriers put between them by the colonists and Khartoum successive regimes. They must not accept less than the total liberation of their people and country whatever the cost maybe, they must reject all the makeup deals that but make Khartoum less ugly, there is no doubt that they will win and that the whole problem of Sudan will settle thereof and permanently.

All the bias and divisions created by the Sudan minority rulers need to be exposed and revealed, the New Sudan vision need a new set of mind, a mind that is conscious and clear, a mind that know what is the meaning of New Sudan in term of structure and substance, the new Sudan could be the old Sudan if we successfully and democratically transform it on the bases of attractive unity , or either if we fail, the seceded new Sudan could be Union of African Sudanese States, South Sudan, Nuba Mountain, Darfur and Blue Nile or if Darfur and Nuba Mountain decide on their own the New Sudan could be south Sudan alone, it depends completely on the free will of all Sudanese, Africans and Arabs, Muslims and Christians and that will be exercised in the projected elections of 2009 and referendum of 2011 if the minority rulers in Khartoum didn't decide to take the country back into chaos and wars. Well even in the later situation, there is really certain thing that is assured and that is that there would be something new out of this struggle and as a result of the ongoing change and no doubt that, the New born Sudan will be one of the above.

However, in the march and the struggle to realize the New Sudan, it is of imperative that all the hidden agenda of Khartoum rulers Arabization scheme must be unearthed with focus on the its short and long term objectives and goals and what mechanism did it employed to succeed in the decades long domination of the indigenous Sudanese and why this Arabization project success and influence did vary in the various African Sudanese communities in Southern Sudan, Nuba Mountains, Blue Nile and Darfur.

The vision of New Sudan is true and is the dream of all Sudanese; however, without a clear explanation and particularly with the current low level of political awareness among the poor people of Sudan it is likely to fail. Confusion and misunderstanding of the very vision of the New Sudan has led to bloody internal wars and conflicts within the liberation movement itself and which did have contributed greatly in a grave setback of realization of this vision. A good example of this was the internal fighting within the SPLM/A form its very inception between the so-called separatists and unionists. In fact, that wasn't the case, but it was the ambiguousness of the New Sudan vision Vs primitive political awareness of its bases that has led to that conflict and if there were more explanation by what was meant by the term of New Sudan, it could save the movement a lot of headache and lost in term of support and manpower. For some, the call for liberation of all Sudan was seen unrealistic as well as an easy pretext of rival politicians within the movement, many Southerners think that they didn't went to bushes to fight for liberation of all Sudan.

In the march and the struggle to realize the vision of New Sudan, an excellent management in execution of the vision is imperatively needed through a strong and responsible leadership, in the lack of the later, the new African consciousness in Sudan won't realize its collective goals and objectives. Therefore, it is necessary that a collective vision have to be drawn and clearly explained, a collective mission need to be pursued and pressed on, but above all a collective coordinated leadership need to be in place to carry out this noble mission and cause.

The change in Sudan will happen through empowering the masses of poor Sudanese about the facts that are behind this miserable situation that they have been facing for decades. People of Sudan need to know that they are fighting for their rights, freedoms and a new country that is built on just and equal sound co-excision, and that won't happen without completely changing the system in Khartoum in term of concepts and Ideologies. The poor people of Sudan won't get their country back neither any real betterment will happen to their freedoms and rights if the roots of problem are not addressed honestly. Some may think and see us emphasize on race and religion as a call for racism or discrimination against some race or else, in fact that is completely not true but we believe strongly that we can't avoid mentioning race when the race or religion are in the very center of the Sudanese problem. The Sudan dilemma needs all Sudanese to be true to the realities on the grounds and that are in fact the causes of this acute dilemma.

Sudan dilemma need no partial solutions that are not interconnected or consistent as a whole exit strategy or oversell solution, any separate peace deals here and there that are signed by the Khartoum rulers with so many factions of the fractured Sudanese opposition are but just a temporary ticket for the Khartoum regime to empower itself and maintain its control on power. Therefore, any other peace deal in Darfur or eastern Sudan must be but an integrated part of the Comprehensive Peace Agreement (CPA).

The Sudan dilemma doesn't need temporary drugs that just druggist our people will and shift the course of their just cause to a different sphere, but all its needs is a real final effective solution for the whole problem, a solution that must solve and settle this problem permanently and forever. It is not necessary whether this overall solution comes in different consistent processes or integrated peace deals, this is not the case, the case and the real important case here is that this bloody and protracted problem must be put to halt permanently and at all the cost, it is not acceptable neither it is wise to wind back to the same problem after the temporary drugs are gone

It is very important for people of Sudan to be realistic to shorten the road and the cost on the way to New Sudan realization and no doubt that they will be tested by a lot of superstitions, illusions and so many barriers that Khartoum successive regimes has planted deeply in their brains and behaviors, no doubt that these bias are the real setback in our quest toward a strong unified liberation movement that will realize the New Sudan vision of dignity, democracy, prosperity.

For African people of Sudan and Sudanese in general, it is the right time for total unity of purpose as well as destination, it is the right time for the shortsighted among us to stop creating more wounds and divisions and welcome the gallant Darfur into the realm of African freedom and consciousness

**Sudan has to accept the truth and the truth shall set it free**

There is no doubt that something is really wrong with Sudan as a state since its inception and mostly this has something to do with the system of governance and those who have designed and set this system. Simply because there is no logic or wisdom that can support all this madness and bloodshed that this country has been in for decades.

However, all this long bitter and continuous misery is but a product of a fierce fight between the truths and false in Sudan, between justice and injustice, equality and inequality. Therefore, it is imperative that we define and explore this bitter truth and when was it decided to be denied and twisted and why, and more importantly how it is being denied as well as defining the false that is being pursued to replace the truth and how it is being executed and defended and why?

This topic is about the truth that is being denied in Sudan and so it shouldn't be a surprise to reader attention that I have mention the word truth more than any word, and in the other hand, I want to first acknowledges that it is not my intention to use any race words or vocabulary of the world in this topic but in this real world, you have no alternative when these attributes are the real constants or the facts that are causing the problems so I do apology for those God people in Sudan and around the world we do see all human kinds not by color of their skins

The false that is destroying Sudan and bringing it down to its knees was put in place when the departing British and Egyptian colonists decided to put the Arabs minority as the new heirs of power and the new colonists to the vast majority of Black Sudan under the pretext of independence, giving them the right to rule the majority of black people by all the techniques of twisting false to be true and true to be false. Since this time This minority have invented all sort of art of twisting and denial of truth through brutal systems of governments, military coups and sometime shaky and proxy democratic government, this is the reason why Sudan didn't have a chance to be ruled democratically because real democracy will have led to the ultimate truth that they are denying, the rule of majority of African Sudanese.

Those who are expecting real democracy to take place in Sudan have a long way to go and to convince this minority to accept the truth, this minority has in its history tried to form a political majority based on religion as their last resort to change the clear face of truth, they tried to deny and twist all the truth in history books, creating false systems of domination of one race or tribe to another, systematic mis-education and misleading, mass killing and uprooting, dividing the majority of African Sudanese in the name of religion and tribe. Though, this is when the truth was denied and its continues denial and twisting became the art and the way of ruling Sudan and its vast African majority, and this is where everything then went wrong in Sudan and the roots of all past and present conflicts, misery and bloodshed in Sudan.

Sudan was ruled up to now by an iron fist dictatorship through minority dominated military regimes that has nothing but to make rule of this minority a bitter reality on our vast innocent African majority, the shameful side of scenario is that this military vast manpower are Africans commanded by this minority. So according to this bitter reality, the victims of this systematic war of killings and uprooting are Africans, Muslims be them or Christians' and one keen mind also should not be surprise why this vast majority of black Africans are so divided and in this weak and poor stage of socio-economic or political development.

This is but the result of the systematic downgrading and domination policies and actions of these minority rulers. Sudan is too rich but all these riches are exploited to benefit just this minority and therefore the world should spare us from the ugly image that is imposed on us, and instead it should look deeply on the real roots of Sudanese dilemma because the mighty God never created us to be in this shameful stage. But it is this powerful and false minority system that has made our lives and the future of our children a misery and a hell.

It is not the first time in the history of human kinds that the false have defeated the truth even briefly, and particularly in the time when there are no defenders of truth and when the false become more powerful and have it all. Many past and present civilizations and kingdoms where built on falsehood and suppression of the truth.

It is this bitter reality of history that motivate all evils systems in the world to pursue the same way and Sudan minority system is just a good example of these kinds. Another aspect of this misery is the dream of these minority rulers to have all the land of the rich Sudan, this is another front and the foundation of all evils that happened and still happening in Sudan to indigenous African owners of the land. To achieve this objective a process of disowning has been in place since the so-called Sudan independence and all this injustice, inequality, domination, slavery, mass killing and uprooting and so on are but just ways and means of this process.

This minority is not alone and is so powerful, backed by its international allies who are so rich and possess a strong influence in all the international politics and decisions; they have the shine of money as well as the mockery of all evils. I pity on the poor indigenous of Sudan, how their luck came to be connected and associated with the most devilish system and rulers in the modern history of humankind I have no doubt that the children of southern Sudan, Nuba and Darfur, will mark my words that all their brighter hopes in good life and glorious future was ruined and turned into misery and hell by this minority and its backers.

We are just defenders of the truth that is being denied and twisted by the powerful evil machine of minority rulers in Khartoum. But, no matter what the truth is the final judgment and what is all the life pillars and creation is built upon, the stream of blood and sacrifices will never stop, neither the poor and good people of Sudan will ever give up to the false to be true, it will take decades and may be more for the truth to prevail in Sudan, simply because there is no such a thing called wisdom or humanity in the heart and conscience of this minority. Their greed and impunity have made them blinds, their humanity and conscience is dead neither they even know the God that they are using. It did work for some time for the minority rulers to shield its racist face behind the pretext of religion but the truth has prevailed and the genocide of Darfur's Muslim African ethnics groups has made it clear that the problem in Sudan is racist at first place.

So how come they are killing the children of the very God they are claiming to be believers. Nobody need to be told or lectured about how this devilish system in Khartoum is working or about its power capacity neither their expertise nor their knowledge about the world. They are Hitlerisms of Sudan; their goal is to wipeout the black people of Sudan systematically and slowly or at least reduce them to be a minority. Armed and empowered by the Sudan stolen goods and resources and no doubt they have their markets and customers and accordingly their devilish power is growing. But the people of Sudan know very well that false will never become true because this false has ninety-nine out of one hundred percent supporters neither it become true because it got all the stolen power resources, it is just a matter of time for the false to fall and the truth to prevail and this is our unshakable faith.

It does not need dictionaries or encyclopedias to know what has been going in Sudan until now; it is just about false being pursued and executed by all means and powers to be true. It is about truth being denied by all means and powers to be false. If democracy is the right system of the government then without doubt the vast African black people of Sudan have the right to rule their land and the other side of this truth is that the minority Arabs Sudanese are full Sudanese citizens that nobody even claiming that they should be denied their rights or to be put as second citizen because they are minority, their origin or religion.

This truth is telling us that Sudan must be formed on equal and just bases that will make it possible for all the God people to live in it with dignity, freedom and prosperity, and the same truth is telling us that enough is enough accept it or not, and make a decision so you Sudanese can stop all these curses, death, hunger, diseases, fear, madness, and hatred, unfortunately our hearts seem to be lost or our ears don't even function or hear any more neither our minds seem to have a little bit of wisdom to restore the lost balance or the gone sobriety.

The same truth is telling us that you Sudanese are blessed with a beautiful fertile land that is watered by a good river from its northern point to its southern, a land that is full of gold, honey and all the above and hidden vast resources yet with few people. The same truth is telling us that you are all children of God who created you in all these beautiful colors and tongues so you can see the mighty and the love of your creator yet you have misunderstood the message and instead you are fighting yourself to death.

There are numerous African countries with vast African Muslims or Christians majority yet they are led by Muslim or Christian president respectively. And in many Sudanese and in south in particular, there are cousins who are Muslims and Christians yet they are one family. Religion is not the problem in Sudan but is being use as a cover for racism. It is true that every race has the right to protect itself and live its culture and all its social norms and life yet it doesn't have any right to deny other races from the very same rights.

The Arabs Sudanese minority can protect itself with other peaceful means or could be guarantees protection by a fair constitution of Sudan but it doesn't have to invent all this falsehood and misery in Sudan in order for it to rule and dominate the African majority or out of its fears of domination. The shameful thing is that this process of mass killing and uprooting is happening in the day light and as the whole world watches and without a little common sense, the minority rulers are populating the emptied and burned down towns and villages of Darfur with Arabs ethnics groups from neighboring African countries after their systematic killings and uprooting of the innocent African Muslims ethnics groups.

Therefore, let the world know that it is the racist policies of all Khartoum successive regimes that did have counterproductive consequences and planted this racism disease in all Sudanese societies. There is no good in corrupt rulers with corrupt systems and this is how most of Sudan if not all become paralyzed with racism, tribalism and corruption because our ruler is one of a kind. When equality, justice, and freedom all prevails, Sudan unity will automatically be in place, when there is no room for injustice and grievance and only when there is no room for discrimination under any form, Sudan will, without doubt, be a real united states on the map of the world and a helping force for humanity to recon to in other areas of misery and conflicts around the world.

In fact, when Sudan become a healthy state that accommodates it's all citizen on equal and just basses, it will never be a matter of conflict whether it's an Arab or African that should rule, it will be a matter of being a good leader. let us all swim in the vast river of Sudan of equality and justice and freedom where the term Arab and African will just give birth to the new Sudanese identity of dignity and freedom.

Otherwise, when it is hard for all of us to digest the various differences of race, religions, cultures and so on of all that make us in this stalemate situation, let us peacefully decide and accept to depart peacefully, there is no need to enforce any either of us to change their identity, race or culture neither it justify for any of us to impose their race, culture or religion upon others. let us also accept that the resources that God did bless us with should be shared and divided peacefully though even that we will depart for the sake of reality and truth and peace let us don't forget that we are just Sudanese that have been defeated in other way by the reality of bitter truth that we cannot mix up or co-exist.

However, both separation and unity are just an outcome of our readiness to accept the truth. They are all options to solve the problem of Sudan, and let us be true to ourselves and ready to pay the cost in order to solve this problem permanently, it is the responsibility of all Sudanese to decide the future of their country and to execute the change they want. Every action or word from anyone of us is but a step toward either unity or separation, so it is imperative that each of us should know to which one is contributing.

The truth is constant, you can twist it for decades but still will never change its realty, it is better of all the Sudanese to act now before it is too late and accepts the truth and truth will set thee free. A normal, healthy and sound conscience will weigh the truth and accept it no matter what We Sudanese need to accept the truth in order for us to be one peaceful and prosperous nation, and for justice, equality, and fairness to prevail. let us accept the truth that we are all equal and nobody have to be brought down because of his/her skin color, tribe, religion, gender or any form of discrimination, let us accept the truth that the violence is not a God message neither it is the objective of creation and that greed, hatred, apathy are the roots of all evils and ills and that without love it is impossible for all of us to be one Sudanese nation

It took millions of innocent souls just for humanity to abolish slavery, colonialism, holocaust, racism, domination yet the Sudanese didn't learn yet. The history of human kind is an open book to learn from, it is clearly and loudly telling us that no matter what, it is the truth that will win at the end, you can stop the defenders of the truth from defending it by all forms of your aggressive powers, by killing, imprisoning, torturing terrorizing them, yet the truth will just get more powerful, it took millions of innocents lives for Sudanese in south and north to make the shaky Comprehensive Peace Agreement (CPA) and it will take others million in Darfur because the minority rulers are far away from wisdom.

Omer El-Bashier and his party must accept the truth now and not tomorrow, the truth that enough is enough, and that the bloodshed in Sudan in whatever name it is or covers is false and untrue, neither the killing of millions in the name of Arabs expansion nor race elimination is true, neither the greed for land or resources justify any killing of God own made souls. Fifty years of denying and twisting the truth are enough, it is time to accept the truth and only this truth shall set Sudan free.

## Better for Khartoum not to test the will of freedom fighters

By Chuar Juet Jock

October 28, 2007 — Khartoum cannot have them both, it got to choose one of two, to hate us and let go or to love us and we chose to stay but it cannot hate us and force us to stay or to co-exist within its hatred system against our own will or to expect us to choose inferiority, sub class humans and citizens, there is no holy war that can suppress people will, dignity and quest for freedom, never, and in the light of this, it is better for Khartoum to save millions of lives of Sudanese youth in south and north, to avoid the upcoming war, it take leaders with wisdom and reasoning to make peace not people with childish reactions like the so-called Dr. Mustafa Osman Ismail. No doubt that his being an advisor to president Bashir is one of reason that fuels the chaos and fire, a man who always doesn't even know the consequences of his own words, and no doubt again that Sudan is cursed to have such a leader like him. But Mustafa Osman or whatever his name is got to know one thing, you don't need to test the oppressed keen will and quest for freedom and clearly it is better for his Khartoum system to think twice and not to test our unparalleled will for freedom and readiness to fight for it

Logic and wisdom are good; they are the foundation of a healthy and a sound mind, and blessed are those nations and countries that are led by leaders who do possess some of these two reasoning elements, because peace, justice, equality and all that high aspirations and Godly values that the humanity needs to co-exist and live in peace are but associated products of logic and wisdom. A permanent liar and a well trained professional in the art of deception and mockery, Mustafa Osman Ismail and his de facto Khartoum regime has nothing left to cover their ugly face, and must accept the consequences of their own mockery games

Faced with the reality of political crisis triggered by its very own tyrants officials irresponsible deeds and that forced the SPLM to withdraw from the then so called Government of National Unity (GoNU) in fact it is a government of national dismay, the National Congress Party (NCP) has only two options left, either to rush again to unfounded war with south, opening an all-out war and digging its own death grave or to come back to its long lost conscience and credibility (if it did ever had any) and willingly decide to implement the terms of Comprehensives Peace Agreement (CPA) it did signed with the SPLM on January 9, 2005, fully and honestly

Yes, there is a dare need for peace and yes the poor people of Sudan are not even wishing to fight another bloody war, that is true, but in the face of the bitter reality of continuous defiance and tyranny of NCP, they would have no option. The gloomy situation in Sudan is not a creation of innocents Sudanese masses neither the provoked racial and religious wars have something to do with people of Sudan that we know very well. They are wars and conflicts that are imposed on them by the minority rulers in Khartoum to further their unrealistic agenda and that have no connection neither with a better future or welfare of Sudanese people, though how the Sudanese became displaced and prisoners in their own countries and refugee in all countries of the world and a sound mind in Arabic and

Muslim world could simply identified the nature and ideology of this regime, what kind of government system in Khartoum that did make Israel became better refuge for the poor African Sudanese Muslims leave alone Christians than their own stolen and invaded Sudan, the Israel that we were told by the same minority media drums of lies that, hell but not Israel.

What type of government system that has been in conflict with certain ethnics of its very own people for two successive decades, systematically killing, uprooting them and having the free hand in transforming Sudan to the worst place a human can dream to live. For African Sudanese, Muslim or Christians alike, Sudan was made by this regime the worse than the Germany of Hitler. What is this system overall goal and objective? Isn't it easy for the world to identify the system in the iron fist control of Khartoum through this mass killing and uprooting of African people of Sudan? If so than any peace negotiations with this regime is just but a complete lie, a tactic and strategy of buying time, a make up to an ugly inhuman face.

For those confused minds of ours and who criticized the SPLM pullout I simply do direct this question, why would SPLM stand on the way of full implementation of CPA? An accord that it fought for and negotiated and accepted as the least possible agreement for creation of new Sudan of unity on new sound bases, The CPA is a program of timed processes that if implemented fully in good faith and through excellent management it would lead to the Sudan that is the dream, at least, of all Sudanese. The agreement is what is possible for Sudan to co-exist as a country, united or separated, through the free will of its people and the NCP did sign it willingly and soberly. With the full implementation of the CPA, Sudan will never be the same as the late leader Dr. John Garang did put it. Sudan will change for better and it is this change that the minority in Khartoum and their backers around the world want to stop, because this change is a threat to their selfish interests and definitely this change will create new equal and just platforms of power sharing and equal participation in running the country affairs, this change will lead to democracy, elections, rule of majority, this change will give back the Sudanese people their stolen rights and freedoms. Why would the minority rulers in Khartoum fully implement the CPA, since the very CPA would shift the power base from them?

Who is really being threatened by the full implementation of the CPA? Answering this question will clearly have identified the forces that are hindering and sabotaging the full implementation of CPA and these forces are not the hardliners within the NCP alone but there are old elements within Khartoum ruling circle that sees CPA as a threat to their interests, they oppose NCP rule but they are unwilling to change Sudan too, they want the change to be associated to their old short visions that have given the chance to NCP to reach to the power.

As southern Sudanese we are not going to be angels of perfection over night as some of us may have wish, we still have a long way to go to heal the damage done to our society in terms of structure and substance, we still have to come out from the long dominated characters and brains to a more independent, healthy brains and characters. Those who see our problems of tribalism, corruption and others as justification to prefers the domination of Khartoum oppressors then our immature own government have a very short sighted and selfish interests, the CPA itself has given a chance for each Sudanese to joint either north or south system. In south we have our northerners that do enjoy the system we do have and vice versa. so please if you are southerner and you think you inclined to the northern system just simply joint it but don't impose it on the southerners, we are in fact living the reality of one country two systems

In seriously and effectively dealing with the NCP, whether in peace or in war, no single political party that will be better than the SPLM itself that has fought the successive regimes of Khartoum, the NCP itself is not just only a local Sudanese movement but a part of an international movement that is executing non Sudanese agenda. Its pure aim is to occupy the total land of Sudan; they want all the African Sudanese uprooted or killed so the vast rich Sudan can be a source of funding of their endless war with the west. They are very strategic and they know how the world politics works and they are well trained in deception in any time of space, lying in the name of God is just a philosophy, they have nothing to do with God neither with Sudanese people but they see Sudan as the source of wealth that need to be seized by all the cost.

The NCP can bring the whole China Arms machines to protect the oil fields but will not even provide a relative security to poor African Sudanese in Darfur, instead it is using this oil money to funds its Arab expansionist project by the systematically killing and uprooting of African people of Sudan. With this vast wealth they will create a military machine that will not only crush the African people of Sudan but a funding base that funds all the terrorists' agenda of their kind and pursue their march into the rest of Africa. With this oil money, the NCP is not just only a part of all the problems in black Africa but a main facilitors for all the unrest movements here and there in Africa. Truly, those who are blaming the SPLM pullout are those who don't have a clue about the history, aims and objectives of NCP and how this racist party works. A final peace will not be attained through escaping the reality that we are dealing with wars lovers and inhuman ideologists that don't sees the world as we see it but it will be attained through a clear cut victory upon the evils machine and it is just a matter of time.

In the light of this bitter reality the SPLM must not believe in a final trustworthy peace agreement with the NCP, but let it go the extra miles with NCP, laugh when they laugh and grin its chins when they do, you never know when the devil finally did or will decide to change, but all options must be on the table, just like it did, the SPLM must know when it have to start, pause, stop or terminate the game. In the quest for final peace and democratic transition in Sudan, it is of imperative that the SPLM/SPLA have to play the game of politics very well, by being fundamentally a peace and change maker through politics and dialogue while being up-to-date in terms of military readiness as well as intelligence gathering, financial resources and political awareness and mobilization of its bases. It is the responsibility of SPLM/SPLA to defend the southern gate of Africa and therefore it will need to strengthen itself and create not only a movement that is really capable to provide a new agenda for new strong Sudan but for the whole Africa, it will need viable allies in intelligence gatherings and military operations and in the light of this our foreign relations with the rest of Africa must be solid as well as the rest of our international ones, we must contain the NCP everywhere and engage it everywhere. The SPLM is a movement with sacred cause and it will continue to shine and thrill as long as its sticks to that cause and it did prove with the recent pullout that it is still the people's movement

In the case of Darfur, the history and the nature of NCP make the negotiations useless, with such a minority regime that has nothing to give but lies, false and fake promises. it is not a surprise to us at all that the gallant Darfur fighters did decide to boycott the proposed peace negotiations in Libya, learning from the SPLM pullout, it is better to search for realistic alternative instead of wasting time with a system that is built on lies, mockery and deception. In fact, the poor Sudanese need to think seriously about real effective and efficient ways to deals with the minority rulers in Khartoum. Sudan will never be the same and the people of Sudan must not retreat nor surrender because their victory against tyranny and authoritarian of the few in Khartoum is certain and near.

Khartoum rulers need to face the reality that the poor Sudanese people won't give up the fight neither surrenders nor retreat, their destiny will be like any tyrants and dictators who have killed millions of their own people, the truth about the Sudan will prevail, neither the widowed women will forget their murdered husbands nor the orphans' children won't forget their murdered parents, nor the uprooted masses won't erase the bitter memories of their burnt villages, killed relatives. In this technological era, the modern world history is well kept and recorded through videos and other sophisticated devices, and clearly the NCP has nothing to hide, its naked racist and inhuman bloody face is well known around the whole world. It is really a good chance for them to seize this moments of peaceful opportunities for the problem of Sudan to solve, it is imperative that they come back to their Sudanese conscience, it is never too late for Sudanese people to forgive neither it is too late for the Sudan of dignity, unity, freedom, democracy to prevail and time will tell.

In a Nutshell: Opinions & Articles During South Sudanese Civil War

Chuar Juet Jock

**ISBN-13: 978-1523702657**
**ISBN-10: 1523702656**